All Species of Knowledge

All Species of Knowledge

A Voyage of Discovery, Failure, and

Natural History in the Pacific Ocean

DAVID IGLER

OXFORD
UNIVERSITY PRESS

OXFORD
UNIVERSITY PRESS

Oxford University Press is a department of the University of Oxford.
It furthers the University's objective of excellence in research, scholarship,
and education by publishing worldwide. Oxford is a registered trade mark of
Oxford University Press in the UK and in certain other countries.

Published in the United States of America by Oxford University Press
198 Madison Avenue, New York, NY 10016, United States of America.

CIP data is on file at the Library of Congress.

ISBN 9780197777688

DOI: 10.1093/9780197777718.001.0001

Printed by Marquis Book Printing, Canada

The manufacturer's authorized representative in the EU for product safety is
Oxford University Press España S.A. of Parque Empresarial San Fernando de Henares,
Avenida de Castilla, 2 – 28830 Madrid (www.oup.es/en or product.safety@oup.com).
OUP España S.A. also acts as importer into Spain of products made by the manufacturer.

For Noah and Sam,
intrepid explorers

CONTENTS

LIST OF ILLUSTRATIONS

ACKNOWLEDGMENTS

This research began a decade ago and benefited from the help of archivists and librarians around the world. Early in the process I was inspired by the gracious support of an archivist at the Alexander Turnbull Library in Wellington, New Zealand, *Aotearoa*. I had traveled there to view Ludwig Choris's lithographic volumes *Voyage pittoresque autour du monde* (1822) and *Vues et paysages des régions équinoxiales* (1826), which I knew were the best versions of these two rare books found anywhere. I arrived at the library in the midafternoon looking forward to a few days of research before returning to Auckland, only to be told by the archivist that the library was soon closing for the Anzac Day celebrations and would remain shut during my short stay in Wellington. I apologized for my American ignorance of the Anzac Day closure and then expressed my desperate need to view these two books, at which point she ran for the basement and within minutes returned with the Choris volumes. "I'll turn the pages, you take the photographs," she commanded with the authority of an enthusiastic drill sergeant. Those images remain on my phone ten years later, and I have an extraordinary archivist to thank for going well beyond her job description. My fascination with Choris's lithographs initiated this research project, and the artist's work remains at the center of the book.

A large cast of helpful archivists, librarians, and curators have made this work possible. I thank Chris Finis of Reese & Company, Christine Hult-Lewis at UC Berkeley's Bancroft Library, Yvonne Reimers of the Museum für Naturkunde (Berlin), Schamarra Smith at the Honolulu Museum of

Art, Alejandra Gaeta and Katlynn Friedman of the Autry Museum of the American West, Matt Daniel Mason at the Beinecke Rare Book and Manuscript Library, Ted Walbye of the Getty Research Center, Ping Yang of the Australia National Library, and Nicole Arnold at my home institution, UC Irvine. Other librarians (whose names I've embarrassingly misplaced) lent assistance at the Alaska State Archives, the British Library, the University of Auckland, Occidental College, and the David Rumsey Historical Map Collection at Stanford University. Our work as historians would be impossible—or at least far less pleasant—without the help of the professionals who manage the archives.

Fellow historians have generously offered their time and expertise in reading draft chapters and educating me about topics far from my areas of expertise. My sincere appreciation goes out to Ryan Tucker Jones, Lissa Wadewitz, Sam Truett, Josh Reid, Andrés Reséndez, Anne Hyde, Kevin Dawson, David Josephs, Dan Lewis, Ron Tyler, Doug Smith, Doris Lonk, Steve Hackel, Peter Mancall, Richard White, and two anonymous readers for Oxford University Press. Marie-Theres Federhofer and Anne Greenwood MacKinney—two scholars on the other side of the Atlantic whom I've never met in person—lent assistance when it was most needed. I am honored by the knowledge shared by two community elders and canoe-building educators, Larry Raigetal (Guam) and Alson Kelen (Marshall Islands), as well as the cartographic expertise of Ben Pease. A very special thanks to my editor at Oxford University Press, Susan Ferber, who encouraged me throughout the writing process.

Many colleagues at UCI read portions of this manuscript and lent their assistance in other tangible ways. I want to thank Jeff Wasserstrom for incisive feedback, Sarah Farmer and Ian Coller for help with translations, Alex Borucki for advice about the Slave Voyages database, Susan Morrissey and Heidi Tinsman for their support as department chairs, Laura Mitchell for an initial gem of an idea, Andrew Highsmith for life inspiration, and David Fedman for reading suggestions. Special kudos to Sharon Salinger, who in "retirement" tramped across Paris to a small archive to photograph pages from a two-hundred-year-old diary. I'm sorry I couldn't put those indecipherable pages to better use.

Bill Deverell generously read most of these pages and provided mentorship since the time I was a postdoctoral fellow. My own mentoring of graduate students has offered truly rewarding experiences as an academic, most recently with Stephanie Narrow and UC President's Postdoctoral Fellow Caroline Collins. Two former graduate students, Eric Steiger and Jennifer Staver, provided research assistance long before this project took shape. My fellow traveler in the profession, Michael Willrich, has been a constant source of support, humor, and occasional depravity since we were sixteen years old. My partner (and physician extraordinaire) Cynthia Willard deserves credit and love for most of the good things in my life, not the least of which is our two sons, Noah and Sam. For their ceaseless comedy and comradery, this book is dedicated to them.

Introduction

Grand Ambitions for a Motley Crew

The Russian brig *Rurik* sailed into a surprisingly large bay northeast of "Beering's Straits" on the first day of August 1816, prompting Captain Otto von Kotzebue to reflect on the journey since its departure from St. Petersburg one year earlier. He estimated they had traveled more than twenty thousand nautical miles on the small ship—from the North Atlantic to the southern tip of the Americas before heading to the middle of the Pacific, at which point the *Rurik* turned north to the Kamchatka Peninsula. As the ship sailed above the Bering Strait in the broken icepack and strangely calm waters of the Chukchi Sea, Kotzebue's imagination sparked as he felt a steady current pulling the *Rurik* toward the American coastline. This bay did not appear on any of the charts he carried. Captain James Cook had bypassed it in 1778, and with this knowledge in mind Captain Kotzebue felt confident in claiming and naming his discovery: Kotzebue Sound. But he also felt a deeper emotion:

> I cannot describe the strange sensation which I now experienced, at the idea that I perhaps stood at the entrance of the so long sought N[orth] E[ast] passage, and that fate had chosen me to be the discoverer. I felt my heart oppressed; and, at the same time, an impatience, which would not let me rest, and was still increased by the perfect calm.[1]

Kotzebue ordered the crew to cast the anchor and then, to the delight of the *Rurik*'s two naturalists and the artist, he requested boats be prepared with adequate supplies for an overnight stay on shore. For these men of science and art, the work of gathering knowledge could commence on the northernmost terra of the Americas.

Once on shore, artist Ludwig Choris followed Kotzebue's armed entourage to the summit of a nearby hill to view the surrounding country. Kotzebue sighted tall mountains to the north and a vast plain stretching out to the east. A large river bisected the plain and disappeared into the horizon. "As far as the eye could reach," Kotzebue observed, "everything was green; here and there were flowers in blossom, and no snow was seen but on the tops of the mountains at a great distance." While Kotzebue searched the horizon for signs of the "long sought" Northern Passage and the naturalists gathered flora, Ludwig Choris watched the quiet approach of five "baydarres" (canoes) on the water.[2] Each vessel carried eight to ten paddlers, "all armed with lances and bows." The men landed on the shore below the hill. Wielding his sketchbook and pencils, Choris eagerly joined the group chosen by Kotzebue to "meet the Americans."[3]

The sketches of "the Americans" drawn by Choris in the coming week culminated years later in a lithograph titled *Habitans du Golfe de Kotzebue*, published in Paris as part of his volume *Voyage pittoresque autour du monde* (1822). The lithograph depicted four individuals, three men and one woman, deliberately arranged to display distinct physical characteristics: chopped hair, facial tattoos, earrings, cheek plugs, and one man's powerful forearm capable of paddling a watercraft for lengthy distances in the open sea. One individual's steady stare provides the focus of the group portrait. He glares aggressively at the artist, and Choris redirects the man's gaze to the viewer, to the wealthy patrons who purchased *Voyage pittoresque*, and to future generations of readers who would look upon this widely reproduced lithograph. Choris left the meaning of the man's deliberate stare to the viewer. But his own mind fashioned the facial expression from a macabre incident that transpired during their short stay at Kotzebue Sound.

These Iñupiat individuals held an ancestral relationship to the surrounding lands and waters stretching back more than one thousand years. They called this place Qiqiktagruk.[4] Naturalist Adelbert von Chamisso felt confident in his ability to understand the Iñupiat, whom he called

Figure I.1 *Habitans du Golfe de Kotzebue.* Louis Choris, *Voyage pittoresque autour du monde* (Paris, 1822). This group portrait of Iñupiat individuals derived from Choris's sketches and watercolor paintings prior to appearing in *Voyage pittoresque autour du monde.* Expedition illustrators were generally instructed to depict the physiognomy of Indigenous people, a practice Choris grudgingly followed at times but also resisted in many instances. "Profiles," he informed Adelbert von Chamisso after the voyage, "do not think that I take pleasure in drawing them!" His portraits of Indigenous people place particular emphasis on clothing, body art, facial expression, and tools, such as the quiver of arrows included in this image. The new craft of lithography allowed for Choris's highly detailed illustrations. Courtesy Internet Archive. Unless otherwise noted, all lithographs come from the Internet Archive's digital version of the volume held by the Getty Research Institute.

"Eskimos."[5] They arrived, he wrote, "as is only right for brave men, equipped for war but ready for peace." Chamisso offered gifts of needles, tobacco, and knives, and he observed that they "seemed to understand trade very well." Over the course of the next week different Iñupiat groups approached and bartered with the *Rurik*'s personnel, and Chamisso noted their friendliness as well as their caution around the "intrusive strangers."[6] Nonetheless, the naturalist felt unsatisfied with the meager results of their barter. He desired an artifact beyond simple trade items.

Before departing from Kotzebue Sound, Chamisso searched for an artifact of importance to natural history, and he found it at the site of a hilltop burial mound. "Our greedy curiosity rummaged through these gravesites; the skulls were removed," he recounted in a voice completely devoid of personal responsibility. Years later Chamisso regretted the grave desecration, referring to their exploit as "what had better been left undone."[7] Yet on the day of the grave robbing his scientific longing for human skulls guided his actions. The *Rurik* quickly departed the next day, before the Iñupiat discovered the ransacked gravesite of their ancestors. The artist Choris had participated in the theft, and in the days ahead he worked on many sketches of the Iñupiat people with this deplorable episode in mind. Choris admitted to disturbing the "tombs" and the "interred...objects which they had prized during their lives and which had served them with success."[8] He also sketched one of the plundered skulls that sat before him on the *Rurik*'s worktable. The accusatory stare cast by the central figure of *Habitans du Golfe de Kotzebue* was hardly a coincidence. Choris deliberately created the man's expression to depict his anger at what the intruders had done. Choris felt the man's contempt for years to come, until he produced the final lithograph for *Voyage pittoresque*.[9]

The *Rurik*'s small complement of officers, naturalists, artist, and crew had remained at Kotzebue Sound for little more than a week to collect information about their surroundings before sailing west across the Chukchi Sea to the coast of Asia. They planned to return the following summer to pursue the expedition's primary goal: the "Purpose of Exploring a North-East Passage," as stated in the subtitle of Captain Kotzebue's published journal. Kotzebue was deeply committed to this "Purpose," although other "discoveries" would ultimately play a much larger role in his final report. Those on board the *Rurik* had their own ambitions for the voyage. The naturalists envisioned discoveries of unknown plants, animals, minerals and fossils, human behaviors and languages, and insights on Indigenous cultures—all the elements of natural history to which they invested their lives. Meanwhile, Ludwig Choris developed his craft of visually rendering natural landscapes, flora and fauna, and Indigenous people for his European audience. The expedition's other members, mostly Russian naval sailors, anticipated advancement and reward for surviving the harrowing three-year circumnavigation of the globe. A group of Aleut translators and paddlers also sailed on some portions of the *Rurik*'s voyage, and four of them remained on the ship all the way to the journey's end in St. Petersburg. Finally, a skilled navigator named Kadu from the Caroline Islands joined the expedition for a year in pursuit of his own quest for knowledge of distant seas and foreign people. His daily engagements with the personnel shaped their worldviews and influenced some of the work they produced after the expedition. For a voyage designed to discover the world's greatest remaining geographic enigma—the Northern Passage—the Kotzebue expedition was notable for its small, inquisitive, and untested staff. They comprised a motley crew of individuals who held their own reckonings of success.

DISCOVERY, KNOWLEDGE, AND FAILURE

Research libraries around the world hold hundreds of volumes bearing titles similar to *A Voyage of Discovery*. The "voyage" part is indisputable in the sense that an oceanic expedition set out and, in most instances, safely returned. The "discovery" part, however, often betrays the author's inventiveness and challenges the reader's imagination. The claim of "discovering" implies the anticipated outcome of these voyages, although the failure to discover something of value was arguably a more common result. This point holds true for scientific practice in general, as well as other disciplines of critical inquiry.[10] Especially in regard to voyages designed to locate the Northern Passage, a constant refrain of "failure" greeted the European voyagers who returned from their missions. "Total failure," wrote England's loudest advocate for Arctic exploration, John Barrow, in 1819, upon the return of the latest two ships that failed to locate the passage. He believed the disillusionment was not his alone, but instead a "disappointment we [all] experience."[11] Barrow proposed a simple solution to the collective frustration: his nation must launch its next round of northern expeditions.

In examining voyages of discovery, one must begin with the understanding that the "discovered" places and revealed things were already well known to the Indigenous communities who lived there. A heralded discovery, in this sense, said as much about the worldview and arrogance of the discoverer as it did about the discovered geography, species, or new-found people. One might also question the genuine value of many acclaimed discoveries.[12] As recent scholars contend, voyages of discovery functioned as information-gathering ventures that were intended to produce new knowledge for European science, commerce, and imperial ambitions.[13] Rather than simple discovery, a set of multifaceted questions comes to the fore: what knowledge was acquired, from whom, and by what means was it circulated to a larger audience? Who creates knowledge, and whose interests does it serve?

Geographic discoveries, especially for Europeans, typically led to an imperial claim to the physical location, whether or not an Indigenous group already possessed it. Apart from staking claims, discovery held other meanings: it represented a collective process between individuals and groups who shared information, between disparate systems of knowledge and ways of knowing, and between those who asserted a particular claim and the audience that accepted or rejected it. In the post-Napoleonic era of the *Rurik*'s voyage—and following scores of Pacific expeditions in the late eighteenth century—new geographic discoveries were few and far between. As a result, expedition naturalists and their fellow travelers increasingly focused attention on gaining knowledge beyond geography. They observed natural entities over extended periods of time in the hope of developing new theories about species, hydrography, or geology. They pushed the boundaries of natural history in different directions, including ethnography, political economy, and the pseudoscience of phrenology.[14] Naturalists could blithely disregard their failure to discover a monumental feature like the Northern Passage when, they believed, their own process of gathering and circulating knowledge produced tangible and innovative findings. Those individuals who sailed on the *Rurik*—from Kadu to Adelbert von Chamisso to Ludwig Choris—fervently believed in the value of the knowledge they brought home and presented to their audiences.

Voyagers had pursued the Northern Passage since the 1500s. Most commonly referred to as the Northwest Passage for its assumed connection between the Northwest Atlantic and the Northeast Pacific oceans, its existence eluded generations of capable navigators until Roald Amundsen's small Norwegian ship *Gjoa* broke through an icy channel from the direction of the Atlantic Ocean in 1905 and found a Pacific whaling vessel on the other side.[15] Prior to Amundsen, some of the most resolute European explorers utterly failed in their attempt to discover, claim, and name the elusive waterway linking the two oceans. Cabot, Drake, Hudson, Cook, Malaspina, Vancouver, and many other famous explorers had all failed to find the passage. Otto von Kotzebue would challenge the fates with the *Rurik* expedition. He failed to find it, which is only one component of this story. Instead of that singular geographic discovery, the *Rurik* returned to St. Petersburg in 1818 with a cargo hold full of artifacts, new theories about flora and fauna, journals, drafted scientific articles and reports, sketchbooks and watercolors, conjectures, claims, and stories—all the stuff of natural history and visual ethnography.

Histories of oceanic expeditions generally end when the ship returns home. However, it was through the afterlife of a voyage that participants accomplished the most significant work. During this period, circuits of knowledge could intersect, and scientific information filtered into the public sphere. The afterlife of the *Rurik* offers an especially vivid example of this process, as a coordinated network of individuals developed and circulated its scientific, humanistic, and artistic productions. The resulting work anticipated or engaged with newly emerging fields of nineteenth-century science, discussions of human difference, and investigations of the Pacific Ocean. Kadu, who arrived home to the Marshall Islands before the voyage's end, was the first to "unpack" his discoveries and experiences for a rapt audience.[16] Kadu had traveled far in the ocean and had seen new places, and he had much to report to his peers and elders. For the other voyagers, it would take years and even decades to process, publish, and publicize the *Rurik*'s gathered intelligence, some of it truly remarkable. Scholars continue to study the expedition's material today.[17]

In tracing the voyage of the *Rurik*, this book offers a close-up view of natural history as practiced on a "floating laboratory" in the Pacific Ocean.[18] The ship's personnel acquired specimens, data, ethnographic impressions, and stories in many locales—the coastal Americas, the northernmost Pacific

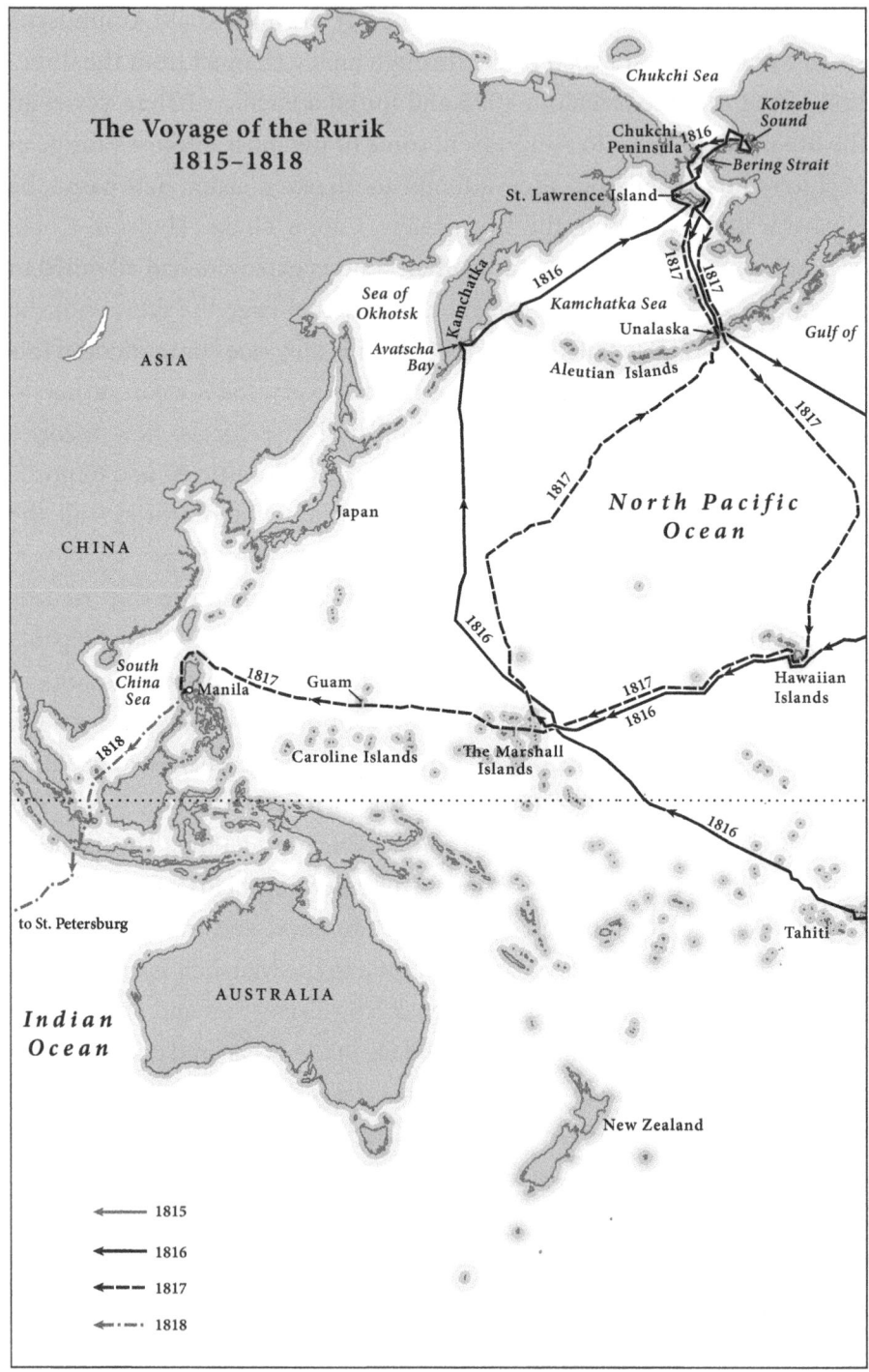

Figure I.2 Map of the Voyage of the *Rurik*. Cartography by Ben Pease of Pease Press.

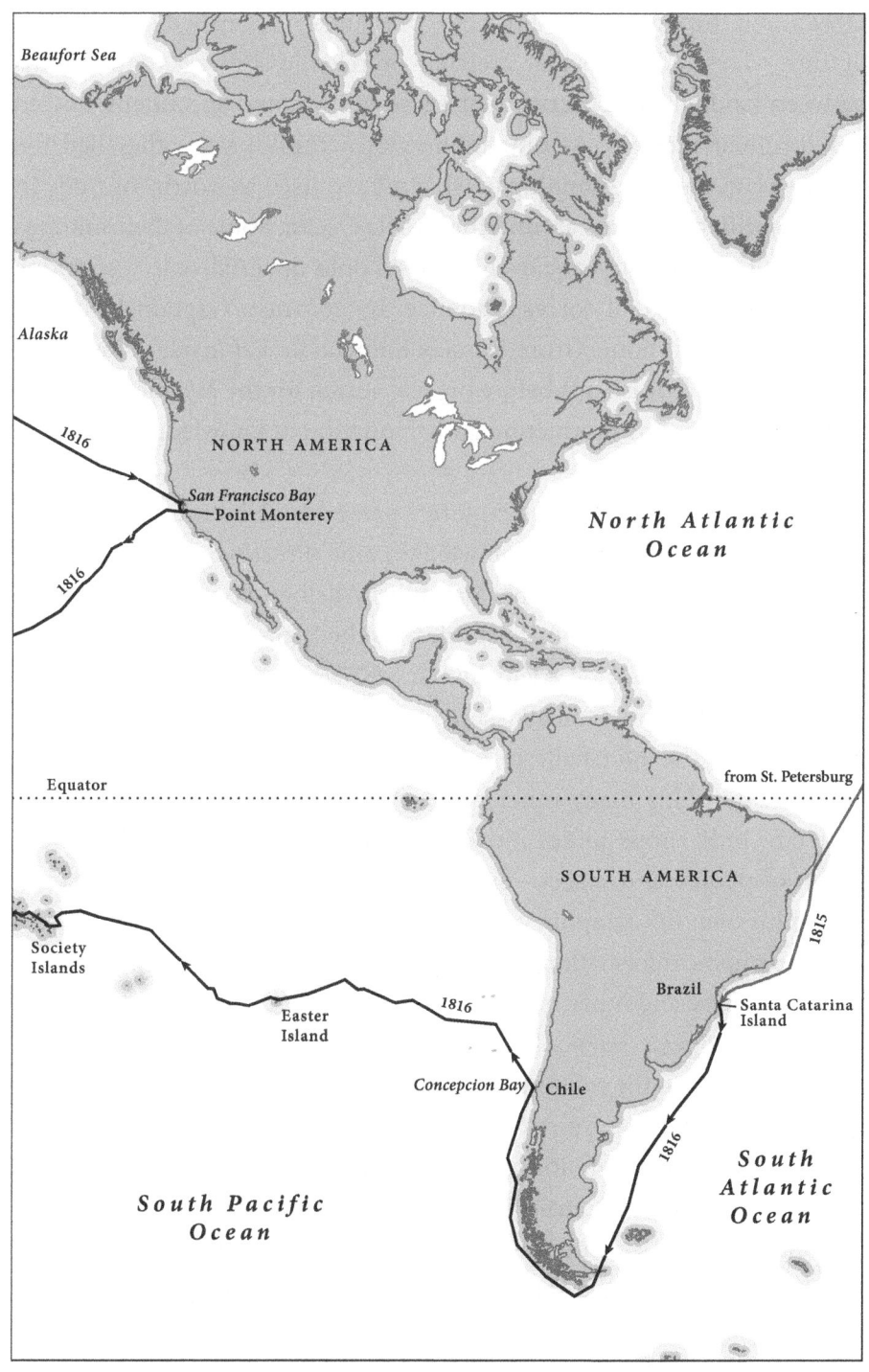

Beaufort Sea

Alaska

1816

NORTH AMERICA

San Francisco Bay
Point Monterey

1816

North Atlantic
Ocean

Equator

from St. Petersburg

SOUTH AMERICA

Society
Islands

Brazil

1816

Santa Catarina
Island

Easter
Island

1815

Concepcion Bay   Chile

1816

South Pacific
Ocean

1816

South
Atlantic
Ocean

Ocean, and throughout Oceania's "sea of islands."[19] They had long periods of time—days and nights that stretched on relentlessly, weeks and months between landfall—to observe their surroundings and specimens, and to develop their theories. As practitioners of natural history, they had the unique privilege of responding to what offered itself as worthy of study in radically different places around the Pacific Ocean. Some of their findings would not appear for years; even then, it could materialize in a scientific journal or a personal correspondence. By contrast, Captain Kotzebue immediately sent home (from Russia's Kamchatka Peninsula) a report of newly "discovered" islands before his real search for the Northern Passage had even begun. The production and circulation of knowledge transpired on different timelines.

What was true for previous explorers proved equally true for this expedition: much of the gathered knowledge came directly or indirectly from Indigenous people. For example, naturalist Adelbert von Chamisso's treatise on northern Pacific whale species resulted from the highly detailed information provided by Aleut hunters; Kotzebue's investigation of the political structure of Marshall islanders was based on the intelligence parceled out by the Marshallese; Johann Eschscholtz's *Zoologischer Atlas* (1826), among his many other publications, contained knowledge presented by Indigenous guides and elders; Ludwig Choris's visual documentation of people and places—circulated and published by authors even before his own lithographic volume appeared in print—contained layers of ethnographic information strongly influenced by the people he sought to depict. In these and other instances, the natural history conducted on the *Rurik* as "European" science bore the strong imprint of Indigenous experts. Similarly, some of the routes taken in this book were based on knowledge generously shared by present-day Indigenous authorities in the fields of navigation, sailing technology, and language.[20]

Beyond the primary purpose of searching for the Northern Passage, the expedition's financier, Count Nikolai Petrovich Rumiantsev, also designed the voyage to assess the status of Russian, Spanish, and other imperial powers in the Pacific.[21] He wanted to better understand the position of the

Russian empire after the Napoleonic Wars and what role (if any) remained for the Russian American Company in terms of commerce and colonization.[22] The *Rurik*'s personnel, none of whom were truly Russian except the sailors, responded to the request for an imperial assessment with pointed critiques of colonialism everywhere they visited. They had observed colonized Indigenous populations in Russian Alaska, Spanish California and Chile, and Portuguese Brazil. They also visited the Hawaiian Islands and came away with mixed reactions to the kingdom ruled by King Kamehameha I. The *Rurik*'s personnel wrote about all of these places, but in the end, they offered Count Rumiantsev very little to support a new strategic role for Russia in the Pacific. The Marshall Islands, by contrast, offered an example of an Indigenous archipelago almost entirely devoid of European influence. Kadu's knowledge presented a glimpse into this world, one he shared sparingly. His perspectives offered a critical rejoinder to colonialist assumptions of Indigenous subordination; his expressed worldview reflects what historian Bronwen Douglas calls a "countersign," or Indigenous presence, that appears in the voyagers' numerous reports.[23]

The *Rurik*'s journey represented a singular voyage of discovery conducted between 1815 and 1818, but its mission followed in the wake of countless transoceanic expeditions. Those voyages preceded the *Rurik* by more than three hundred years in the Atlantic Ocean, much longer in the Indian Ocean, and longer still in the Pacific Ocean as practiced by ancient seafarers. Pacific voyagers, according to recent scholars, had to contend with an extreme waterscape of uncertainties as well as Indigenous cultures they little understood.[24] In all these ventures, oceanic exploration offered voyagers a proving ground where the human imagination collided with known and unknown worlds, where survival, profit, and imperial ambitions intersected. Like previous voyages of discovery, the *Rurik*'s real value would be assessed upon its return, to St. Petersburg in 1818. At that point a new phase of the venture commenced. Unpacking the voyage required a concerted effort, one every bit as coordinated as the assembly of the expedition's personnel three years earlier.

ASSEMBLING THE PERSONNEL

The Financier. Count Nikolai Petrovich Rumiantsev maintained his wealth and ambitions for the Russian empire despite his humiliating demotion from Chancellor in 1814. His offense was hard to deny. Rumiantsev held strong sympathies for France at a time that Napoleon's army had invaded Russia and burned large parts of Moscow during its brief occupation. Resentment, even hatred, for the Count circulated among his government peers. Apart from his Francophile leanings, Rumiantsev had led a life of service to the empire, rising through the ranks from Russian Foreign Minister to President of the State Council, then Minister of Commerce to the position of Chancellor. As a young man he had studied at the University of Leiden and developed relationships with European scientists and philosophers. Rumiantsev was a polymath and avid collector of maps, coins, art, and books, with specific interests in natural history, philosophy, geography, and exploration. His wealth rivaled that of any Russian noble family, but unlike his peers, Rumiantsev invested a good portion of his fortune in science and discovery.[25] He partially financed Russia's first circumnavigation of the globe (1803–1806) under the command of Captain Adam von Krusenstern, whose voyage account was quickly translated into seven languages due to Rumiantsev's patronage. Ten years later and "no longer [holding] any influence in the Government," according to one visiting consul, Rumiantsev desired a new expedition "of the highest importance to science."[26] He and Krusenstern had discussed the expedition for years, and the end of European warfare offered a new opportunity to make discoveries.

Russian to his "courtly" core, Rumiantsev embraced an enlightened Europe and longed for a more prominent role for Russia in the world.[27] In his previous official capacities, he had urged Russian ministers—and even Czar Alexander himself—to claim its rightful place among European nations. Rumiantsev acted on many fronts to advance Russia's potential: he convinced the Emperor to send an ambassador to Japan in 1804; he rebuked the United States for initiating a "clandestine trade" with Russia's colonized populations in the North Pacific; and he urged the Russian

American Company (RAC) to support a broad mission of Pacific exploration rather than its singular pursuit of fur trade profits.[28] He viewed the
United States as a rising power in commerce and maritime affairs, and he
closely monitored political events in that country through his ambassador
in Washington, DC, Andrei Dashkov. Rumiantsev cheered the American
victory over the British in the War of 1812, if only because he held no affection for the English.[29] The Count knew of British naval plans for Arctic
exploration and its renewed search for the Northwest Passage, while
Russia's own Naval Ministry had neither the ambition nor the resources to
carry out a similar endeavor. Rumiantsev would launch the *Rurik* well
ahead of the British expedition, and he hoped to claim a major discovery
with his own name firmly attached to it.

For a Russian noble, Rumiantsev may have been among Europe's most
forward-thinking and globally oriented individuals. His varied interests
attracted intriguing offers from near and far. From the US Minister to
Russia, John Quincy Adams, he heard of a fascinating and novel inven-
tion, "a kind of launch or ship to navigate on rivers even against the wind
and currents by means of fire and steam." Would the Count recommend
the American inventor Robert Fulton and his "steam-boat" to the Emperor
for a patent in Russia? Yes he would, Rumiantsev replied, because he was
interested in all useful nautical inventions. From Kamchatka he received a
personal dispatch from Irish-born trader Peter Dobell, who offered commercial intelligence on Manila, Canton, Hawai'i, and Japan. Could they
discuss matters vital to "the interests of Russia" if Dobell survived his long
trek across Siberia to St. Petersburg?[30] The Count's reply does not exist, but
his promotion of Russian trade certainly made him welcome such a meeting.

And yet, what did his financing of the *Rurik* expedition represent, given
that the world's explorers had pursued a northern passage for more than
three hundred years? On a practical level, Rumiantsev desired to counter
British plans to pursue Arctic exploration, while he also wanted to assess
the strength of Spanish colonial holdings in places like Alta California.[31]
Shunned in the highest echelons of government, Rumiantsev could
demonstrate his personal power by gathering strategic intelligence. On a
deeper level—where philosophy, hope, and science intermingled—Count

Rumiantsev dreamed of announcing major discoveries in the "natural history in that icy land" of the North Pacific.[32] A discovery on that level would award him worldwide recognition.

The Promoter. Estonian-born Adam von Krusenstern first went to sea in his early teens, and he committed the rest of his life to maritime and scientific endeavors. His family title descended from Swedish aristocracy, but his parents possessed none of the wealth implied by the title. Instead, they struggled to sustain a respectable existence on a fledgling estate in Estonia, as Baltic Germans absorbed by the Russian empire in the eighteenth century.[33] Krusenstern sought advancement throughout his early life. He graduated from the Russian Naval Cadet Corps before he turned sixteen, served in the Russo-Swedish War (against his Swedish ancestors' side), and sailed on British naval and commercial ships in three different oceans during the 1790s. Krusenstern acquired modest wealth along the way, and more important, he amassed knowledge and experience in matters related to exploration, geography, hydrography, and commerce. Like every other aspiring explorer, Krusenstern zealously studied Captain James Cook's three voyages in the Pacific and even convinced the Russian Naval command to publish translations of Cook's journals.[34] Krusenstern's extensive experience in the world's oceans made him an obvious choice to command Russia's first circumnavigation (1803–1806) on the flagship *Nadezhda*, with Yuri Lisiansky commanding the *Neva*.

Successful circumnavigators—those who survived the voyage and had useful findings to report—moved in very exclusive European networks upon their return. Krusenstern excelled in this activity more than any of the numerous Baltic Germans under Russian employ. He published articles in learned journals, secured election to scientific academies in five countries, and corresponded with the editors, publishers, and promoters of scientific exploration. Krusenstern sent copies of his three-volume voyage journal to the Royal Society President Sir Joseph Banks in 1812, who made sure English translations quickly followed for use by the Admiralty.[35] Krusenstern also kept the British Admiralty abreast of "what the Russians are about" with Arctic exploration, because this was hardly privileged information, and in the end, Krusenstern would need British assistance to launch a new circumnavigation.[36] He viewed Pacific commerce as part and parcel of Russia's explorations in the great ocean; it was time, he wrote in 1813, "to rouse Russia from that state of slumber" in commercial matters that European nations had "endeavored to lull her."[37] Like Rumiantsev, Krusenstern wanted respect for Russia as a European empire, befitting the nation that had stopped Napoleon's army in its wintry tracks.

Krusenstern recognized the dismal state of the Russian Navy and its moribund shipbuilding industry. His own circumnavigation on the *Nadezhda* was conducted on a refitted British slave trade vessel. Russian ships were "literally rotting" in the main naval shipyard at Kronstadt, making his relationship with the prosperous Rumiantsev the only viable path for a new expedition.[38] As the main promoter of the *Rurik*'s voyage, Krusenstern also knew the expedition required a purposeful rationale, which he articulated in a forty-page introduction to Kotzebue's published account. "For three successive centuries," he explained, "the connection between the two oceans has been sought in vain" by the "greatest navigators of all nations." With the war's end, Count Rumiantsev would support the search for a passage "at his own expense" for the betterment of humankind and the "highest importance to science." Krusenstern proudly accepted the honor of working with the Count while offering hope that the expedition "may not be a vain enterprize."[39] He would continue to promote the expedition's findings well after its conclusion.

The Commander. Otto von Kotzebue lived much of his life in a paternal shadow he could not escape. His father, August Friedrich Ferdinand von Kotzebue, relished his personal fame as one of Europe's leading dramatists. He authored more than two hundred plays and was also prolific in family matters: August fathered eighteen children with three wives, each of whom were related to Adam von Krusenstern. Everyone in Europe knew of August von Kotzebue, while those people who had reason to mention his son Otto typically identified him in reference to the father. Krusenstern, for instance, explained his choice of Otto von Kotzebue to lead the *Rurik* expedition based on his naval experience and, of equal importance, his relation to "the celebrated writer."[40] Similarly, Sir Joseph Banks noted the *Rurik* voyage in the Pacific with a simple detail: "a Son of

Kotzebue had the Command of it."[41] It certainly mattered which "Son of Kotzebue" commanded the vessel, since there were so many, but the father's name served as the principal identifier in Banks's mind. Even the *Rurik*'s naturalist, Adelbert von Chamisso, received his commission on the voyage through a personal connection to the elder Kotzebue, a man Chamisso heralded as "the poet of the world."[42] Otto even had trouble leaving his famous father behind when the *Rurik* set sail from Europe: an oil painting of August hung in the Captain's great cabin for everyone to see and comment upon—which many did. Once Otto returned from the *Rurik* expedition, it was August von Kotzebue who garnered widespread public attention. A young German nationalist named Karl Ludwig Sand murdered the famous writer for political reasons. Otto watched the public beheading of Sand just days after he finished drafting his voyage account. The elder Kotzebue had offered to edit his son's manuscript, which Otto regretted not sending to him sooner.

Perhaps because he lived in the shadow of his father's fame, Otto von Kotzebue sought to achieve his own acclaim through naval service, leadership, and ultimately geographic discoveries. Like Krusenstern, Kotzebue was a Baltic German who hoped successful exploration would secure his place in the Russian empire. He began at the age of sixteen, serving as a cadet on Krusenstern's circumnavigation of the globe. He studied the arts of charting, sounding, and shoreline navigation during this voyage and gained additional training upon his return in 1806. Kotzebue read the published works of the great explorers while continuing his commission in the Russian Navy and awaiting the opportunity to command a voyage of his own.

Kotzebue was well prepared when Krusenstern offered him command of the *Rurik* in 1814. He had gathered an impressive library of books and charts, including the works of Pacific navigators and specialized texts about seldom-visited locales, such as the Penrhyn Islands.[43] With Krusenstern's assistance (and the Count's pocketbook), Kotzebue acquired British-made instruments and accessories, because the two men knew that making discoveries required the best modern instruments money could buy. They selected sextants, compasses, marine barometers, hygrometers, and aerometers designed by the "justly celebrated" English craftsman Edward Troughton; telescopes made by Charles Tully & Sons; two chronometers manufactured by Paul Philip Barraud; an "extensive collection" of maps by the London publisher Horsburgh, Arrowsmith, & Purdy; surgical instruments; a "life-boat" of British naval construction; and, among other supplies, "eatables of every kind." They procured assorted preserved meats in sealed "tin boxes" containing gravy "which penetrates the meat."[44] Kotzebue also grasped the importance of reporting his discoveries as quickly as possible, which he would do less than a year into the voyage via a communiqué sent to Rumiantsev from eastern Russia. Rumiantsev and Krusenstern made sure Kotzebue's earliest reports received publication in German and Russian journals.[45] Claiming a discovery hardly mattered unless it was published and distributed in learned circles.

The Naturalists. At least since the 1760s, voyages of discovery employed a category of traveler variously known as gentleman of science, natural philosopher, scientific, physician, botanist, natural historian, titular scholar, or, more commonly, "naturalist." Trained to some degree in natural sciences and the "collaborative enterprise" of Linnaean science, the individuals' interests ranged widely from humanistic philosophy to the emerging scientific disciplines of the early nineteenth century, such as botany or geology.[46] Krusenstern's first choice for the position, botanist Carl Friedrich Ledebour, withdrew for health reasons. Neither of the two naturalists who soon joined the expedition, Adelbert von Chamisso and Johann Eschscholtz, seemed especially well prepared for making scientific discoveries, while a third naturalist, the disagreeable Morten Wormskjold, began the voyage but quit when the *Rurik* reached Kamchatka. The boisterous Chamisso was best known as a poet and writer, although he had recently studied botany and linguistics at the University of Berlin. The more reticent Eschscholtz earned a practical degree in medicine even though he preferred the study of nature beyond the human body. Insects especially fascinated him. Neither man had previously stepped foot on a ship, much less sailed on the open ocean. These two naturalists developed a positive synergy: throughout the *Rurik* voyage and for the following decade, their individual interests in the human and natural worlds intersected in a generative fashion that neither could have anticipated.

Adelbert von Chamisso frequently made fun of his own ambiguous "national character." Employed by Count Rumiantsev to sail on a Russian-funded voyage, Chamisso self-identified as "the Russian who was only a German and as a German really only a born Frenchman, a *Champenois*."[47] Chamisso repeatedly distanced himself from anything having to do with the Russian empire, instead asserting a provincial French identity rooted in a nearly vanished noble ancestry. Chamisso's family fled their Champagne estate during the French Revolution, eventually settling in Berlin in 1796. His minor title and ongoing education allowed Chamisso certain opportunities: service as one of many pages to the Prussian Queen Friederike Louise, lessons at a French Gymnasium in Berlin, and officer training in the Prussian Army before he left to join the ranks of underemployed Berlin Romantic writers. He hitched his cart to wealthy patrons and key literary figures in both Germany and France while developing his craft as a poet, essayist, and editor of the literary journal *Musen-almanach* ("Muses' Almanac").[48] Finally, in 1812 Chamisso sought training in the natural sciences, where his Romantic sensibilities fused with a desire to "devote myself to the study of nature."[49] In 1814 his close friend Julius Eduard Hitzig learned of the need for a naturalist on board an upcoming Russian voyage to the Pacific. Hitzig happened to know August von Kotzebue, who forwarded Chamisso's recommendations to Krusenstern, who endorsed him to Rumiantsev. The under-trained naturalist received his commission to join the venture just weeks before it departed.

If unknown in European scientific circles, Chamisso had recently attracted widespread acclaim in the literary world with the publication of a fairy-tale novella that strangely prophesized his *Rurik* adventures. In *Peter Schlemihl's Remarkable Story* (published in 1814 as *Peter Schlemihls wundersame Geschichte*), Chamisso's protagonist sells his shadow to the devil in exchange for a "firmly stitched purse" capable of producing unlimited gold coins. Lacking a shadow, Schlemihl becomes a nonperson, nearly lost in the world until the devil offers to return his shadow for the price of his soul—an offer he rejects. Schlemihl rids himself of the magic purse and with his last few coins purchases an old pair of boots from a shop-boy who knowingly wishes him a "prosperous journey." The boots are magical, of course, and they allow Schlemihl the power to bound at the speed of light around the globe: over flaming volcanoes and snowy mountains, across the Bering Strait and over Southeast Asia as far as Borneo. Through his travels, Schlemihl arrives at the realization that studying nature holds the key to knowledge, happiness, and enlightenment. At the tale's end, the protagonist devotes himself to scientific inquiry and publishes a series of groundbreaking works on flora, fauna, and geography.[50] That Chamisso's escapist novella would culminate in a celebration of natural history is hardly surprising given his concurrent studies at the University of Berlin. But the fact that his fictional creation undertook a journey around the Pacific (including the Bering Strait and Oceania) in pursuit of natural history—before he had even learned of Kotzebue's planned voyage—was bizarrely prescient.

Chamisso boarded the *Rurik* a year later with no magical boots but boundless enthusiasm for natural investigation. Like the young Joseph Banks, who served as the naturalist on James Cook's first Pacific expedition, Chamisso anticipated a rare opportunity to observe nature in its varied forms and scales, from tiny zoophytes to massive marine mammals, to the volcanic mountains encircling the entire Pacific. Similar to Banks's experience with Cook, the study of Indigenous people would quickly consume Chamisso, because they embodied his Romantic ideal of the "natural man," a mixture of freedom and happiness within a traditional social hierarchy.[51] Whether investigating culture or botany, Chamisso desired to "wrest secrets" from nature. He was exhilarated by this activity, as he told his friend Julius Hitzig just months into the voyage: "I am breathing new experiences in through every pore at every moment."[52]

Less is known about the second naturalist, Johann Eschscholtz. The son of a struggling Estonian notary, Eschscholtz read zoology from an early age before taking the more secure career path of medicine at his parents' urging. He studied at the University of Dorpat under Karl Ledebour, who helped secure Eschscholtz's position on the *Rurik* as a surgeon, a role that frequently overlapped with naturalist on voyages of discovery. Ledebour remarked that Eschscholtz "is diligently studying drowning and leg fractures because Kotzebue wrote me that this often happens on ships."[53] Eschscholtz jumped at the opportunity to join the expedition. His only other job offer came from the small ironworks town of Zlatoust located in the Ural Mountains one thousand miles east of Moscow. Eschscholtz chose the uncertain fate of a Pacific voyage over the security of serving as doctor to the people of Zlatoust. He met Chamisso in July 1815, and for the next three years the two naturalists shared a berth the size of a small broom closet.

The Artist. Ludwig York Choris joined the *Rurik*'s personnel at the invitation of Count Rumiantsev, an active patron of St. Petersburg's Academy of Fine Arts, where Choris had studied during the previous year. Voyages of discovery required a visual record of people and places, flora and fauna, coastal views and geological wonders. More than a simple visual record, Rumiantsev desired a quality "portfolio" of the *Rurik*'s travels and discoveries, an artistic work worthy of presentation to European leaders.[54] Choris, though only twenty years old when he boarded the *Rurik*, did not disappoint his patron when he published *Voyage pittoresque autour du monde* (1822) and, four years later, *Vues et paysages des régions équinoxiales* (1826). The former volume is among the finest collections of travel lithographs and visual ethnography of the nineteenth century.

Like Johann Eschscholtz, Choris rose from humble origins due to his talent and supportive mentors. Born in the Ukrainian town of Yekaterinoslav in 1795 to ethnic German parents, Choris was the son of a lecturer at the University of Kharkov. Both parents died early in his childhood, at which point a university colleague named Dietrich Jacob Christian Matthes took in the young Ludwig.[55] He studied at a local gymnasium before moving to St. Petersburg with Matthes for further artistic training. Matthes arranged for Choris to accompany an expedition to the Caucuses in 1813 led by German botanist Friedrich Marschall von Bieberstein. For Choris, this rare opportunity to travel offered exposure to natural history and landscape illustration. Upon Choris's return to St. Petersburg, Matthes continued to assist the artist with his work and professional introductions. It would be years before the artist met the great explorer and naturalist Alexander von

Humboldt, who inspired his landscape renderings as well as his second (and ill-fated) expedition to South America. But Choris had already begun to imagine his career in Humboldtian terms, and he dedicated his second volume of lithographs to the explorer.

In their descriptions of the *Rurik*'s officers, gentlemen, and crew, both Kotzebue and Chamisso initially referred to Choris as simply "the painter."[56] Any painter on a voyage of discovery—especially one in search of the fabled Northern Passage—had some impressive artistic forebears to contend with, not the least of whom were the British painters John Webber and William Hodges. Veterans of Cook's second and third expeditions, respectively, Webber and Hodges each had extensive training (Webber in Paris and Bern, Hodges in London), notable reputations, and years if not decades of experience prior to their Pacific voyages.[57] By contrast, the twenty-year-old Choris seemed more like an apprentice than a professional artist ready for the task of visually rendering the grand vistas and diverse populations of the Pacific. But enlisting a renowned artist for a dangerous three-year expedition proved untenable—and Choris was eager to go. With Krusenstern's endorsement, Kotzebue welcomed him to the captain's table, and the two naturalists quickly formed a collaborative relationship with the man who Chamisso affectionately called "Login Andrevich Choris."[58]

The Indigenous Navigator. More than a year into the voyage, an enthusiastic traveler and expert navigator named Kadu joined the expedition. The setting was the island atoll of Aur, part of the Ratak chain of the Marshall Islands, located more than two thousand miles southwest of the Hawaiian Islands. Kadu immediately became a focal point of interest and investigation for the naturalists, artist, captain, and crew. He knew a great deal about oceanic travel, and he piloted the *Rurik* through the dangerous shoals of the Marshall Islands. Chamisso, for his part, developed an intimate attachment to Kadu, a man he viewed through his intellectual prism of Romantic naturalism. At times Chamisso and his companions took Kadu quite seriously in terms of the knowledge he had to offer, but they also seemed to regard Kadu as a human palimpsest—a living embodiment of natural histories and stories they could refashion and employ for their

Figure I.3 *Kadou, habitant des îles Carolines.* Kadu joined the *Rurik* expedition in February 1817, and traveled on the ship for the next year. During this time he visited the Aleutian and Hawaiian Islands, and he also witnessed the solid ice pack preventing the ship's advance north of the Bering Strait. A skilled navigator, Kadu was the first Caroline or Marshall islander to explore a large portion of the Pacific Ocean and return home. Choris's lithograph shows Kadu's tattoos, shell necklace, elongated earlobes, and hair bun in a traditional Marshallese style. By contrast, the reproduction of this portrait by engraver John Heaviside Clark (Fig. 2.1) and published in Kotzebue's voyage narrative presents Kadu in European clothing, which he frequently wore while on the *Rurik*. Courtesy Internet Archive.

own texts and discoveries. Kadu left no textual record, because he did not write, which challenges researchers with what historian Tiya Miles terms "the conundrum of the archives."[59] However, his stories and perspectives were extensively recorded by the *Rurik*'s personnel.[60] Everyone on the voyage wrote about Kadu, allowing his voice and expertise to emanate in a refracted way into the historical record. His physical features became well known by virtue of its appearance in many publications following the voyage.

The known facts of Kadu's life appear in the writings of Kotzebue, Chamisso, Eschscholtz, and Choris. He hailed from the coral atoll of Woleai in the Caroline Islands, and by an early age he had participated in trading voyages on outrigger canoes to numerous islands, including Guam, more than one thousand miles to the northwest. The last of these voyages went awry during a storm, casting Kadu and three companions adrift for months in what a Yapese chant calls the "ocean of uncertainties."[61] They survived on collected water and fish, but without a sail they could hardly navigate their outrigger canoe. Eventually they washed up on Aur in the Ratak chain of the Marshall Islands. The people of Aur initially viewed Kadu with suspicion—or so writes Chamisso—but an *iroij* (chief) named Tigidien saw value in the young beachcomber because he knew of distant islands, possessed foreign navigational skills, and told stories about Europeans even though he had never met one.[62] He even spoke a few words of Spanish by virtue of his previous voyage to Guam. In the isolated and politically divided realm of the Marshall Islands, Kadu represented a world traveler with knowledge to share. The *iroij* Tigidien allowed Kadu to stay, and there he found a partner and became a father. In 1817—three or four years after he arrived in the Marshalls—the *Rurik* appeared and Kadu seized the opportunity for a new voyage.

How anomalous was Kadu's voluntary enlistment with this European voyage of discovery? On the one hand, Indigenous islanders assumed a variety of roles on most European exploratory voyages as pilots, cartographers, interpreters, navigators, sexual consorts, and many other positions—often, and perhaps most frequently, against their will.[63] Captains sometimes abducted Indigenous people from shore for a specific reason, at which point their fate became anything but certain once they fulfilled a proscribed task. Some individuals willingly joined these voyages as guides or emissaries, the most famous being the Ra'iatean navigator and *arioi* (priest) named Tupaia, who provided Cook with indispensable geographic knowledge and translation skills in Oceania. Lesser-known Indigenous participants on European voyages included "Joseph Freewill" from a small Indonesian island, Comekala from King George's Sound, a Māori named Te Pahi, and the Hawaiian man Kualelo—all of whom signed on to Pacific expeditions. Kadu brought useful skills similar to these individuals, but his own motivation seemed strategic and personal: to gain the experience, status, and knowledge of exploration on a European vessel. He would put this experience to use upon his return to the Marshall Islands.

The Crew and Vessel. In addition to these key members of the ship's personnel, the *Rurik* carried a small crew and only two officers under Captain Kotzebue. The eclectic bunch included the following: Gleb Shishmarev, who served as Kotzebue's First Lieutenant and would be granted his own polar expedition in 1820; the irritable Ivan Sakharin and naturalist Morten Wormskjold, both of whom left the *Rurik* when it reached Kamchatka; the humorous First Mate Petrov, who traveled with a monkey named Elliot; a blacksmith named Ziganzoff, who died in Chile from consumption (and possibly spread the lung infection to others); a sailor named Shafekha, who deserted the ship in Chile, which led the crew to honor a pet pig with the name Shafekha; and assorted sailors from the Russian naval service. Together, and with only minor acrimony, these expedition members coexisted on a 180-ton, one-hundred-foot-long sailing vessel for three years at sea.

Krusenstern faced limited options in choosing a vessel. As he explained, Count Rumiantsev "could not expend" a "considerable sum on such an enterprize," because he "already dedicates the greater part of his revenues to the most expensive scientific and many patriotic undertakings." A voyage of discovery—even one executed on the cheap—could be scaled to size. Rumiantsev and Krusenstern planned a light ship for a small crew with the rationale of easy maneuverability in the icy North Pacific and the shallow shorelines of Oceania. A ship constructed of oak meant additional cost due to the Russian Navy's exclusive claim to the timber, so Krusenstern contracted with Finnish builder Erik Malm in Abo, who fashioned the ship with Finnish fir even though, as Krusenstern admitted, "it seemed a hazardous experiment" to use a soft wood for a three-year circumnavigation.[64] The two-masted *Rurik* cost thirty thousand rubles, far less than any previous exploratory vessel, and Krusenstern equipped it with eight mounted guns for defensive purposes. With a cannon salute and the Russian flag flying above, this modest vessel began its voyage on July 23, 1815. Captain Kotzebue noted the day in his journal: "I bid adieu to my native land for many years, and perhaps for ever."[65]

The narrative that follows resists straightforward chronology for a few reasons. Most important, certain people (such as Kadu) and themes (colonialism, visual representation, and the study of species) require specific and sustained attention, and therefore the middle chapters focus on these subjects in a temporal manner that occasionally overlaps. Chapter One examines the first year of the expedition from its European departure to the initial reconnaissance of the Bering and Chukchi Seas, including the Indigenous groups and landscapes. The second chapter moves six months ahead in the voyage to the Marshall Islands, where Kadu encounters the *Rurik*, and the expedition's personnel assess the Ratak islanders. With Kadu as the central focus, this chapter moves geographically from the Marshall Islands to the ice-bound North Pacific, where the *Rurik* made a second attempt to locate the Northern Passage. The third chapter investigates colonialism in three distinct places visited during the voyage: Russian Alaska, Spanish Alta California, and the Hawaiian Islands. European voyagers had authored reports about these sites for at least four decades, but no one had produced a visual record of the Indigenous people and their material culture on the scale or quality of Ludwig Choris's work. Chapter Four examines the study of species as central to the practice of natural history. The naturalists Chamisso and Eschscholtz gathered extensive knowledge about species in different environments, and Kadu also shared in the quest for insights about the natural world. The fifth chapter addresses the "afterlife" of the expedition for each of the main participants, a process that began with Kadu's return to the Marshall Islands and continued with the European personnel producing written accounts, announcing discoveries, and visually rendering the entire voyage. This book concludes with a consideration of failures and discoveries in oceanic exploration, as well as the ongoing pursuit of natural history.

In the long history of scientific exploration, few voyagers produced as much natural history as did those aboard the *Rurik*. Its eighteenth-century expedition predecessors, who sailed from England, France, and Spain among other countries, claimed an assortment of geographic and ethnographic discoveries that remapped and peopled the Pacific Ocean in astonishing ways. Nineteenth-century voyagers shared these ambitions for monumental findings, yet they also served the particular interests of a new and more specialized science that progressively compartmentalized the natural world and categorized its human element by race. The *Rurik* expedition embarked on the cusp between these two eras of discovery. Apart from the captain's objective to locate a Northern Passage, the *Rurik* expedition was an immersive journey in the possibilities of an enduring natural history. Its scientific, artistic, and narrative results represented a natural history of wonder, Indigenous knowledge, and holistic thought.

All Species of Knowledge: A Voyage of Discovery, Failure, and Natural History in the Pacific Ocean. David Igler, Oxford University Press. © Oxford University Press 2026. DOI: 10.1093/9780197777718.003.0001

Claiming Discoveries from St. Petersburg to the Bering Sea

On September 7, 1815, the *Rurik* cast anchor in a calm stretch of England's Plymouth Sound called the Cattewater. During the next week, Captain Kotzebue busied himself with the tasks of securing local provisions and synchronizing the ship's chronometers. While on shore, Kotzebue enjoyed a lengthy visit with George Whidbey, one of Plymouth's most distinguished residents and a good friend of Adam von Krusenstern. Whidbey had sailed as First Mate on George Vancouver's 1792 circumnavigation, and for his able service Vancouver had given Whidbey's name to Puget Sound's largest island. He possessed a clear memory of their reconnaissance of the North American coastline, including the fact that George Vancouver had failed to discover a Northwest Passage in the latitudes above Puget Sound. Kotzebue planned to search well north of Vancouver's area of exploration, and he therefore characterized the meeting with Whidbey as "agreeable and instructive." If nothing else, he felt uplifted by meeting one more officer who survived the ordeal of a three-year voyage around the world.[1]

The ship's small scientific and artistic corps spent their time in Plymouth purchasing supplies and searching the tidewaters for interesting species. Ludwig Choris acquired more sketchbooks, while Adelbert von Chamisso obtained a few volumes in natural history. His most notable acquisitions included works by German scientists Peter Simon Pallas and Johann Georg Gmelin. Both volumes would assist Chamisso and Johann Eschscholtz with a significant scientific discovery in the early part of the voyage.[2] Chamisso, whose passion for the arts rivaled his interests in science, also attended Plymouth's local theater. He watched acclaimed Irish actress Eliza O'Neill perform in two different stage productions. Her performance in *Romeo and Juliet* disappointed him, but Chamisso praised her lead role in *Menschenhass und Reue* (*The Stranger*), a famous German tragedy written by the celebrated playwright August von Kotzebue. If Captain Kotzebue attended this showing of his father's play, he failed to mention it. More than likely, he desired to sail away from the public acclaim lavished on his father. The elder Kotzebue possessed widespread celebrity in England, where his publications received more English translations than those of all other German authors combined.[3]

Departing from Plymouth in early October, the officers and crew of the *Rurik* bade farewell to a continent still reeling from the Napoleonic Wars. The wars had left many millions dead, wounded, and disabled—the horrendous outcome of combat, disease, starvation, and mass atrocities. From Portugal in the west to Russia in the east, from Sweden south to Egypt, the warfare shattered European norms and nations as it produced new alliances and formulations of state power. The man at the center of the decades-long war, Napoleon Bonaparte, capitulated to Britain following his armies' defeat in the Battle of Waterloo in June 1815. Napoleon formally surrendered on board the *HMS Bellerophon*, which held him during the summer of 1815 in Plymouth Sound before his transportation to the island of St. Helena. Chamisso expressed mild disappointment for missing Napoleon in Plymouth by a matter of weeks. The "man of destiny," he wrote, "who had once subjected and ruled the world," was known to walk the *Bellerophon*'s decks in the late afternoon. Plymouth sightseers in small boats tried to catch a glimpse of him. A "multitude" of voyeurs, Chamisso claimed, were "intoxicated with the sight of [Napoleon]," an oddly positive view for the naturalist given his family's exile from revolutionary France and his brief service in the Prussian Army.[4] But Chamisso descended from a minor French noble family, and he possessed an ingrained regard for authority and traditional social hierarchies. He may have viewed Napoleon as the embodiment of a once-strong French empire.

During the next ten months, the *Rurik* sailed south through the Atlantic Ocean, rounded Cape Horn, and tracked northwest across the entire Pacific Ocean. The expedition would cross the Bering Strait in late July 1816, with the goal of reconnaissance and preparation for a second season of targeted Arctic exploration in the summer of 1817. A spirit of discovery animated the officers and crew during this initial stage of their voyage. But what did "discovery" actually mean for them? For Kotzebue, the only member of the *Rurik* to have previously circumnavigated the globe, discovery meant the ambitious goal announced by Count Rumiantsev and Adam von Krusenstern: locating the "North-east" Passage. And yet even Kotzebue understood that claiming other discoveries—one might say lesser findings—could justify his expedition if he failed to find the passage. The captain accommodated himself to this possibility even before the *Rurik* crossed the Bering Strait.

The idea of discovery held other meanings for the naturalists and the artist. Like previous scientific travelers, they had little sense of what they might encounter, find worthy of study, and eventually claim as a discovery. Even those naturalists who carried highly detailed "instructions" from their sponsors rarely viewed the orders as much beyond a general roadmap.[5] These were curious intellectuals who, in large part, understood their purpose as the study of nature and humanity as a whole. Naturalists in this era certainly recognized distinct scientific fields pertaining to categories of plants, animals, rocks, hydrography, geography, and human types, and yet most of them in the early 1800s appreciated the porous borders of knowledge encompassed by the term *natural history*. They asked questions. They failed with most of their answers, at least according to later generations of scientists who devised different answers. For Chamisso, Eschscholtz, and Choris, the expedition offered an opportunity to develop their talents within natural history, artistic representation, and the exploration of knowledge. They would spend the next three years on their individual journeys of daily observation and investigation. But they also worked collaboratively, and beyond that, they gained much of their knowledge from interactions with Indigenous people, who possessed their own understandings of the natural and spiritual worlds.

ENCOUNTERING SALPS AND SLAVERY

While the real work of any Pacific expedition waited until the vessel crossed into the Great Ocean, the initial months at sea in the Atlantic offered learning opportunities for all personnel. The *Rurik*'s captain and crew acquired experience with the new ship in the open ocean, and the naturalists had to learn how to function as scientists in the exceedingly tight quarters of a pitching ship. Given the *Rurik*'s small size, Chamisso and Eschscholtz created a makeshift laboratory on the long table also used for daily meals. Dissecting and preserving specimens proved especially challenging in this cramped setting, as described by one midshipman who sailed years later on a Pacific voyage.

> The *Scientifics* cut up & dissect and overhaul, and use a magnifying power the better to see, and make drawings & paintings, and search their books, and write down learned descriptions and invent unpronounceable terms.... And they have dead & living lizards, and fish floating in alcohol, and shark jaws & stuffed turtles.... [S]uch sweet looking objects as doubtless scientific eyes to behold. Catch any of them in my *room*—no, no!—I'll *visit*, when I have curiosity in that way.[6]

Apart from this midshipman's aversion to the sights and smells of marine species in various stages of dissection and decay, he accurately perceived an essential aspect of the "Scientifics'" labor: it entailed group work. Fortunately, Chamisso, Eschscholtz, and Choris immediately established a strong collaborative relationship. According to Chamisso, "[we] studied, observed, and collected together...in complete harmony, we never distinguished between mine and thine." Meanwhile, the third naturalist, Danish botanist Morten Wormskjold, struck everyone as abrasive and condescending. He considered Chamisso a mere "natural philosopher" rather than a trained scientist.[7]

The *Rurik* first made landfall at the Canary Island of Tenerife en route to the southern coast of Brazil. The naturalists took a three-day "excursion" across this subtropical island and collected dozens of plants and insects while also offering observations of the people: "very inquisitive," Chamisso decided, but "extremely poor and ugly." He rarely minced his words or prejudices. They gazed at the snowy peak of Mount Teide, one of the world's tallest island volcanoes, and they made mental comparisons to the European mountains they knew. They attempted to imagine the towering glacial peaks they would soon observe in the North Pacific.[8] Choris described Mount Teide as "majestic" up close and easily visible from eighty miles distant at sea.[9] Chamisso consulted the publications of naturalists who had previously visited the volcanic island, including Alexander von Humboldt and Leopold von Buch. In particular, Humboldt's *Travels* (1805) provided Chamisso with the idea of volcanoes as earth-forming and dynamic mountains—a theory he would later use to delineate the Pacific Basin in its entirety. They all read Humboldt as a guide to understanding the natural world, and some of their future work was clearly inspired by the famous German naturalist, including Chamisso's extended essay "A View of the Great Ocean."[10]

By the time the *Rurik* left Tenerife for Brazil on November 1, 1815, the naturalists and artist had established a work rhythm in the ship's tight quarters. They shared an appreciation for the investigative process itself, an appreciation that came to define their individual studies as well as their group work. Even minor undertakings became animated collective endeavors: "On the 14th of November," Eschscholtz wrote, "after we had passed the Cape Verd[e] islands, we caught three sharks (*Squalus glaucus, L.*)." They all took part in the dissection, if only for the novelty of dismembering a large fish for the first time in their lives. They collected all manner of strange creatures pulled from the sea using a jerry-rigged "net of canvas on a pole" to assist their harvest.[11] Somewhere in the vicinity of Tenerife they caught and dissected a colorful Portuguese man-of-war (*Physalia physalis*), which Choris sketched and painted from different perspectives.[12] Years later Choris titled his completed lithograph of the creature *Vers marins* (sea worm), and his caption confirmed the collaborative process of their dissection.

In mid-October Chamisso and Eschscholtz pulled from the sea a different and exceedingly strange creature. Though neither naturalist knew it at

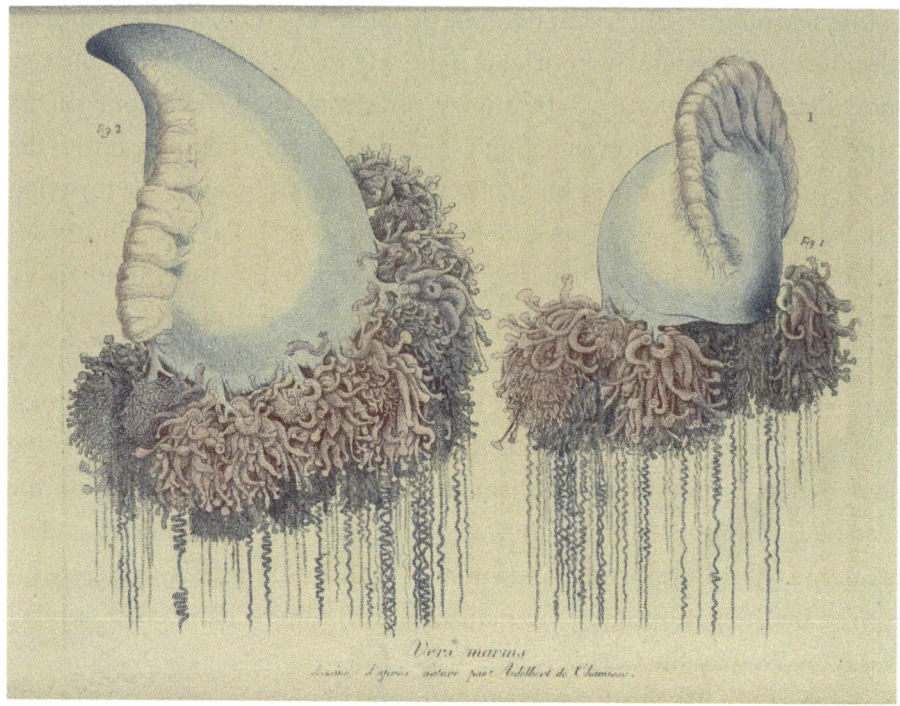

Figure 1.1 *Vers marins, dessiné d'après nature par Adelbert de Chamisso.* Choris's caption credits Chamisso for the initial sketches of this Portuguese man-of-war: "drawn from nature by Adelbert von Chamisso." The artist occasionally noted such collaboration in his captions, indicating that Chamisso, Eschscholtz, and Choris studied, classified, and rendered objects in a group setting that benefited from their individual skills. Eschscholtz, for instance, understood taxonomy better than the others, and he would classify hundreds of new species during his career. The subject matter of *Vers marins* suggests a metaphor for the naturalists' collaborative process. The Portuguese man-of-war, like other species in the *Siphonophorae* order, is a "colony" organism composed of four different animals (zooids): the dangerous tentacles, the reproductive organ, the digestive tract, and the gas-filled float. The colony's survival depends on the health of the individual parts. The Portuguese man-of-war drifts and shifts along the ocean's surface according to the wind and current, not unlike a sailing vessel with its colony of mechanical and human components, such as the naturalists themselves. Courtesy Internet Archive.

the time, this specimen would provide their most novel theory about the malleability of species. "On the 16th of October," Eschscholtz wrote, "we saw for the first time two kinds of *Salpæ*." The creature's long and translucent body propelled itself by ingesting and releasing water, and it possessed an oddly indeterminate shape. Chamisso had no idea at this point of its scientific meaning, but he nonetheless described the mysterious specimen in a letter to his Berlin companion, Julius Hitzig, once the *Rurik* reached Brazil. He wrote that, on a calm sea, the "sun coaxes [these] lowly animals of the sea to the surface of the water, and [we] can easily gain possession of these most fascinating enigmas of nature."[13] Like many naturalists, Chamisso loved enigmas.

The two naturalists could have simply described the strange sea worm and moved on with their other studies. Instead, they preserved it in a saltwater tank for observation and began looking for additional salp specimens. The salp puzzled the naturalists, because their observation revealed something undoubtedly bizarre: it seemed to manifest itself in two very distinct physical appearances.[14] In its most conspicuous form, the long snake-like creature drifted under the ocean's surface like a translucent and slithering jellyfish, "chained together almost like polyps." And yet upon further investigation—which required multiple salp samples harvested from various places in the Pacific—Chamisso and Eschscholtz discovered that this long organism was assembled from dozens of individual and interconnected salps. Furthermore, the salps were truly peculiar, because the two distinct physical forms appeared to alternate with each generation. In one generation, it appeared as an extended body of component parts, while its next manifestation resembled individual small jellies. How could this be? Later scientists would call the process "metagenesis," but Chamisso described it this way: "It is as if the caterpillar bore the butterfly and the butterfly then in turn bored the caterpillar."[15]

Chamisso and Eschscholtz pondered their enigma throughout the expedition. Like other naturalists on long voyages—such as Charles Darwin aboard the *Beagle* or geologist James Dwight Dana on the USS *Vincennes*—the *Rurik*'s scientists had ample time to collect, observe, and form hypotheses. Perhaps as much as anything else, they had extended periods to simply ponder the enigmas of nature. Chamisso, who was more intrigued than Eschscholtz by the salp question, pored over their limited libraries for information on the jelly-like creatures. Months later and quite fortuitously, at the Russian outpost on Kamchatka, he found a copy of Louis Augustin Guillaume Bosc's 1802 study *Histoire naturelle des vers* ("Natural

History of Worms"), which helped him to further identify the organism.[16] Chamisso had kept some salps alive in a small seawater tank, and he observed the metagenesis cycle until they died, at which point he preserved the animals in alcohol. According to scholars Matthias Glaubrecht and Wolfgang Dohle, without "continuous observations it would have been impossible to describe the whole life cycle of salps as [Chamisso] did."[17] By the end of the voyage Chamisso had nearly completed his findings for publication.

The salp research lay in the future as the *Rurik* sailed south from Tenerife to the coast of Brazil in the early winter of 1815. The daily regimen of shipboard life remained a novelty for everyone, and moments of levity prevailed when high seas did not violently toss the small ship. In a lighthearted parody of their desire for new discoveries, Chamisso announced a novel finding as the *Rurik* sailed southwest. "I *discovered*," he exclaimed, "that in the 'Bride of Corinth,' one of Goethe's most perfect poems, one of the jewels of German and European literature, the fourth stanza has one foot too many!" Chamisso reported his literary detection in a letter to a German publisher, though he no doubt also announced it to his table companions. They may have been amused—or not—based on their appreciation of German literature as well as their tolerance for Chamisso's peculiar sense of humor. Either way, Chamisso found it "amusing" that "a native-born Frenchman had to travel around the world to announce [this discovery] to the Germans."[18]

On November 23 the *Rurik* "crossed the line" of the equator into the southern hemisphere, which represented a significant rite of passage for all sailors. For this occasion, Captain Kotzebue allowed a day of celebration highlighted by the staging of a play called *The Peasant's Wedding*, written by the captain's mate, Petrov. The sailor-actors "performed with suitable irony," grumbled the acclaimed writer Chamisso, who followed little of the dialogue due to his inability to understand the Russian language. The day's festivities climaxed with a "solemn" ritual performed by "Neptune," Kotzebue reported, who "baptized everyone who had not crossed the line before, and I was the only one that had not to undergo that ceremony."

Kotzebue marked the festivities by ordering the cook to open a tub of "sour-krout" for all to enjoy.[19]

Arriving on the southern coast of Brazil in mid-November, the *Rurik's* personnel looked forward to weeks of collecting specimens in a South American jungle while Captain Kotzebue replenished supplies for the coming months at sea. These were privileged European travelers who accepted as a right their freedom to roam the land, the independence to speak their minds, and the liberty to conduct their work. However, on Brazil's southern coast they encountered the institution of chattel slavery for the first time in their lives. In fact, they found themselves at the epicenter of the world's largest and most inhumane commerce: the trans-Atlantic slave trade.[20] The *Rurik* made landfall at Santa Catarina, immediately south of Rio de Janeiro. During the previous three centuries slavers had taken more than ten million enslaved Africans across the Atlantic Ocean, with over four million of those captives destined for Brazil. In the year of the *Rurik's* arrival, more than two hundred ships carrying human cargo crossed the Atlantic, and over half of those vessels were destined for ports on the coast of Brazil. Most of the vessels landed at Rio and its southern satellite ports, including Santa Catalina. On this coastline of "ravishing beauty," where Chamisso, Eschscholtz, and Choris desired to wander without constraints, they witnessed a human condition entirely devoid of the freedoms they possessed.[21]

While the men saw the institution of slavery all around them, the staggering dimensions of this maritime trade seemed well beyond their reckoning. The cargo of each slave ship contained an average of 357 survivors of the Middle Passage, while 10 percent of the captives purchased on the coast of Africa did not survive the trans-Atlantic voyage.[22] The geography of this maritime traffic had recently shifted. Southern Brazil was the center point of slave trade shipping: the largest share of slave ships in 1815 no longer originated from European ports but instead from Rio de Janeiro itself. The Portuguese owners of the ships focused their attention on specific slave markets in West Central Africa. Between 1808 and 1856, more than 90 percent of the captives destined for Brazil (some 933,000 individuals) were purchased in the West Central Africa markets of Luanda, Cabinda, and Benguela, with additional captives acquired in the southeastern African region around Mozambique. Some countries had legally abolished direct participation in the trans-Atlantic slave trade during the previous three decades, but the slave traders of Rio de Janeiro had expanded their operations prior to national independence in 1822 (Brazil would not abolish slavery until 1888). The *Rurik* had arrived at not just a South American slave port, but also at the most active site in the transoceanic commerce of human beings.

While they considered themselves enlightened and inquisitive individuals, the *Rurik*'s personnel made only cursory observations of slavery, often in relation to the landscape itself. Kotzebue noted the "inhuman treatment" of the enslaved Africans, while Chamisso remarked on the "unsubdued" natural "paradise" in which Brazil's slavery prospered.[23] Eschscholtz reported that they collected 237 types of plants during the stopover at Santa Catarina, but he expressed frustration that "we could only ascend [the hillsides] as far as the slaves had opened a way with the axe."[24] The wild landscape, he intimated, was made accessible only by the labor of enslaved Africans. Slave labor also sculpted the landscape of the valuable rice plantations, according to Kotzebue, but to achieve profits "[slaves] are driven to their work with a whip." Chamisso came the closest to explaining the horrendous racial violence that drove the region's plantation economy. He queried a local planter about the cost of enslaved workers. The planter responded that a "prime" enslaved male valued at "two to three hundred piasters" could labor for some years until death, at which point the enslaved individual would be replaced "by a new purchase." From this information Chamisso grasped the fact that plantation production required a continuous supply of new captives. Each year at Santa Catalina, Chamisso concluded, "five to seven ships full of negroes [are required] to supply the place of those who die on the plantations."[25] He may have seen the arrival of two Rio-owned slave ships, the *Serpente* and the *Diligente*, at Santa Catalina during the *Rurik*'s stay. These two ships each carried over four hundred captives, and yet they represented only a small sample of the trade in 1815, which entailed thirty-seven vessels arriving in southeast Brazil with over ten thousand human beings in their cargo holds.[26]

Captain Kotzebue was the only person on board to have previously visited a slave port. He had spent the month of January 1804 in this locale as a member of the Krusenstern circumnavigation. Kotzebue left no record of his previous visit to Brazil, and Krusenstern's published voyage account offered only one passing reference to the enslaved population of Santa Catarina.[27] Alexander von Humboldt's writing could have enlightened the *Rurik*'s naturalists on the institution's hideous nature. "Slavery," Humboldt wrote in *Personal Narrative of Travels*, "is no doubt the greatest evil that afflicts human nature."[28] A vocal abolitionist, Humboldt's views might have encouraged a humanist like Chamisso to study slavery in greater detail and describe its inhumanity from personal observation. Instead, he and his fellow naturalist Eschscholtz remained uncharacteristically reserved about the conditions they witnessed.

CLAIMING DISCOVERIES IN THE GREAT OCEAN

During the next seven months the *Rurik* traveled the entire length of the Pacific Ocean, from Tierra del Fuego to the Bering Strait, almost fifteen thousand nautical miles of shifting winds and currents, random dangers, and layovers at small islands. The ship followed in the wake of previous European voyagers going back in time to the sixteenth century, and Kotzebue frequently consulted his library of explorers' journals and charts for useful intelligence.[29] Kotzebue feared any delay, he explained after a brief stop at Rapa Nui (Easter Island): "I was obliged to take the shortest course to Kamtschatka, in order to reach Beering's Straits" during the warm summer months.[30] But his desire to stay on schedule could not interfere with the possibility of claiming new geographic discoveries, however minor or dubious those discoveries might be.

Kotzebue declared numerous island discoveries during the next five weeks. He recorded all the pertinent circumstances in his journal: the first sighting of land, the island's coordinates, the existence (or not) of inhabitants, and the name he bestowed on the place. When he published these findings, Kotzebue offered a rationale for each claimed discovery and why he was the rightful discoverer. Adam von Krusenstern would lend support for those claims in his essay "Analysis of the Islands Discovered by the Rurick."[31] Given Kotzebue's failure to achieve the voyage's ultimate objective (the Northern Passage), his stake in these island discoveries carried a heavy burden.

As the *Rurik* approached the chain of Polynesian islands now known as the Tuamotu Archipelago, Kotzebue stationed a sailor at the masthead "to whom I promised a reward for every new discovery." He eagerly awaited "the cry of Land!," at which point, "I was thinking already what name I was to give my island." On April 16 he marked a first discovery and, with some hesitance, named it "Doubtful Island," because Dutch explorer Willem Schouten had described an island at that latitude exactly two hundred years earlier. Kotzebue doubted it was the same spit of land Schouten had named "Dog Island," nor could Kotzebue step foot on his claim, because he could not locate a safe landing place. But he felt confident enough to consider the island a new discovery. Three days later a crewmember spotted a larger island, and Kotzebue "was quite certain that I could with justice call it a new discovery."[32] This time he desired a ceremony to claim the island, which again had no safe landing spot due to heavy surf and a surrounding coral reef. Two sailors successfully reached shore, soon followed by the Captain and naturalists who desperately clung to a small raft secured to a boat with ropes.[33] They discovered uninhabited huts and fishing tools, and Kotzebue concluded that some group of people must use the island seasonally. He opened a bottle of wine for a joyful ceremony of possession, and they drank to the health of Count Rumiantsev, naming the island in his honor (Romanzoff Island, known today as Tikei). At nightfall the landing party returned to the *Rurik*, and Kotzebue recorded the precise coordinates of his discovery. He awarded the sailor who first spotted the land six piaster coins.

The discovery of new islands continued in the coming days. First came a small and seemingly uninhabited place that Kotzebue named "Spiridoff"

(Takapoto), after his former naval commander, Admiral Grigory Spiridov. The next day, while sighting the Palliser Island chain discovered by James Cook in 1774, Kotzebue saw "a number of small coral islands, covered in wood, and joined by coral reefs." Since Cook had neither named nor marked these spits of land on his published chart, Kotzebue "declared [them] to be a new discovery." One day later he glimpsed more land in the east, and he named the small island group "Rurick's Chain" (Arutua), even though he had not closely inspected the grouping. "[I]t is sufficient," he concluded, to know that "it exists." At this point Kotzebue could identify some islands already named by previous navigators (such as Cook and Schoeten) while other islands remained unremarked upon by his predecessors due to their unimpressive size. On April 25 he sighted "Dean's Island" (Rangiroa), as it was labeled on the 1798 map of the South Pacific drawn by London cartographer Aaron Arrowsmith (and based largely on Cook's reports), and the next day "a group of small coral islands" appeared that "without a doubt was a new discovery." He named this island group for Adam von Krusenstern, "the man with whom I made my first voyage round the world."[34]

Kotzebue claimed further discoveries as the *Rurik* sailed through the well-mapped Penrhyn Atoll and then to the northwest, skirting just east of the uncharted but already named Marshall Islands. He felt a pressing need to reach Kamchatka en route to the Bering Strait, while he also professed his great success in eastern Polynesia: "I add no proofs that the discoveries are new; the greater part of my readers will not dispute my assertion, and Captain Krusenstern will have the goodness to convince the others, by giving a short view of this, as well as the subsequent discoveries."[35] In fact, Krusenstern's "short view" amounted to a lengthy essay on Kotzebue's discoveries, offering a stirring validation of the explorer's success. Before the *Rurik* had even returned, Krusenstern had published some of these findings in one of Germany's oldest scholarly journals, *Göttingische Gelehrte Anzeigen*. A second set of accounts from Kotzebue arrived in mid-1817, and Count Rumiantsev instructed Krusenstern to have the new information quickly published in the Russian journal *Syn Otechestva*.[36] Krusenstern wanted confirmation of the island discoveries prior to the *Rurik*'s arrival in St. Petersburg. He closely compared Kotzebue's information with the charts and journals of other explorers before concluding which islands constituted an "*entirely* new discovery" in contrast to those islands that "*may* therefore be looked upon as a new discovery." In one case, Krusenstern applauded the naming of an apparently unknown island (Kotzebue named it "Krusenstern"), even though it already possessed a name: "it is called by the natives Ailu."[37] A prior Indigenous name and claim to an island hardly discounted Kotzebue's discovery of it, Krusenstern appeared to suggest. He praised the captain's "undaunted courage" and compared him to the famous explorer, "the celebrated [Matthew] Flinders."[38]

Kotzebue and Krusenstern promoted these island discoveries with full knowledge of—and perhaps because of—the expedition's principal failure to locate the "North-East" Passage. For his part, Chamisso expressed skepticism of the veracity of these discoveries. "Learned hydrographers," he wrote, could "compare the low islands which we saw" with the gathered knowledge of "former navigators" as well as the "chart of Tupaya"—an intriguing nod to the Ra'iatian navigator Tupaia, who had provided indispensable geographic information to Captain Cook fifty years earlier.[39] The captain's island discoveries, Chamisso suggested, were already part of the known world to the people of the Pacific.

DISCOVERIES OF THE SEA PEOPLE

Some discoveries claim new geographic, cultural, or scientific knowledge in relation to existing information or hypotheses. A different type of discovery is more personal in nature, representing an individual awakening to unexpected worlds of experience. Kotzebue desired the former type of finding: a claim that he was first. Chamisso, Eschscholtz, and Choris, however, began embracing the other type of discovery as they sailed across the Pacific and encountered Indigenous groups. They each knew of specific Indigenous communities by reading the publications of explorers, and they also knew of "Natives" in the abstract through the lens of natural Romanticism.[40] But they encountered real people in their travels—people who displayed fear, hostility, curiosity, and sometimes even cautious affection.

Despite the tremendous diversity of Pacific Indigenous groups who inhabited lands from the Aleutian Islands to the Tuamotu Archipelago, these "sea people" shared a common tradition of seafaring. Their daily activities and sustenance owed much to their skills in the sea, while many of their ancestral cosmologies evoked a kinship with the ocean itself—the place Māori called *te moana nui a Kiwa*, or "the Great Ocean of Kiwa."[41] Though living on land, some of their principal technologies and lifeways contributed to a cultural identity as "people from the sea."[42] The two naturalists and the artist repeatedly documented the skill and ease with which Indigenous people utilized their sea craft. They studied the multiplicity of Indigenous sailing vessels: simple or extravagant dugout canoes, single- and double-hulled outriggers, individual and multiperson *baidarkas*, sea craft under sail and other craft propelled by multiple paddlers. They measured the length of Native boats and marveled at the artistry of design. They also came to recognize the dexterity and speed of Pacific islanders on the water. "These sons of the sea," Chamisso explained upon meeting a group under sail miles from shore, "hurried on ahead of [the *Rurik*], and dropped their sails to await us."[43] Once home, Choris carefully documented the variety of native vessels with a dozen lithographic prints of sea craft from the Tuamotus, the Marshall Islands, Hawai'i, California, and Alaska. In *Entrevue avec les habitans des Iles Penrhyn*, Choris offered a stylized depiction of Penrhyn islanders in single-hulled canoes approaching the *Rurik* in late April 1816.

Apart from the naturalists' awareness of Indigenous seafaring culture, they also discovered a level of fear and animosity exhibited by some groups as the *Rurik* progressed in its northward voyage. The fear was far from universal. Instead, it appeared in specific places and resulted from past violent experiences with Europeans in general and, in the North Pacific, with Russians in particular. In late March both Kotzebue and Chamisso had recorded the "fear and distrust" of islanders at Rapa Nui (Easter Island), who had experienced capture ("blackbirding," as it was known at the time) by an American ship ten years earlier. The Rapanui hid their women and

Entrevue avec les habitans des Iles Penrhyn

Figure 1.2 *Entrevue avec les habitans des Iles Penrhyn*. Unlike many of his lithographs, Ludwig Choris composed this "meeting with the people of Penrhyn Islands" (Tongareva) to underscore a narrative of European power and maritime mastery. The *Rurik* rises high above the waterline, where a half dozen single-hulled canoes approach the ship's stern. An Imperial Russian Navy flag flies high above the partially naked islanders on the water. Both groups display peaceful gestures despite the apparent martial advantage of the Russian ship. However, Choris failed to depict the actual tension of this specific encounter. According to Kotzebue, "[t]he Rurick was soon surrounded by twenty-five boats. Some of the boats which had from twelve to fifteen men on board…their being armed with lances, gave them courage" (Kotzebue, 1821). Chamisso counted thirty-six boats surrounding the *Rurik*. Choris thought the men had a "wild look" ("*air farouche*") because of their long hair, ceremonial scarring, and near-nudity, but he was generally impressed by their stature and lack of fear (Choris, 1826). All three writers agreed upon one fact not evidenced in the lithograph: the *Rurik* had been quickly encircled by native seacraft expertly rowed by "well-built" men. Islanders, they realized in this early encounter, could easily challenge their safety. Courtesy of the National Library of Australia.

children and, according to Kotzebue, "pelted" their landing party with stones.[44] The *Rurik* received a similar reaction at the Mulgrave Islands in May, where the islanders refused to conduct trade on board the ship due to their mistrust of the foreigners. Once the *Rurik* reached Kamchatka in July, Chamisso discovered that numerous communities in the Far North feared Russian ships due to ongoing depredations by the Russian American Company. In the "dreary north" with its "gloomy veil" of fog, Chamisso opined, they met people who lived "under a new foreign [Russian] yoke" and dreaded the arrival of outsiders.[45]

These initial encounters with Indigenous groups piqued the interest of the naturalists and the artist. During the following year they would have more sustained and amicable meetings with the people of the Aleutian, Hawaiian, and Marshall Islands, as well as Native Californians in the San Francisco Bay region. They would spend almost a year on board the *Rurik* with the Carolinian islander Kadu. Through these interactions, they discovered that Indigenous people possessed extensive knowledge of many things they wanted to study. The question remained whether they possessed the capacity to understand and value what Natives had to say.

MAKING KOTZEBUE SOUND

Arriving in June 1816, the Kotzebue expedition spent almost a month at the Russian settlement of St. Peter and St. Paul, located on the shore of Avatscha Bay, Kamchatka Peninsula, eastern Russia. "Here," Chamisso joked in reference to his role on a Russian-sponsored voyage, "I first stepped on Russian soil; here I was to make my first acquaintance with Russia."[46] The crew set about the arduous task of repairing the *Rurik*'s battered copper bottom while the naturalists explored the surrounding country. The unhappy naturalist Morten Wormskjold left the expedition "for various reasons," according to Kotzebue. Wormskjold claimed an interest in writing a natural history of Kamchatka, but for everyone else he had simply worn out his welcome on the expedition. Kotzebue sent a dispatch across Siberia to Krusenstern, who published it six months later in *Journal des Voyages*, the main European journal of exploration. The ship's crew, Kotzebue wrote, carried out its work with great dedication ("beaucoup d'application"), and he anticipated success in the coming season of exploration.[47] The irritable Second Lieutenant Ivan Sakharin also departed from the expedition due to health concerns, which left Kotzebue with only one fellow officer, Lieutenant Gleb Shishmaref. "This is certainly the first voyage of discovery happily [conducted] by only two officers," Kotzebue commented.[48] Shishmaref and Kotzebue got along famously due to their shared service in the Russian Navy, but the lieutenant's subsequent actions suggest he held a different opinion than the captain's characterization of a happy conclusion to the voyage.

At Avatscha Bay the expedition members met Aleut people for the first time, including a translator named Afzenikov, who "served" the Russian American Company. Chamisso described him as a "very experienced, very understanding man."[49] What did Chamisso know about Afzenikov and, for that matter, about other people of the Far North? At this stage in the voyage, he knew very little. Even the term *Aleut* could be misleading, as Russians used it in reference to a broad cross-section of groups including Unangan, Alutiiq, Kodiak, and Eskimo people.[50] Over the course of the coming year Chamisso, Choris, Eschscholtz, and Kotzebue would learn much more about the impoverished living conditions of many Aleut, and they also came to understand some aspects of the complicated relationships among different Native groups in the Arctic region. They would witness and comment upon the Aleuts' subjugation by the RAC, intergroup hostilities, extensive trade relations, and the occasional kindly reception to the *Rurik*'s appearance. But that knowledge lay in the future as the voyage departed from Kamchatka after a month's stay. Chamisso began his investigation of the northern people by collecting artifacts, the first of which were human remains.

Making its way north through the Bering Sea, the *Rurik* first sighted Bering's Island, previously named for "our renowned, but unfortunate navigator, Beering, who found his grave here," wrote Kotzebue. The next major island came into view just below the Bering Strait, wedged between the continents of Asia and North America. The Yupik islanders called the island *Sivuqaq*, while Vitus Bering had christened it St. Lawrence. Russian visitors mistakenly called the people *Tschukutskoi* or *Chukchi* (due to their relationship with the people of the Chukchi Peninsula). Choris described a cautious reception: a boat "manned by eight islanders advanced towards us," Choris wrote, and "they accompanied us as we went ashore." Through the Aleut translator Afzenikov, Choris and Kotzebue learned about the island's geography, which the Yupik divided between East (*Kilalilakgh*) and West (*Tchibokakgh*). The people desired tobacco, and they offered in exchange clothing made of red fox pelts and walrus intestine. The next day several islanders came on board the *Rurik*, greeting the officers by rubbing noses and spitting in their hands before rubbing each other's faces. "It was the greatest mark of distinction they were able to give us," Choris commented.[51] This distinction may have come at a high cost to the islanders. One Russian sailor had already died of tuberculosis on the voyage, and a second crewmember left the ship in Kamchatka due to a lung infection. It was entirely possible that pathogens moved from the Europeans to the Yupik community through this greeting ritual. At the end of the second day Choris jotted a cryptic detail in his diary: "Chamisso found a very old human skull."[52]

Chamisso had botanized his way up a rocky mountain that he likened to the "High Alps of our Switzerland." He found the skull on this hike, and he offered two different accounts of the discovery. In his "Remarks and Opinions of the Naturalist," Chamisso wrote: "We have found skulls on the plateau of the island, [located] in the fragments of rocks at the foot of the mo[u]ntains, but not the monuments made of drift-wood, which are erected on the American coast, to mark the burial place of the dead . . . and protect it against wild beasts."[53] In this account, Chamisso indicates that Eschscholtz may have accompanied him on the venture ("we have found") even though Choris's diary gives Chamisso sole credit for discovering "the very old human skull."[54] Chamisso also claimed that the skull lay amid "fragments of rocks" rather than at an identifiable burial monument "made of drift-wood." In other words, he took the artifact not from a burial ground but instead from a location littered with rocks and rubble. This was hardly an instance of grave desecration, he argued, and he expressed no guilt or embarrassment for taking the skull.

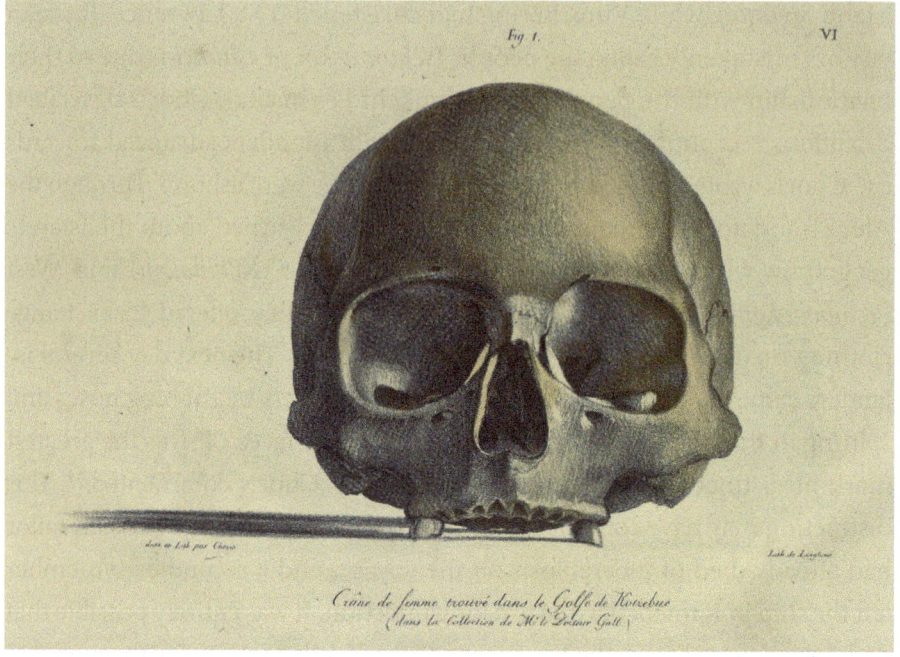

Figure 1.3 *Crâne de femme trouvé dans le Golfe de Kotzebue.* What knowledge did European scientists hope to gain by studying a human skull? In preparing for the *Rurik* voyage, Chamisso consulted with the French naturalist Georges Cuvier, a specialist in zoology, paleontology, and comparative anatomy. Cuvier encouraged Chamisso to acquire human skulls, because he believed they offered evidence of human traits and racial characteristics. Choris presented the French phrenologist Franz Joseph Gall with a skull upon his arrival in Paris after the voyage. This gift secured the artist patronage from Gall, who contributed a written analysis of the skull to accompany the lithographs in Choris's *Voyage pittoresque.* According to Gall, the skull acquired at the Gulf of Kotzebue (shown above) revealed a depressed frontal lobe, which to him indicated "weak development in the faculties proper to man." By contrast, Gall praised a second skull for its "beautiful high forehead"—a feature that suggested "excellent character and knowledge" (Choris, 1822). Gall's own pate possessed an unmistakably high forehead. Chamisso brought home a collection of three skulls, which he contributed to the Berlin Anatomical Museum, along with other artifacts. One of these skulls exists today in the collections of the Anatomical Institute at the Charité in Berlin. Labeled "A 685" (also "AN 3901" and "N.C.1138"), it includes the inscription "*Aleute v[on]. Unalaschka*" and "*v[on]. Chamisso*" on the forehead. Modern-day analysis of the skull suggests it was quite old, possibly belonging to a "Neo-Aleut" individual who died as much as one thousand years ago (Glaubrecht, et al., 2013). Courtesy Internet Archive.

Years later Chamisso offered a different telling of the episode. "Alone and undisturbed" as he "botanized" this day, "I found a human skull, which I took along carefully concealed under my [collected] plants." Though "found" on the ground like any other specimen, Chamisso knew that human remains were unique, and he therefore concealed the skull from any Yupik observers as he returned to the ship. Somehow, he reasoned, this skull must not be sacred to the islanders, because "[m]ost people, like our northlanders, bury their dead and consider the graves to be sacred. Only through a rare happy accident can the traveler and collector gain possession of skulls, which are of the greatest importance for the history of the human race."[55] In this telling, Chamisso acquired the skull purely by happenstance, and he presented a scientific rationale ("the history of the human race") for removing it from the island. His skull collection would increase modestly once they reached Kotzebue Sound, as previously described in the Introduction.

The *Rurik* departed from St. Lawrence Island on July 29, and two days later the expedition passed through the Bering Strait. Under sunny skies the crew could easily view the coastlines of both Asia and North America thirty miles distant from each other. Kotzebue took pleasure in sighting a fourth island adjacent to three other islands named by James Cook in 1778. "I took it for a new discovery, I called it Ratmanoff," he wrote. Chamisso, for his part, pronounced this rock formation as something less than an island and more akin to "pillars of rock standing alone in the middle of the strait."[56] Kotzebue kept the *Rurik* on a northeast course directly parallel to the American continent to increase the likelihood of further discoveries. The ship entered a small bay that Kotzebue quickly named Shishmaref in honor of his only remaining Lieutenant, followed by the naming of a low-lying island he called Sarichef (Inuit residents called it *Kigiktaq*). The island's inhabitants had retreated from view at the approach of the *Rurik*, only to return once the Captain's small skiff separated from the ship. A tense exchange between the parties ended peacefully, but "the Americans" left no doubt that they did not welcome Kotzebue's people, whom they recognized as Russian.[57]

Sailing northeast the following day, the Captain finally discovered a geographic feature grand enough to honor with his family name. Indeed, the bowl-shaped "Kotzebue Sound" on the Chukchi Sea struck the expedition members as thoroughly remarkable: it measured forty miles across at the entrance, contained protected anchorages, and encompassed a low coastline with towering peaks on the horizon. The Iñupiat had lived around the bay they called *Qiqiktaġruk* for thousands of years.[58] They maintained extensive trade relations with groups on the American and Asian sides of the Bering Strait. The "habitans" of the Gulf of Kotzebue sketched by Choris not only knew the Inuit community who confronted Kotzebue at Shishmaref Bay on the previous day, but more than likely, those Inuit had notified their Iñupiat neighbors of the *Rurik*'s arrival in these waters. While only a few European voyagers had navigated north of the Bering Strait by the time of the *Rurik*'s arrival, the Indigenous groups around the Chukchi Sea were fully aware of Russian traders, their goods, and the opportunities and dangers they posed.

Kotzebue was elated with his discovery of the bay. He struggled to describe the "strange sensation" he felt upon entering this protected bay, because it just might contain the "long sought N. E. passage" to the Atlantic Ocean. He marveled at the idea that "fate had chosen me" to locate this grand geographic feature. Though soon disabused of the notion that Kotzebue Sound would reveal the Northern Passage, the captain contented himself with the fact that they had "found a place of refuge" for the next year's effort to discover the passage. He described a beautiful coastline, green as far as the eye could see and dotted with wildflowers, and he cherished the idea that "no European has ever visited" it.[59] Kotzebue proudly bestowed place-names on geographic features, including Chamisso Island, Eschscholtz Bay, Cape Deceit, and Asses' Ears (named for two peaks in the distance), and then he immediately used his invented place-names in his journal as if to validate their existence and his claim to discovery. Kotzebue Sound encompassed all of these geographic markers, and he, rather than his famous literary father, had made the discovery. It hardly mattered that James Cook had sailed directly west of the bay in 1778, and Charles Clerke may have sailed into it. Neither man had explored or named it. Kotzebue relished the intelligence he gathered through interactions with "the inhabitants of this country" and, thinking more grandly about the future, proposed "our government might establish several settlements on the coast of Beering's Straits to the north" for the benefit of the fur trade.[60] His proposal failed to gain traction in St. Petersburg due to its impracticality.

The naturalists' brief and fragmentary interactions with the Iñupiat prevented the exchange of much useful knowledge about the people themselves. The few dozen individuals who met Kotzebue's group represented thousands of Iñupiaq-speaking people on this northernmost shelf of North America.[61] They had fashioned a lifestyle in this exacting environment based on family ties, mobility, hunting, and an expansive trade system. Kin-based communities spread across more than one thousand miles of shoreline and inland waterways, forming an intricate social web united by barter and seasonal migration patterns. They gathered resources during the warmer months for the long and dark winter seasons, hunting caribou, moose, and other quadrupeds for meat, bone, and fur. Iñupiat families came together at seasonal trade fairs located across the territory from the village of Sheshalik on Kotzebue Sound to Kaktorik on Barter Island in the Arctic Sea, with Native traders arriving from as far away as the coast of Siberia. When the Bering Sea's icepack opened in summer, the Iñupiat took to the waters for bowhead and beluga whales, seals, walrus, and other marine creatures. The region's natural bounty was readily useable to the northern groups, who had learned to live within the environment's extremes and vicissitudes.

Rather than ethnographic information about the people, Kotzebue primarily desired geographic information. A group of Iñupiat described a large river (either the Noatak or Kobuk) running in a northeast direction from their territory, but Kotzebue had no practical way of exploring a waterway that ran inland for hundreds of miles. He asked an elderly man about the length of the river, to which the man responded with a pantomime of nine days' paddling. The captain brought home this information with the intriguing suggestion that a large bay might be found at the other end of the river.

VISUALLY REPRESENTING THE FAR NORTH

Since the time of the *Rurik*'s departure from England the previous October, Ludwig Choris had conscientiously developed his craft of sketching and painting in watercolor, often working as the ship pitched to and fro on the open ocean. He sat at the naturalists' worktable and rendered their dissections and specimens; he also spent long hours on deck delineating coastal approaches and waterscapes. He spent the most time on his drawings of Native people and their material culture. At best, those images had the capacity to not only accurately render Indigenous people, but also to convey Indigenous perspectives and knowledge. His initial sketches could change substantially when years later he reworked them as lithographs for *Voyage pittoresque*. For example, his watercolor of an earth-covered glacier devoid of human presence took on a different meaning when he turned it into a lithograph featuring four human forms, including himself.

The *Rurik* left Kotzebue Sound in mid-August and crossed to the Asia side of the Bering Strait. The ship "cast anchor within sight of a Chukchi village situated on a hill," Choris wrote, and "[t]wo boats [from the village] immediately came alongside us."[62] The expedition would remain with this community for a week, during which time the artist produced dozens of sketches and watercolors of the villagers in their summer habitation. An elder of the community welcomed the artist into his home; he was "an old man who appeared to exercise authority in this place, for, at the slightest sign which he made, everyone was eager to obey him." Choris described the man's evident power as that of a "father" to all "the inhabitants of this village," and the artist appeared especially interested in presenting the people as an extended family.[63] In *Tchouktches et leurs habitations*, he depicted a Chukchi family standing in front of the village to reflect its domestic nature. Various publications would reproduce this lithograph in the coming decades, most likely because it seemed to display a domesticity similar to European ideals.

The Chukchi seemed responsive to the questions posed by Choris. They described their seasonal migrations as a strategy to balance winter

Figures 1.4a and 1.4b "Glacier dans le Golfe de Kotzebue au delà due détroit de Behring," watercolor; and *Vue des Glaces dans le Golfe de Kotzebue*.
Choris's watercolor depicts a forbidding and wild Arctic landscape. It is devoid of human presence despite the site's habitation by Iñupiat people since time immemorial. The artist significantly altered this scene in its lithographic form by placing himself in the foreground and three figures in the background. The human figures lend scale to the landscape, but they also domesticate and secure this peculiar landscape for nineteenth-century viewers. Courtesy of Louis Choris Paintings and Sketches, Beinecke Library, Yale University; courtesy Internet Archive.

Figure 1.5 *Tchouktches et leurs habitations.* While Choris's group portrait of Iñupiat emphasizes their physical difference from European appearances, this Chukchi family scene contains elements largely familiar and reassuring to a European audience. In the foreground stands a nuclear family with clear gender roles, including the male hunter and the female who cares for the child. Their clothing is not only functional for the cold climate but also contains stylish adornments, showing the people's aesthetic desires. The skin-covered huts show a village community in relation to work: the men carry spears for the hunt, while females tend to domestic production. Two multiperson canoes (*umiak*) cut through the inlet in the background, suggesting the importance of the marine hunt to the Chukchi. Choris noted that "a throng" of villagers welcomed them after some initial hesitance on the shore (Vanstone, 1960). On this eastern edge of the Russian empire, Choris seems to suggest, village life for the Chukchi bore similarities to patriarchal peasant life in Europe. Courtesy Internet Archive.

necessities with summer opportunities. Choris asked them (through the Aleut translator Afzenikov) about their relations with the groups who lived across the Bering Strait. The Chukchi elder described those people as the "American" enemies. "He told us that his nation was continually at war with the inhabitants of the coast of America.... [The Americans] attracted strangers to their women in order to kill them."[64] The specific causes of this conflict may be lost in translation or even community memory, but what seems striking in this elder's perspective is an understanding that longstanding trade relations across the Bering Strait did not necessarily create friendship, trust, and familial mixing. The tension was real, and such tensions may in fact define the history of Eurasian, Indigenous, and Russian trade relations during this period.[65]

In the Far North, Choris sketched Native watercraft, paddles, tools, spiritual icons, and habitations as visual documentation of Indigenous technologies and cultures. Some of his sketches and lithographs revealed collections of artifacts, such as the various "objects" carved by the Iñupiat: a seal, a human figure, a polar bear, adornments on a visor, and a hatchet blade. In other works, he focused on a single item, such as the intricate carvings on a set of walrus tusks. Here, Choris presents a story within a story: an object that offers the viewer an example of Indigenous crafts-manship as well as stories of community life and history. The ivory tusks show the hunting of whales, tracking of moose, spearing of walrus, and people adorned in differently colored fox skins. The carved tusks simulta-neously served aesthetic, utilitarian, and mimetic functions.

What did the expedition members make of this carving and, by exten-sion, similar examples of Indigenous material culture? Captain Kotzebue appeared to write them off as simple Native curiosities. He collected many Indigenous items during the voyage, presenting them to his Russian spon-sor upon his return to St. Petersburg. Choris and the naturalists, however, closely studied the ivory etchings and other Indigenous products for aes-thetic and cultural clues about the people of the Far North. Choris made every effort to precisely reproduce the symbols and figures etched by the Iñupiat carver, because he recognized them as culturally specific texts rather than mere ornamentation.[66] His rendering of the Iñupiat walrus tusk, like his depiction of the Chukchi village, offered knowledge about Indigenous work, survival in the elements, the priority of the hunt, and community life beyond the boundaries of Russian colonialism. The lithograph of the tusk made legible an Indigenous story and perspective despite its production by the European artist Choris.

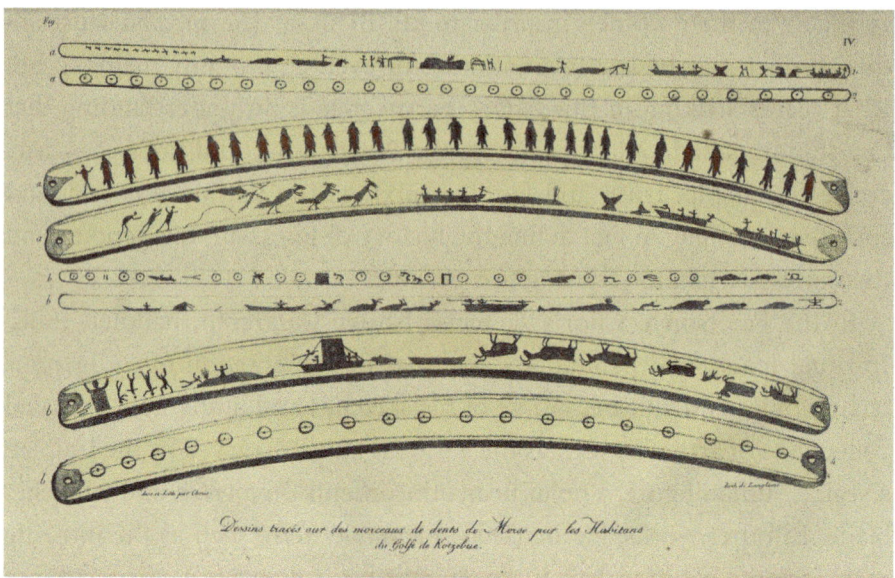

Figure 1.6 *Dessins tracés sur des morceaux de dents de Morse par les Habitans du Golfe de Kotzebue.* The art of ivory and whalebone carving among the Iñupiat and Inuit people goes back thousands of years. Here, Choris depicts what might be the first example of an Iñupiat bone carving acquired by Europeans. It exemplifies what Dorothy Jean Ray calls the "old engraving style" of pictographic forms showing the daily activities of people and important wildlife (Ray, 1977). By contrast, late nineteenth-century "scrimshaw" frequently depicted European ships or coastlines created specifically for foreign buyers. Choris writes: "Perceiving that we did not have much to their liking, and that we eagerly desired their clothing, their ornaments, and their weapons, they would not sell us furs, and brought us all sorts of objects sculptured from walrus teeth, and pieces of these teeth on which they had drawn designs." The *Rurik* personnel traded "ordinary knives" and "small glass beads" for the carved ivory, but the Iñupiat "desired large beads similar to those which they had" (Vanstone, 1960). Courtesy Internet Archive.

RATIONALIZING NORTHERN PEOPLE

As the *Rurik* completed its initial northern exploration at the end of August, expedition members remarked upon their guarded reception by people in the Far North. Their interactions with different Indigenous groups had transpired without conflict, and they anticipated a hospitable welcome when they returned the following summer. Choris recognized who set the terms of any future meeting. The Chukchi's "conduct was very friendly," he noted, but "they all had cutlasses at their sides." Their numerical superiority over this group of foreign voyagers perhaps made those cutlasses unnecessary, but the Chukchi had learned the necessity of weapons due to their prior experiences with Russians.[67] Choris observed that the village men guided them everywhere in their territory, and "when we returned [to the *Rurik*] several boats accompanied us, and we made them a present of tobacco."[68] The Chukchi, like the Iñupiat, closely surveilled this group of foreigners and viewed any relations with them in transactional terms.

Kotzebue certainly understood the numerical strength of their Native counterparts, but he offered a different perspective on the power relations. He noted how the Chukchi happily provisioned his men with dressed reindeer, not realizing that the villagers might have been offering a gift of provisions to encourage the ship's departure. Kotzebue viewed the Natives as childish in their fears (of a mirror, for instance) and ineffective in their attempts to intimidate him. When a group of Chukchi visited the ship just prior to its departure, the Captain proudly displayed the painting of his famous father that hung prominently in his cabin. "[T]hey considered the portrait of my father as the image of a saint, bowing and crossing themselves before it like the Russians," Kotzebue wrote.[69] What these individuals actually thought about the painting remains a mystery, but they clearly understood the Captain's expectation and behaved accordingly. Kotzebue's severely patriarchal worldview—perhaps ingrained by his own father—left him little room to understand the people as individuals, nor did he suspect their ability to adopt a certain role based on their prior experiences with Russians. They mostly wanted his ship gone.

Chamisso regarded Kotzebue's perspective on the Chukchi as naïve at best and dangerous at worst. "The Chukchis," he wrote, "received us...in a friendly manner, but with a solemnity that deprived us of all freedom." Chamisso felt watched, guarded, and contained in all his movements by the well-armed villagers. He praised their status as "an independent people...subservient to no one." Yet Chamisso also noted the conditional nature of the Chukchi's independence: the Russian settlements along the Aleutian Islands and Kamchatka Peninsula posed distinct dangers while also offering the benefits of trade goods, such as weapons. The Chukchi, he continued, "recognize Russian sovereignty only inasmuch as they pay the tribute in the market places, where they trade with the Russians to their mutual advantage."[70] Even though Chamisso bristled at the way they surveilled his movements, he respected how they vigilantly guarded their communities and "rejoice[d] in their inborn freedom." Such was the "peculiar characteristic" of humankind, the naturalist concluded.[71]

After a year at sea and successfully navigating halfway around the globe, the *Rurik* departed from the RAC headquarters at Unalaska Island on September 15, 1816. "[W]e passed before Unimak Island and headed for California," Ludwig Choris explained in a casual voice, as if his contemporary readers would readily grasp the geographic and colonial differences between these two places.[72] From California they would stop in Hawai'i before sailing farther west to the Marshall Islands, where they met Kadu. This islander knew nothing of the *Rurik*'s past year at sea or where it was headed. He seized the opportunity to join the expedition for its coming year of exploration.

All Species of Knowledge: A Voyage of Discovery, Failure, and Natural History in the Pacific Ocean. David Igler, Oxford University Press. © Oxford University Press 2026. DOI: 10.1093/9780197777718.003.0002

Kadu's Voyage and a Second Attempt at the Northern Passage

Ocean of reefs, Ocean of Uncertainties,
I split open, I pierce open, this ocean,
this ocean that is mine.

—YAPESE NAVIGATION CHANT

The *Rurik* arrived in the Marshall Islands in early 1817 after skirting the eastern edge of this "ocean of reefs" during the previous year's northbound journey.[1] Within a few weeks the expedition had visited a dozen islands, and the *Rurik*'s personnel was struck by the natural beauty as well as the impressive stature of the islanders. Kotzebue conjured up new names for the individual islands, a practice criticized by Chamisso because he believed the names were "imposed upon them by strangers." Chamisso arrived at his own sobriquet for the entire chain of islands: "The First Province of the Great Ocean."[2] The Marshallese showed interest and warmth rather than hostility to the foreign *dri-belle* (people with goods and foreign clothes), which Chamisso ascribed to their "pure, uncorrupted customs" and "modesty."[3] Kotzebue observed that the people across this archipelago shared a common language as well as hierarchies of ranked leaders, known as *iroijs*.[4] An *iroij* frequently declared their place in the hierarchy upon greeting members of the *Rurik* when it arrived.

Such was the case when an *iroij* named Tigedien from the Aur Atoll announced himself to the *Rurik*'s personnel on February 23. Two young men, Edock and Kadu, accompanied him, and they expertly guided Tigedien's outrigger canoe to the European vessel. After exchanging mutually incomprehensible pleasantries, Tigedien invited the foreigners ashore, at which point Edock prepared the outrigger to return to Aur with the *Rurik*'s landing craft in tow. Kadu, however, refused the leave the ship. Instead, he expressed a clear desire to remain on the vessel and join the expedition when it sailed away from the Marshall Islands. In the coming days Captain Kotzebue consented to Kadu's request, because the islander had already proven himself useful and genial.

Why did Kadu desire to sail on a European vessel? He was born on a small atoll named Woleai in the Caroline Islands, some two thousand miles west of Aur. He was a young and highly skilled navigator raised in an island culture that valued sailing knowledge above all else. Kadu had previously led trading and tribute voyages across the Caroline Islands, charting his course on the open ocean for days at a time. He could read the night sky as a star compass, a navigational method that carried his outrigger from island to island by triangulating the stars.[5] Kadu also understood the power of storms that could send his outrigger into unknown seas—including the great storm that overtook his vessel some years earlier, placed it north of the Caroline Islands, and threatened the lives of his three fellow Woleaian sailors for months on end until they finally arrived in the unfamiliar seas of the Marshall Islands.

Fortunately, Kadu possessed knowledge and experiences to share with the Marshallese he encountered on Aur, including the *iroij* Tigedien. Although Kadu remained a partial outsider on Aur, his foreign nautical skills provided him a measure of security and prestige among the Marshallese.[6] His outsider status may explain why Tigedien chose Kadu to greet the foreigners who arrived on the *Rurik*. Perhaps Kadu would understand something about the ways of these strange people. Maybe he possessed useful knowledge to exchange with them. Later, after joining the *Rurik*, Kadu would carefully consider the information he shared, as well as how he shared it.[7] Almost a year later he returned to the Marshall

Islands with unique knowledge to pass along about the new seas he had traversed and the people he had met.

Kadu's role on the *Rurik* could be characterized as similar to that of other Indigenous individuals who found themselves—either willingly or unwillingly—on board a European ship. His role could be that of a cultural "go-between," or an "Indigenous intermediary," or a "broker" and "translator," or a "native informant."[8] All of these roles, to a greater or lesser degree, imply the employment or exploitation of the Indigenous islander for a specific purpose. Kadu could fill some of these roles because he had done so before, in a different cultural context, upon his arrival at Aur. In the months ahead, the personnel of the *Rurik* queried Kadu on a wide range of topics. They believed they had struck a unique font of knowledge with this Indigenous "source," and they also believed they had formed a reciprocal relationship with their "new authority."[9] To some extent this proved true, as revealed in many of their unpublished reports, publications, and visual renderings of Kadu.

The gentlemen of the *Rurik* viewed Kadu as a unique Indigenous man. Unlike many of the people they had met during the previous year, he seemed unsullied by colonial influences and his desire to join the expedition affirmed their own sense of purpose. He appeared to enjoy their company. His body was graceful and attractive—even his tattoos and elongated earlobes struck the *Rurik*'s officers as handsomely authentic. Dressed in European attire—which they supplied him—Kadu looked like a well-groomed member of an antipodean crew. In Kadu they found support for their view of the Marshall Islands as a whole: a remote and undiscovered place, a romantic setting fashioned by their enlightened minds. Kadu, the authentic *indigene*, could shed light on this exotic world and its realms of useful knowledge.

He traveled on the *Rurik* for most of a year—from the Marshall Islands to the Bering Strait, from Unalaska to the Hawaiian Islands, and then back to his adopted home on Aur. This chapter explores the world from which he came and his journey north to the Bering Strait, while subsequent chapters examine other aspects of his voyage. By year's end, Kadu had explored a tremendous range of oceanic and terrestrial space. Not unlike

Figure 2.1 Kadu, a native of Ulea. This print, published in the first edition of Kotzebue's voyage account, stands in contrast to the lithograph of Kadu that Choris included in *Voyage pittoresque* (Figure I. 2). Most noticeably, Kadu appears in European-style clothes, not unlike the "red vest" portrait of the Hawaiian monarch King Kamehameha painted by Choris (Figure 3.15). The *Rurik*'s officers "presented [Kadu] with a yellow cloak, and red apron" within days of meeting him, according to Kotzebue, and he "walked proudly in his ludicrous finery, without condescending to notice his [islander] companions, who gazed on him with astonishment from their boats, and could not conceive the metamorphosis" (Kotzebue, 1821). Kotzebue's patronizing description failed to consider the possibility that Kadu was mimicking the stiff manners of Europeans, whose clothing and aloof behavior seemed ludicrous to many islanders. John Heaviside Clark produced this print for the English-language edition of Kotzebue's book, which demonstrates how some of Choris's drawings and watercolors circulated in various publications before the appearance of his own lithographic versions. A successful and prolific illustrator, Clark took artistic license to alter Choris's image, including the clothing and the sculpted eyebrows. Print by John Heaviside Clark, in Otto von Kotzebue's *A Voyage of Discovery* (1821).

the naturalists with whom he sailed, Kadu observed his surroundings everywhere he went, and he soon presented this new knowledge to his Marshallese contemporaries.

KADU'S WORLD

To refer to Kadu as a "Pacific Islander" or "Native sailor" reveals little about his origins, training, or identity. His travels on the *Rurik* would expose him to far-reaching experiences throughout the North Pacific, but he was shaped in a very specific locale, a spit of land called Falalap. This two-square-mile coral island is part of the Woleai Atoll, which sits in the Woleai group of the Yap District of the Caroline Islands, the most dispersed island chain of Micronesia.[10] The term Micronesia (along with Polynesia and Melanesia) represents a nineteenth-century imaginary invented by Europeans to divide Oceania into three geographically coherent zones.[11] This larger geographic designation held no meaning for Kadu. By culture and lineage, he was Woleaian, an identity he shared with several hundred residents of the atoll in the early 1800s. A navigator by training, Kadu's rearing exposed him to the extensive Caroline seas and the privileged ancestral knowledge stretching back in time more than two thousand years.

Woleaians referred to privileged knowledge as *itang*. This sacred wisdom explained such things as measurements and time, the alignment of the stars, the locations of far-flung islands, the value of different plants and animals, and the philosophies that ordered the surrounding material and spiritual worlds.[12] *Itang* represented a shared way of knowing and also the "world of spirits" entered by navigators when they sailed.[13] Navigators-in-training like Kadu memorized parts of this knowledge from a very early age through the tutoring of an elder *pelu* (navigator), who often conveyed the information in the form of tales, songs, and even bodily movements. Not surprisingly, when Chamisso or Kotzebue posed a straightforward question to Kadu, he often responded with a lengthy story, song, or chant, which befuddled and sometimes amused the Europeans. The young Woleaian navigator learned the season of the most reliable trade winds (*nifang*) and memorized the shifting path of the stars (*wofalu*). The elder *pelu* placed in front of the trainee small stones on the ground in a pattern to teach the arrangement of the stars. They learned to orient by the star Altair (*Mailap*), due to its position above the Central Pacific and the east–west alignment of the Caroline Islands.[14] Kadu and other trainees internalized this wisdom because it meant the difference between life and death on the open seas. They also recited the names of long-disappeared navigators. They did not desire to share the same fate as those memorialized voyagers.[15]

Navigators held a unique status in Woleai and throughout the Caroline Islands due to their extensive training, but the navigator's occupation also made possible the main socio-political structure of their oceanic world: the *sawei*.[16] Caroline ancestors had formed the *sawei* as a tribute and trade system for one thousand miles surrounding the high island of Yap. Each year a fleet of canoes sailed for Yap with three categories of offerings (land, religious, and canoe tributes) for the chief of Yap's Gagil District, who responded with the distribution of gifts for the canoe representatives. Rather than direct payments, these tributes solidified ancestral bonds and helped facilitate the exchange of trade goods. The *sawei*, writes historian Damon Salesa, organized the "native seas" as a space that "cohered through narrations of distinctly Yapese, Palauan, and Carolinian kinds."[17] The ceremony of the annual voyage followed strict procedures, with canoes from the eastern islands converging on Woleai before proceeding to the islands of Fais, Mogmog, and finally to Yap. Ceremonial gifts and commercial goods included woven skirts and cloth, shell belts, coconut products, rope, turmeric, and food items. Breadfruit formed a staple of material exchange. Yapese currency could also exchange hands, including the shell money known as *gau* and the heavy aragonite mineral called *fei*, both of which circulated around the islands for material and ceremonial value.[18]

The *sawei* affirmed political, economic, and spiritual relationships at the same time it linked the widely dispersed islands in a system of obligations and hierarchies. Kadu entered this interconnected world at an early age when he took part in his first *sawei* voyage. Through experience he learned the ways of distant Caroline islanders and he also gained some exposure to the people and maritime worlds across Micronesia. However, the *sawei* represented privileged information and included secret rituals. Kadu would not discuss these things with the men of the *Rurik* beyond the fact that he regularly sailed to other Caroline islands.

During a time when most people around the globe rarely strayed far from their locality, Kadu's training purposely rejected a provincial life. Kadu traveled far from his Woleai Atoll long before the storm-driven "drift" or "accidental" voyage that brought him and three fellow Woleaians to the Marshall Islands.[19] His annual tribute voyage to the island of Yap exposed him to influences from Melanesian islands, China, and Spain, because Yap intersected with extensive trade routes, and it also had the occasional non-Indigenous resident from European shipwrecks.[20] Those influences included linguistic exposure: Kadu was conversant in different Micronesian dialects, and he could count to ten in Spanish, a fact that stunned the naturalists aboard the *Rurik* when he unexpectedly demonstrated the skill. He also knew the general location of islands far distant from his Yapese orbit, including some islands in the Mariana, Gilbert, and Marshall chains. Kadu had heard apocryphal stories about Yapese navigators taken by storm as far east as Aur and as far west as the large foreign lands (the Philippines). He had previously navigated four hundred miles north to Guam on a trading expedition (where he could barter for items such as iron) and a slightly shorter distance west to Palau—nautical feats conducted in an oceangoing outrigger (*yailap*) that challenged the skills of any mariner.[21] In these and other ways, Kadu possessed a worldly sensibility in a sea of islands that European visitors derisively stereotyped as remote, isolated, and primitive.

For navigators like Kadu, the canoe represented the singular instrument from which their training and knowledge flowed. The forms of eastern Caroline canoes reflected different functions: they produced canoes designated for chiefs (*gawalu*) and non-chiefs (*papa*), distinct canoe types for at least five different ranges of distance (*walúwei*, *manúbwil*, *wamar*, *wäfatul*, and *chósemel*), and canoes propelled by paddle as opposed to sail (as Choris depicted in Figure 2.2). Highly skilled canoe builders shaped their creations from the trunks of breadfruit trees, and they spent months fashioning the

various components of an oceangoing vessel, including the prow, planking, platform, mast, and the complex outrigger that stabilized the vessel at
sea. Builders and navigators recognized the keel as the "heart of the canoe,"
a belief that still resonates today among Indigenous canoe builders.[22] The
builders typically worked in isolation, and they sought spiritual guidance
through chants that "conjoined the sacred and the earthly" realms.[23] They
consulted the navigators during the finishing stage of their creation. Kadu,
for instance, would take a new canoe on a test voyage to assess its maneuverability and strength. Kadu would experience the canoe's unique feel as

Figure 2.2 *Bateaux à voile des îles Radak*. Choris documented the types of Indigenous
seacraft everywhere visited by the *Rurik*. His journal records discussions with Kadu
about navigation and the shape of outrigger canoes from the Caroline Islands, which
he and Chamisso noted were very similar in form to those of the Marshall Islands.
The outrigger with sail depicted in this lithograph was based on information provided
by Kadu. It is small and used for short-distance travel, whereas Chamisso noted that
"the largest of these vessels can carry up to thirty people." The naturalist described
the "two identical ends, both of which are equally adapted to become bow or stern
when it is in motion," while a "hand paddle" would be used to steer the canoe from the
rear (Chamisso, 1836). The triangular sail could rapidly propel the vessel across the
water. This seacraft reflected the contemporary maritime culture of Kadu's people, but
Chamisso also remarked upon the ancestral use of sailing vessels that allowed islanders
to "emigrate" from the western Pacific and "[take] possession of all the points of land
which rise from the Great Ocean" (Chamisso, 1821). Courtesy Internet Archive.

it moved through the sea, and he would experiment with its position reckoning—a process of triangulating (known as *etak*) between two islands, a
star in the night sky, and the canoe.[24] In all these ways a canoe embodied
an instrument of material, scientific, and spiritual power for the navigator.
The navigators depended on its powers for their survival.[25]

Given his navigational experience, canoe technology, and studied
knowledge of the seasons and the seas, what happened on Kadu's voyage
when he and three other Woleaians went adrift? Accidental drift journeys
were hardly uncommon, according to Kadu, who provided Chamisso
with sparse information about voyages gone awry.[26] His outrigger canoe
departed from Woleai in the *nifang* season of 1812 or 1813 as part of a
small fleet that gathered from surrounding islands, and together they
sailed north for two days to Gaferut Island. After stopping at Gaferut, the
fleet again sailed north for three days to Guam, where they participated in
an annual trade fair. An unanticipated storm struck the Woleaian navigators shortly after their departure from Guam. The canoes separated in the
squall, and Kadu's severely damaged vessel was thrown into unknown seas
north of Micronesia. They survived for months in the open ocean by fishing and consuming supplies acquired in Guam. But he shared no other
details of this wretched experience with Chamisso, because he considered
it unlucky to recount misfortune. Kadu and his canoe-mates washed up at
Aur, and there they began new lives in a different island culture.

REPRESENTING RATAK

The *Rurik's* ten-week reconnaissance of the Ratak chain of the Marshall
Islands in early 1817 was the first European survey of this island chain.
Kotzebue's published account of these islands spanned more than eighty
pages, while Chamisso easily doubled that length in two separate volumes.
For Choris, the Marshall Islands presented the opportunity to depict the
scenery and people of an island chain never previously sketched by a
European artist. His lithographs of the Marshalls suggest a hardly touched
island paradise, while also revealing a depth of knowledge drawn from

personal observation and Indigenous informants. Outrigger canoes glide across the coastal waters in front of low-lying islands. Lithe men and women on a sparsely inhabited beach sway in time to an unheard tune. High-ranking male leaders pose for the artist, who renders their tattoos and piercings in close detail for his European audience. In his lithograph *Intérieur d'une maison dans les îles Radak* ("Interior of a house in the Radak Islands"), Choris depicts a naturalized domesticity of children at play; distinct gender roles; and a well-built, open-air habitation. It offers a romantic vision for Choris's wealthy readers and benefactors, who wanted to encounter this exotic beauty from the comfort of their drawing rooms.

Figure 2.3 *Intérieur d'une maison dans les îles Radak.* Choris's lithograph of a Marshall Island home depicted a natural and unspoiled setting—open air and an unobstructed view of the water, nutritious fruit, happy children, and the defined gender roles of healthy men and women. The rats in this home, according to Chamisso, were ubiquitous on the islands, and they destroyed some of the plants and seedlings introduced by the naturalist. By contrast, a reproduction of this illustration created by an engraver for Kotzebue's English-language voyage narrative shows a wilder setting. The home is crowded with additional people, who wear excessive plumage and jewelry, while the background is composed of a tropical jungle encroaching on the dwelling. Choris, who worked from his own sketches and recent memories of the islands, emphasized a light and airy setting, while the London reproduction showed readers a more exotic and forbidding scene. Courtesy Internet Archive.

Choris's depictions showed no visual references to prior contact with Europeans or the symbols of colonialism he included in his images of Hawai'i, Alaska, Alta California, and other places visited during the voyage. This was an unknown place, as Captain Kotzebue made clear in his claim of discovery. When "I discovered" these islanders, he wrote, "their whole attention was engaged with the ship, which they surveyed with astonishment, from the mast-head down to the water." He continued: "That we had begun the new year [1817] with a discovery seemed to us a good omen, and gave us all much pleasure." The islanders' "sensible" behavior impressed Kotzebue, who added, "we observed neither the cries nor grotesque movements with which savages generally distinguish themselves on their first meeting with Europeans."²⁷ Kotzebue's occasional use of the word "savages" angered Chamisso, who came to view the captain as arrogant and unenlightened in the way he characterized many Indigenous groups.

In contrast to Kotzebue's telling, the accounts offered by other members of the *Rurik* confirm that this was hardly a "first meeting" for the Marshallese. Indeed, the islanders seemed to welcome this opportunity to exploit the newcomers. As the *Rurik* sailed into view on January 2, more than twenty canoes encircled the ship, each paddled by five or six men, according to Chamisso. The men demanded iron ("Moll!" or, in Marshallese, *maal*) in exchange for "delicate shell wreaths," suggesting they were more than prepared for trade. The paddlers appeared to carefully assess the strength of the *Rurik*'s small crew.²⁸ The islanders were firmly in control, despite the implied martial advantage of the Europeans' guns and cannon. The supposed novelty of the meeting—a very significant notion to Kotzebue and his claim to discovery—was belied by evidence that the Marshallese had a good idea of how to handle the situation.

The people of the Ratak and Ralik Islands (the Marshalls' two parallel chains of more than twenty islands) had discovered European vessels in their seas centuries earlier. Spanish ships sighted land in the Marshalls during the 1500s and 1600s, but sustained interactions with the islanders were not recorded and only a few of these vessels actually made landfall.²⁹ A Dutch fleet sailed across the northern edge of the Marshalls in 1625 en route to the Moluccas, stopping at Guam for provisions. The British ship

Dolphin under Samuel Wallis's command sighted a pair of the islands in 1767, and, more significantly, two British ships commanded by William Marshall in 1788 not only marked various islands on their charts but also traded with a large group from the island of Mili aboard Marshall's ship, the *Scarborough*. Captain Marshall's report offered enough detail to place his name on charts identifying these islands—a fact known to Captain Kotzebue. Kotzebue conveniently set aside these prior encounters as his vessel intensely surveyed the entire Ratak chain and the personnel interacted with groups of islanders every few days. Kotzebue referred to the islands as "Radack" and "Ralick" (permutations of what the people told him), and he even stuck the name "Romanzoff's Islands" on his expedition's map for the atoll of Wotje. This Russian name never stuck.[30] Thus, not only was Kotzebue's "discovery" a highly dubious claim, but the Ratak islanders knew of Europeans, their vessels, and their most valuable trade items from prior experiences.

Even if Kotzebue and the others could ignore the signs of previous interactions with foreigners, what did this moment of sustained contact represent in their minds? British anthropologists in the 1930s and 1940s referred to first contact as the "zero point." Reflecting on this concept decades later, anthropologist Greg Dening argues: "the zero point was that dividing moment between a *Before*, when an indigenous culture was in its pure form, and an *After* of the encounter, when it was somehow adulterated. The zero point was a dividing line between authentic and inauthentic culture."[31] Dening's reflection captures the mindsets of the *Rurik*'s personnel. In contrast to almost all of the Indigenous people they met during the previous year, these Ratak islanders appeared unsullied by outside influences. The *Rurik* officers could exalt in the seeming newness of their encounters, announce the things they introduced to the islands, and celebrate the cultural authenticity of the islanders.

Ludwig Choris described the "friendly welcome by the natives" in the first week of January and the rituals of exchange that repeated as they shuttled from one island to the next.[32] The islanders presented breadfruit, pandanus, and coconuts as offerings to Choris and the others, while the Europeans reciprocated with presents of iron, seeds, and some domesticated animals. Chamisso feared that the *Rurik*'s imposing size might frighten the islanders, imagining their "surprise" when "they see our giant ship with outspread wings like a seabird move contrary to the direction of the wind that carries it"—almost as if the Marshallese possessed no sailing technology of their own.[33] In fact, they expressed no real concern for the ship beyond the episodes when they helped guide it through a reef to a safe anchorage. Choris described the persistent demand for scraps of iron and small knives in their initial meetings, concluding that the islanders possessed no iron except for the occasional flotsam that washed ashore. One welcoming ritual struck Choris as especially authentic. On January 6, Choris noted in his journal, "we found Rareck" (Rarick), a young, high-ranking *iroij* from the island of Wotje. Rarick immediately boarded the ship and introduced Kotzebue to the friendship ritual of exchanging names. "I was now called Rarick, and he Totabu, as he could not pronounce my name in any other manner," Kotzebue wrote. He felt personally honored by this gesture and awarded Rarick "plenty of presents" to solidify their unique friendship.[34] Rarik then turned to Chamisso and conducted the same friendship ritual with him.

Apart from friendship, Kotzebue desired specific information from Rarick regarding the extent of this island chain and how to safely navigate through the dangerous reefs. Rarick described the length of the Ratak chain before asking another man to sketch a map on a scrap of sail—an exercise Kotzebue and Chamisso learned to repeat whenever they found a willing and knowledgeable Marshallese informant. The geographic information they gathered helped establish the extent of the Marshall Islands, but even more significant for the safety of the *Rurik* was the detailed intelligence on safe channels, shoals, and barrier reefs. Outrigger canoes frequently guided the ship through the shoals and reefs, and Kadu would assume the roles of pilot and interpreter in late February after he joined the *Rurik*.

Chamisso found a clear meaning in these apparently harmonious encounters. These "sons of the sea," he wrote, became "friends without reservations.... In them I found pure, uncorrupted customs, charm, grace, and the gracious bloom of modesty."[35] Choris concurred with his colleague's assessment. Almost all of the artist's visual depictions of the Marshallese project their openness with the foreign visitors. For their part, the Marshallese showed very little caution toward these foreigners, because nothing in their limited experience with outsiders inclined them to do otherwise. Previous meetings had not been marred by violence, the taking of captives, or the introduction of foreign pathogens. Most important, these outsiders possessed things desired by the Marshallese, primarily things in the form of iron. The islanders' friendly reception veiled their true desire for iron and weapons—a byproduct of the inter-island conflicts affecting Marshallese society. The *Rurik* expedition blithely sailed into these local politics.

The inter-island and leadership tensions became more apparent when the *Rurik* arrived at the Aur Atoll, where the *iroij* Tigidien, Kadu, and Edock climbed aboard the ship. The *Rurik*'s personnel spent three days on the island, during which time Tigidien made clear his need for iron and weapons. Kotzebue supplied Tigidien with lances and other iron pieces, as he had done previously when he met Rarick. Kotzebue even brought the ship's forge to shore to demonstrate the shaping of weapons and hooks.[36] Years later Chamisso vehemently criticized this arms trade ("Mr. von Kotzebue gave Tigedien weapons! Lances and grappling hooks!"), because, as he learned, it soon led to increased conflict among island leaders.[37] But at the time Chamisso only noted how the "lust of dominion and conquest has extended its curse" to the islanders and "fate" had allowed the Europeans to supply weapons for their "feuds."[38]

Those "feuds" represented the local politics entered by the *Rurik*. Tigidien, Rarick, and other high-ranking *Iroijs* were all subservient to an ambitious young *iroij* named Lamari, who had consolidated his authority over the islands by means of violent assault against any local leader who opposed him. Furthermore, Lamari was gathering his resources and allies for attacks against people on the Ralik chain of islands.[39] Iron weapons from the *Rurik* could play an important role in this warfare, similar to the way European technologies assisted King Kamehameha's consolidation of power in the Hawaiian Islands. However, these local politics were difficult for the *Rurik*'s personnel to decipher. Kotzebue had no idea whether the weapons he left at Aur would be used in support of Lamari's ongoing warfare, or possibly against him. Lamari had murdered Aur's highest-ranking *iroij* "without any provocation" some years earlier, and Tigidien feared Lamari, according to information supplied by Kadu during the voyage.[40] Kadu would have his own strategic decisions to make when he returned to the Marshall Islands.[41]

Choris may have best captured the subtle tensions among Radakian elders with his portraits of two *iroijs*, Rarik and Labeloa. Rarik exudes benevolence with a cautious expression, while Labeloa appears menacing as he grasps a three-pronged spear. Neither man appears entirely at ease with the artist taking their likeness, even if Choris would have spent only a few moments drawing them on paper. His sketches would soon become watercolor paintings, and later the artist reproduced them in lithographic form.

In the months ahead, Kadu provided certain intelligence about these and other island leaders. While in the Marshall Islands, the *Rurik* mostly desired his language skills and navigational experience for the dangerous shoals of the low-lying islands. They also queried him about Marshallese sailing techniques. Kadu knew enough about Marshallese maritime culture to distinguish it from his own training in the Caroline Islands. The Marshallese practiced a form of "wave navigation" (or "swell navigation") in their vessels, a skill of sensing very subtle wave patterns (known as *kōkḷaḷ*) produced by the current's interactions with far-off islands, including the smallest landmasses too distant to be seen by the naked eye.[42] The *kōkḷaḷ* pattern allowed navigators to locate land, while the *dilep* wave channel showed the navigator a pathway leading from one island to the next. Marshallese navigators—then and today—model this navigational system with a *wapepe*, or hand-made "stick chart," constructed from pandanus roots and twine. The resulting latticework shows the "wave field" surrounding an island as well as the expected path between islands. Present-day Marshallese navigators and canoe-builders continue to use the *wapepe* as pedagogical tools for their apprentices, according to master canoe-builder Alson Kelen.[43] Kadu certainly witnessed the stick charts in the hands of young trainees, and he may have wondered why they were not memorizing

Figures 2.4a and 2.4b *Larik, Chef du groupe des îles Romanzoff;* and *Labéléloa, Chef du groupe des îles Koutousoff smolensky.* Expedition artists sought not only to sketch the physical appearance of Indigenous individuals but also to capture the person's essential character. Choris met Rarik (Larik) during the *Rurik*'s first week in the Marshall Islands, while Labeloa encountered the expedition ten days later, when both *iroijs* joined the officers for a meal aboard the ship. Rarik, according to Chamisso, "was especially distinguished by gentleness and good humor," while Labeloa struck the naturalist as more reserved and possibly hostile. The two portraits show Choris's attempt to characterize the individuals' distinct demeanors. Chamisso celebrated their "hereditary ruling class" as the proper "nature of things," but he also sensed tensions among the *iroijs* at this moment in time, and the expedition may have amplified the tensions by providing iron weapons to certain leaders (Chamisso, 1836). Courtesy Internet Archive.

star patterns as he had done during his years of apprenticeship. Regardless, he would have quickly recognized the tradition of trained navigators passing on knowledge to chosen apprentices, who themselves became respected navigators as they grew older.

In mid-March—and with Kadu in place as the ship's temporary pilot— the *Rurik* carefully maneuvered through the shallow channels and atolls of the northern Marshall Islands on its way to the Bering Sea. The value of having an experienced navigator on board was not lost on the officers and crew. Chamisso offered the most telling comment when he contrasted the "scientific research" of the most "learned hydrographers" with the more helpful knowledge possessed by a well-trained Indigenous guide. Kadu's language and navigational talents impressed the captain, and he utilized both skills in the northern Marshall Islands. Kadu "confirmed" or "corrected" the ship's direction "and every new path was diligently followed" by Captain Kotzebue.[44] Kadu greeted and conversed with paddlers of canoes as the *Rurik* continued its route through the islands. But like Tupaia's experience with James Cook five decades earlier, the practical value of Kadu's skills diminished once the *Rurik* departed from Micronesian seas. Thereafter a different process of knowledge exchange began between Kadu and his foreign shipmates.

EXCHANGING IMPERFECT KNOWLEDGE

The month-long journey from "the pleasant world" of the Ratak Islands to "the gloomy north" of the Aleutian Islands was filled with questions and cross-examinations. Kadu charmed the Europeans with his easy manner and interest in their travels. They valued his presence on board the ship, and each of them reflected on Kadu in their reports, journals, and drawings. At best, the officers attempted to understand Kadu to gain knowledge about the world from which he came. At worst, they subjected him to occasional ridicule and hazing—not uncommon practices directed at a newcomer on a ship—because they viewed him as different and submissive. Throughout, Kadu pursued his own interests as the *Rurik* struck a course into a northern ocean he did not recognize. He would collect objects of value, and he stored information that might prove useful when he returned home.

The personnel arrived at a means of communication with Kadu through trial and error. Since the day Kadu climbed aboard the ship, he had developed ways to make his intentions known through learned words, nonverbal signs, and what historian Celine Carayon terms "paralinguistic communication," which ranged from intonation and volume to songs and gestures.[45] The ship itself already contained a babble of competing European languages. By default, Russian served as the official language spoken between the captain and the Russian crew, but it was hardly the most important language of communication. Chamisso spoke French, German, English, and some Spanish. He failed to learn Russian. Choris knew Ukrainian, Russian, and some English and French (through Chamisso's tutelage), while he penned his journal in a nearly indecipherable script of old German. Kotzebue commanded his crew in Russian, but he shifted to his native German for the others. Naturalist and physician Johann Eschscholtz had German, Russian, and a smattering of English. Latin constituted a shared scholarly language for Eschscholtz and Chamisso when classifying species. Choris sprinkled some Latin characters and words throughout his journal.

Kadu contributed his Carolinian and Marshallese languages to this linguistic jumble, and over the course of the voyage he learned enough of different European languages to express his thoughts. Kotzebue blithely commented: "Kadu soon understood the Russian language, and we, on the other hand, perfected ourselves in his [language]." This was a gross over-statement. Chamisso diligently copied Kadu's Woleaian and Marshallese words into lists with comparisons to the Hawaiian and Chamorro "Vocabulary" he collected during the voyage. The challenge of translating all of these Indigenous sounds for the benefit of his English readers, Chamisso admitted, required liberally borrowing tonal and nasal elements from his own languages. "It is hardly necessary to say, that none of [the linguistic] faults could be avoided," he concluded.[46]

Faults of miscommunication aside, no one seemed particularly con-cerned about their ability to communicate with Kadu. Choris chronicled their conversations in his journal on a regular basis, while Chamisso and Eschscholtz recounted many of Kadu's statements years after the voyage in their private correspondence. Kotzebue directly quoted Kadu with some regularity in his official voyage record. In one instance, as the ship ap-proached a yet-unseen island south of the Arctic, Kotzebue offered this translation of Kadu's voice: "There is certainly land! The birds are flying home to their young ones; and by this we always know how to find an island when we have lost it."[47] Kotzebue surely placed these specific words in Kadu's mouth, but it is also reasonable to assume that Kadu expressed something approximating this sentiment to the captain and, one way or another, had made very clear his knowledge that birds could assist a navigator in sensing an approaching island.

Kadu made clear decisions about the information he offered as well as the method by which he offered it. On the northward journey, the officers queried Kadu about many topics: his home island of Woleai, religious beliefs, island geography, vocabulary, knowledge of Europeans, diet, and so on. Kadu answered in his own time and in his own way. When "new particulars were mentioned [by Kadu]," Chamisso stated about one conversation, "we reproached him for having concealed [those details]." Kadu apparently responded: "You did not ask me that before!" Kadu could grow tired of the questioning, close his eyes, and feign sleep. Other times he would break into song, which mystified his sailing companions until they realized his songs represented a vital means of communication and contained valuable information. "The songs," Chamisso concluded, "which he learnt from the people among whom he had resided, served him, as it were, as a book, in which he sought explanation or confirmation of his assertions."[48]

A poet trained in the internal workings of verse, Chamisso came to understand the value of Kadu's songs as a means of knowledge transmission rooted in his oral culture. In response to a question regarding the conflicts among different Marshallese *iroijs*, Kadu sang about specific leaders sailing to Aur in support of Lamari's fight against a rival *iroij*: "On the beach the people throng!/ Shift the sails round!/ Strike we not on the reef!/ Land out of sight!"[49] In this instance, the accuracy of Chamisso's translation is less significant than his attempt to grasp Kadu's means of communication through verse. Another song repeated by Kadu involved an island called Waghal (Guam), "the land of iron . . . inhabited by Europeans," which Carolinian navigators frequently visited. The details of Kadu's song about Guam included the names of ships, the exchange of specific items, and a man named "Torres" who seemed "glorified" on Woleai. This song "remained an enigma for us," Chamisso commented, until the *Rurik* arrived at Guam the following year and they met the Spanish representative Don Luis de Torres.[50] Kotzebue told Torres that Kadu had left the voyage a few weeks earlier when the *Rurik* stopped in the Marshall Islands. Torres promised to inform Kadu's Woleaian friends of his whereabouts when they next sailed to Guam.

Kadu's songs contained information drawn from the collective Woleaian memory of places, people, and events. One song in particular, Chamisso noted, "preserved the knowledge" of Caroline geography and the names of specific islands, which Chamisso translated as Malilogotot, Wugeuetsagerar, Giep, Vageval, Lomul, and Pullop. He queried Kadu further in order to build a comprehensive list of islands, and he later compared those place-names to a report compiled by Luis de Torres and a second list produced decades earlier by the Jesuit missionary Juan Antonio Cantova, who was killed by islanders west of Woleai for his intrusive proselytizing activities.[51] "Kadu's testimony is of more weight [than Cantova's or Torres's]," Chamisso concluded, due to his actual experiences as a navigator and the collective memory of his people as embodied in the songs.[52] Perhaps Chamisso simply liked Kadu more than Luis de Torres (or the murdered priest Cantova), but he also clearly weighed the three informants' experience in determining their cultural and scientific value.

Beyond linguistic or geographic knowledge, Kadu's interrogators also sought to gain a sense of his ability to reason and react to new information. They did so in various ways. The naturalists typically asked informational questions and took note of his answers. But on a few occasions, they presented Kadu with intentionally false information, such as the suggestion that seals hatched eggs. Kadu refused to believe this joke. At least once they showed Kadu an unexpected artifact to gauge his reaction. Ten days into the northern voyage, Chamisso, Choris, and Eschscholtz produced a display of three human skulls they had ransacked during the previous season of exploration in the North Pacific. Chamisso described the scene that unfolded below deck: "I happened to pull a human skull out from under my bunk...[and] Eschscholtz and Choris did the same thing and moved toward him with skulls in their hands."[53] In the ordinary course of daily events, one does not simply "happen" to pull a human skull on someone without anticipating a startled response, nor do fellow skull-holders unexpectedly advance on that acquaintance without some prior coordination. This staged experiment was clearly meant to gauge Kadu's reaction and instinct.

To the extent that Kadu held unexpressed fears of traveling with a group of strange foreigners—and how could he not?—this moment brought his suspicions to the surface. Chamisso recorded his immediate response. "What is this?" Kadu exclaimed, as he scanned the expectant faces of the two naturalists and the artist. His shocked reaction showed an existential fear for his own life, which surprised the Europeans, because they had convinced themselves of Kadu's easy comfort with them. They explained the scientific reasoning for collecting human skulls and, according to Chamisso, they "had no trouble at all in getting across to him that we were interested in comparing the skulls of the variously formed human races and peoples with each other." To the extent Kadu understood any of this information, the racist "science" of phrenology must have seemed utterly absurd.[54] It may have struck him as an incomprehensible way to reveal anything meaningful about human difference, a concept he certainly understood as it pertained to separate island groups, languages, and cultures. But race, as a constructed category and supposed hierarchy of difference, likely held little meaning for Kadu.

In this instance, the naturalists exploited Kadu as a human subject in a macabre ethnographic experiment. Why did they do it? They wanted to gauge Kadu's reaction to the skulls, because they saw him as a "pure" Native unsullied by colonial influences.[55] But what *was* a Native islander, they seemed to ask by provoking Kadu with their exhibit of plundered skulls. These were questions primarily about Kadu's indigeneity.[56] While they frequently made broad claims about Indigenous groups in general, they clearly viewed Kadu as an individual and someone worthy of close study. His bodily symbols and behaviors fascinated the naturalists and artist—the many tattoos that adorned his body, the ease with which he sang songs about the "air" of his home island, and the fact that Caroline islanders could marry "several women" if they consented.[57] But what other exotic habits did Kadu possess? Did he believe in multiple gods? Would he eat human flesh? Did he, by any chance, collect human skulls? This was the purpose of the skull display: to see if Kadu might respond with a savage-like instinct at the mere sight of the skulls. Kadu failed the test. Instead, he displayed fear for his own safety and revulsion at the possible source of the skulls. In failing this initial test, Kadu revealed to the observers that his instincts were not entirely dissimilar from their own, although his respect for human remains certainly set him apart from European naturalists, many of whom collected skulls. To end this tense moment, Kadu told Chamisso he would attempt to secure a skull from Ratak for their collection. He never did so upon his return to the Marshall Islands.

A reliable and willing informant at times, Kadu could also undermine their research with misinformation. During their northern journey, the topics of cannibalism and human sacrifice surfaced, which was hardly surprising given European naturalists' fascination with these practices.[58] Kadu, according to Chamisso and Choris, stated that human sacrifices took place in the Caroline Islands and, furthermore, that adult captives were eaten on some islands. But Kadu admitted he had never witnessed either activity.[59] What Kadu actually said and how they transcribed his meaning remains a mystery. However, the intended message that cannibalism and human sacrifice existed was clear. Kadu offered Chamisso a more precise level of detail in reference to islands in the Ralik chain of the Marshalls: "Human flesh is eaten at Repith-Urur," he supposedly reported, and the people of "Malilogotot" did the same.[60] We can only guess at Kadu's motivations for providing this false information to the artist and naturalist. It may have been an attempt to amuse, confuse, or belittle his audience. He may have been fearful for his life—the skulls certainly gave him cause for alarm—and therefore wanted his inquisitors to fear the behaviors of some islanders. He may have been passing along gross stereotypes of enemies; for instance, the information he offered Chamisso about the flesh-eaters of "Repith-Urur" and "Maliligotot" referred to the known adversaries of his Marshallese hosts on Aur. He also may have aimed to direct these Europeans away from his home Caroline Islands. Whatever his reasoning, Kadu had a captive audience, and the misinformation he provided shaped the knowledge recorded by his inquisitors.[61] It was hardly uncommon for Indigenous "informants" to offer false information to European inquisitors. Kadu did so for any number of reasons.

THE GREAT STORM AND THE RETREAT FROM THE ICE

The shipbuilder Erik Malm of Abo (Turku), Finland, had designed the *Rurik* for speed on the open ocean and maneuverability in the tight quarters of the Arctic Sea. At 180 tons, its size was extremely small compared to most circumnavigating vessels, while its light Finnish fir framing allowed it to sail high in the water unless filled with sufficient ballast. Many captains would have considered the *Rurik* "crank"—or top-heavy—and therefore prone to upset in a truly violent storm.[62] For more than a year at sea the officers and crew had avoided the Pacific's potential for overpowering seas. Three weeks out from the Marshalls and nearing the Aleutian Islands, the sea was calm enough for the naturalists to conduct their business on deck under a pleasant but cool breeze. They hooked and dissected a 180-pound "moon-fish," which tasted like something "between fish and crabs," Kotzebue reported, and they also netted an albatross with a seven-foot wingspan. On April 5, the captain "took advantage of the calm" to measure the temperature of the water at the surface and also at a depth of 250 fathoms (58 and 48 degrees Fahrenheit, respectively). The "transparency of the water" reached to six fathoms (36 feet), but Kotzebue also commented, "we clearly perceived that we were quitting the fine tropical climates" as the *Rurik* crossed 36 degrees North latitude.[63] Days later, a tempest struck.

Storms in the world's largest ocean arrive alarmingly fast and with a furious intensity. Recall the storm that overran Kadu's small fleet of outrigger canoes years earlier, which quickly engulfed this group of highly experienced Caroline navigators shortly after they left Guam. This weather event was entirely common in the Carolines, and the fact that Kadu's small group survived indicates their ability to handle its moderate intensity. On the other end of the spectrum, the most extreme Pacific storms generate unbearable winds and swells taller than any nineteenth-century vessel.

Individual "rogue" waves can appear during extreme storms and leave devastation in their wake. In 1826 French captain and naturalist Jules Dumont d'Urville experienced "a raging storm...the waves veritable mountains were up to at least 80-100 ft in height," which still pales in comparison to the tallest rogue waves known to crash over the bows of today's immense container ships.[64] Apart from the *Rurik* officers' own reports of the event, it is impossible to know the comparative power of the storm that engulfed the ship as it drew closer to the Aleutian Islands. The *Rurik* had entered the North Pacific's transitional zone of currents as it passed from the North Pacific "Gyre" (a circular clockwise current stretching from Japan to California) and into the counterclockwise flow of the North Pacific and Alaska currents. These intersecting seas, even during a moderate storm, could easily disassemble a 180-ton wooden ship and scatter its planks, cargo, and personnel across the ocean swells.

All four diarists aboard the *Rurik* penned accounts of the storm due to its power as well as the way it contributed to the disappointing outcome of the expedition's ultimate mission. Choris published the briefest description of the event:

> [On April 10,] the wind began to blow with force from the southwest; suddenly it veered to the west and northwest and became a frightful violence. The tempest raised the waves to an extraordinary height. Pushed and swept along by the force of the wind, the breaking of the waves filled the air with excessive and disagreeable moisture. A wave struck the bowsprit and shattered it. This storm lasted for [more than] an entire day. Finally the wind began to die down.[65]

Choris had experienced brief episodes of rough weather on the *Rurik* during the previous year, but the chaotic winds, towering waves, seawater-drenched air, and shattered bowsprit (the long spar jutting from the ship's bow) terrified the young man. This storm of tremendous magnitude threatened all their lives, and Kotzebue ordered everyone but the sailors below deck. Choris, Kadu, Chamisso, and Eschscholtz huddled in the pitching cabin while the Russian sailors struggled to keep the ship afloat.

Chamisso's diary confirms the key elements of Choris's account. He wrote about the "extraordinary size of the waves," the "smashed bowsprit," the windswept swells that made it impossible to see, and the "force of the tempest" that encircled the *Rurik* for two days.[66] In the main cabin—and fearing for their lives—Chamisso's thoughts darkened, and he sought solace in poetry. "Not many German verses are made on or in the vicinity of Unalashka" during a violent storm, he mused:

> So rage, storm, complete your work,
> strew these planks about, even as
> you so easily split the mast,
> so well-fitted and mighty!
> Down below, I think, a man can find peace,
> there he will find rest from all storms.
> What is cracking now? Good! The wave has struck?
> Go away! It has happened, we are sinking. –No,
>
> We are not sinking! We are still being rocked about,
> our narrow coffin carried toward the sky.[67]

Though decidedly below the caliber of his favorite German poets Johann Goethe and Friedrich von Schiller, Chamisso's verse adequately reflects the terrifying predicament of the passengers crammed in a dark cabin as the ship tossed them about. At some point Chamisso and the others may have accepted their fate: either the ship would become their "coffin," or they would "find peace" and "rest" when the storm diminished.

They made themselves useful by securing every object in the main cabin and tending to a young sailor named Peter Prishimoff, who shattered his lower leg after crashing into the gunwale.[68] Kadu wanted to assist the captain on deck, but Kotzebue refused his request. "In these two days [of the storm]," Chamisso recalled, "we got a lot out of Kadu."[69] They queried him about the sudden storm that overtook his own vessel years earlier, and he confessed to far more fear at this present moment. As a navigator of open-air outriggers, Kadu loathed the idea of huddling in the coffin-like enclosure of a ship. "Kadu had been in great terror during the storm" because he feared the "white waves would kill the poor ship," Kotzebue wrote. On a foreign vessel in alien seas, Kadu had no authority in a situation for which he had trained since childhood. He doubted the captain's command of the vessel, Kotzebue admitted, believing "we were now wandering at random about the sea" and might crash into a rocky shore.[70]

Kotzebue described an endless series of high waves during the "fury of the hurricane." It seemed, he commented, "as if a direful revolution was…destroying the whole stupendous fabric of nature" as the "tops of the waves" formed "a thick rain over the surface of the ocean." More than twenty-four hours into the storm he sighted the highest wave yet "[take] its direction to the Rurick, and in the same moment threw me down senseless." Chaos reigned on the ship: the two-foot-thick bowsprit was "dashed into pieces," the helm was smashed in two, and a sailor was thrown into the foaming sea.[71] The sailor grabbed hold of a rope that hung behind the ship and clawed his way back on board. Kotzebue suffered his own injury when a violent pitch of the ship threw him against a gunwale. He severely cracked his chest and passed out—an injury that would influence the fate of the expedition.

The storm gradually diminished during the next twelve hours, and everyone took stock of the circumstances. The physician Eschscholtz dosed two injured sailors as well as the captain with opium, while Lieutenant Shishmaref temporarily took command of the battered ship. Those crewmembers still able to work re-rigged the sails, and the carpenter fashioned a temporary helm. Luckily, the two masts had held firm during the storm despite the loss of the bowsprit, whose remaining parts dangled uselessly from rigging attached to the bow. The copper sheathing on the bottom of the Rurik required immediate attention, but that repair would have to wait until the ship arrived at the Russian port of Iliuliuk on Unalaska Island. The sky briefly brightened as the Rurik limped northeast near the Aleutian Islands, but then it darkened again.

After surviving an extreme storm, Kadu found himself in a northern climate unlike anything he had previously experienced. A light snow fell on the ship deck, allowing Kadu to see "water become a solid body" for the first time in his life. "I never saw him regard anything with more astonishment than snow," the captain commented.[72] For Kadu, this chilly northern ocean with its strange new elements must have seemed like a truly bizarre place. When the skies again cleared, he could see the stark and forbidding islands of the Aleutian chain. Whales clustered around the ship, and seals populated the rocky shoreline as the *Rurik* approached Iliuliuk. Kadu stared at these marine mammals through a telescope while Choris sketched a coastal scene filled with sea lions and elephant seals.

Figure 2.5 *Lions marins dans l'île de St. Georges.* The *Rurik* entered a calm stretch of sea along the Aleutian Islands after it survived a violent storm in the North Pacific. In this lithograph, the *Rurik* sails across a placid horizon, and sea lions appear to observe the ship from a safe distance on shore. In the decades surrounding the *Rurik*'s visit, the Russian American Company slaughtered millions of sea lions and other fur-bearing mammals in the Arctic region. By the time of the *Rurik*'s arrival, sea otters had "suddenly vanished from these parts," according to Kotzebue's report (Kotzebue, 1821). Sea otters represented the most valuable commodity of the hunt due to the value of their fur, and the RAC had aggressively forced Aleut to hunt sea otters to near extinction. The still-plentiful sea lions mesmerized Kadu due to their size, numbers, and loud barking. Chamisso wrote: "On the whole voyage nothing gave [Kadu] more pleasure than the sight of the sea-lions and sea-bears on St. George's Island" (Chamisso, 1821). Courtesy Internet Archive.

The expedition would spend two months on the island of Unalaska to repair almost every part of the damaged *Rurik*. Beyond the sorry state of the rigging, masts, and sails, the copper sheathing "was quite gone in some parts" while other copper "plates still hung on"—requiring the careening of the ship on a rocky beach. Russian American Company agent Ivan Kuskov, who managed this colonial outpost, offered every possible assistance, but Unalaska had little of value to offer a ravaged ship beyond a safe harbor, some planking, and Aleut laborers. Captain Kotzebue secured a group of Aleuts as interpreters and paddlers for the next stage of the voyage north of the Bering Strait.

The captain was still suffering from his injuries as the ship departed on June 29, 1817. He praised the Russian commander of Unalaska for supplying the ship with provisions, which included a few cows tethered to the deck, and he reported that the sailor who suffered a broken leg during the storm "was now able to go about again." Everyone else on the *Rurik* appeared fine following two months of ship repairs and, for the naturalists and Kadu, some intense botanizing on the mountainous island. But Kotzebue was not well—a direct result of the injury he suffered to his chest during the storm, which caused broken ribs and possibly a perforated lung. Choris thought the captain ailed from consumption, but this diagnosis from a twenty-one-year-old artist may lack credibility. Regardless, Kotzebue described a "constant pain in [his] breast," and he occasionally coughed up blood.[73] This was an inauspicious start for launching the expedition's second attempt to discover the world's most elusive geographic feature, the Northern Passage.

Between Unalaska Island and the Bering Strait stretched more than eight hundred nautical miles of open ocean—a relatively quick northward journey with favorable winds. The *Rurik* completed this distance in less than ten days and arrived at an anchorage on St. Lawrence Island— immediately south of the strait—near the same Yupik village the expedition had visited the previous year. Using a telescope from the ship's deck, Kotzebue watched women and children departing from the village while a group of men prepared to meet the visitors on the beach. Clearly, the Yupik continued to distrust any foreign contact, even a scientific expedition they had already met. Kotzebue went ashore with an armed entourage and a few Aleut interpreters for the purpose of gathering intelligence. Specifically, he wanted to know about the state of the icepack immediately north of St. Lawrence Island. "On my question whether the [winter] ice had long left their shores, I received the bad news that it had only left within three days," Kotzebue wrote. "My hope, therefore, of penetrating Beering's Straits was blasted, as I could not expect it would be cleared of ice for fourteen days."[74] This was an odd confession by the captain, considering the public recriminations that would follow. Why would his "hope" be "blasted" if the strait was not yet open but would quite possibly clear within two weeks? During the previous summer's successful exploration, the *Rurik* did not pass through the Bering Strait until the end of July—two weeks from their present date.

Back on the ship, the captain steered to the northern tip of St. Lawrence Island for a better view of the sea ahead. From that location "at 12 o'clock at night," Kotzebue wrote, "we perceived, to our terror, firm ice, which extended as far as the eye could see...covering the whole surface of the ocean." He gave no explanation as to why the "firm ice" would evoke "terror," since they already knew the icepack remained at this time. This observation offered a weak rationale for his sudden and controversial decision: the *Rurik* would retreat and abandon its search for the Northern Passage. Kotzebue's primary reason was his worsening health. "My melancholy situation, which had daily grown worse since we had left Oonalashka, received here the last blow," he wrote. "The cold air so affected my lungs, that I lost my breath, and at last spasms in the chest, faintings, and spitting of blood ensued." He sought the advice of Doctor Eschscholtz, who, according to Kotzebue, "declared to me that I could not remain near the ice." The physical proximity to the ice, it seemed, endangered his health. Kotzebue contemplated his desire to "brave death [to] accomplish my undertaking," and then he reflected on the "difficult voyage [back] to our own country" and the "lives of my companions." He felt he "must suppress [his] ambition" for the sake of everyone involved, including himself. From his cabin Kotzebue wrote an order to the crew, concluding: "my ill health oblige[s] me to return to Oonalashka."[75] With no alternative but to follow the captain's order, Lieutenant Gleb Shishmaref struck a southerly course for Unalaska Island. After a quick provisioning stopover, the *Rurik* set a course for the Hawaiian Islands, where the captain could regain his health, the naturalists and artist could continue their studies, and Kadu would meet the ruler of the most populated kingdom in the Pacific Ocean.

No one aboard the *Rurik* appeared content with the captain's decision to abort this season's search for the Northern Passage. Lieutenant Shishmaref would have cherished the opportunity to lead the expedition north of the Bering Strait despite the captain's ill-health. In fact, he would return to this exact place in 1820 in command of the *Blagonamerennyi* (Good Intent) to explore further into the northern seas. The physician Eschscholtz offered the only remarks that might justify the captain's decision. He documented the "spasms in the lungs, and fainting-fits" as well as the "spit blood, though in very small quantities." He concluded that Kotzebue could "expect his recovery in repose on shore," presumably a warm shore far from the icy North.[76] Eschscholtz's clinical description rang hollow if he intended to justify the captain's decision, which he did not. Chamisso received the captain's order to retreat from the ice with great disappointment. He noted the "painful outrage" he felt as a mere "passenger" on the ship who "must make no demands." Chamisso recorded a long and accusatory list of what the captain "could have" done given the circumstances, which ranged from recuperating on land for a few weeks to handing over command of the ship to Lieutenant Shishmaref.[77] Reflecting on the captain's decision years later, Chamisso quoted an English critic of Kotzebue: "[I]t appears to us that its abrupt abandonment was hardly justified under the circumstances stated."[78]

From the moment he turned around the *Rurik*, Kotzebue knew that accusations of failure would circulate in the maritime community and the periodicals devoted to exploration. The captain certainly ruminated on this prospect from his cabin as the *Rurik* made its way to Unalaska Island. Could he claim enough notable "discoveries" even if he had aborted the central mission? He would certainly attempt to do so with his list of new islands in the Central Pacific, the discovery of Kotzebue Sound, and the notable scientific findings made by the naturalists. The rest of the personnel had hoped for another cruise into the Chukchi Sea, even if they doubted the existence of a northern passage. What might they find worthy of study? No one knew, and especially for the naturalists, this was precisely the point. Many concerns cycled through Kotzebue's opium-fogged mind as he recuperated during the return to Unalaska Island. From his berth in the captain's cabin, he could see the portrait of his accomplished father, August von Kotzebue. How would he explain his decision to his father?

Kadu, for his part, would carefully describe these new places and experiences to his Marshallese peers and elders. Only five months into his voyage, he had sailed farther north than anyone from Micronesia, survived a fierce storm, touched ice and snow, approached strange new marine mammals, and met other islanders whose living conditions were radically different from his own. In the coming months he would accumulate additional experiences in the Hawaiian Islands and form new thoughts about his European shipmates. Kadu would report all this information upon his return to the Marshall Islands. But for now, as he sailed south through the Bering Sea, the *Rurik* brought him closer to a more familiar climate and a realm of the ocean that closely resembled his home islands.

All Species of Knowledge: A Voyage of Discovery, Failure, and Natural History in the Pacific Ocean. David Igler, Oxford University Press. © Oxford University Press 2026. DOI: 10.1093/9780197777718.003.0003

Depicting Sites of Colonialism

According to the information given by Kadoo...
—FREDERIC SHOBERL, *The World in Miniature (1824)*

How did the European public gain knowledge about the world's distant populations in the early nineteenth century? Scholars and explorers published their impressions of foreign people in academic journals, books, and travel diaries, which reached limited, if enthusiastic and learned, audiences. Naturalists, many of whom directly interacted with Indigenous populations through their travels, also directed most of their publications to educated readers. But some of them sought a larger audience, because they believed their opinions on matters such as colonialism, human difference, or a newly discovered species held significant value for the public. Naturalists often altered their voice to address a public audience. For instance, Adelbert von Chamisso slipped in the intimate appeal "dear reader" when he shared a personal detail with those who held in their hands a copy of his travelogue *A Voyage Around the World*.[1]

Lay readers of travel and exploration possessed many options in the early 1800s, ranging from the writings of naturalists like Chamisso to penny press periodicals and mass-produced book series.[2] London-based author Frederic Shoberl, best known for his wildly popular translation of *The Hunchback of Notre Dame*, capitalized on the expanding public market of readers with an 1821 book titled *The World in Miniature: Africa*. The "miniature" in the title referred specifically to the book's duodecimo size, but it also suggested the author's attempt to reduce the non-European "world" to easily digestible bites.[3]

Due to the immediate success of his first volume, Shoberl followed up with more than three dozen additional "world in miniature" titles. These books introduced readers to a variety of places and their resident populations of "inhabitants," "savages," and "exotic tribes"—and, by implicit contrast, the "non-exotic European."[4] In 1824, he devoted a two-volume work to Pacific islands, titled "THE STATE OF SOCIETY AMONG THE VARIOUS TRIBES SCATTERED OVER The GREAT OCEAN, *called the* PACIFIC, *or the* SOUTH SEAS." Since Shoberl had no firsthand knowledge of the Pacific, he relied extensively and imaginatively on the information circulated by explorers who had visited these places. He particularly borrowed from Otto von Kotzebue's recently published voyage record and Adelbert von Chamisso's "Remarks and Opinion of the Naturalist of the Expedition." For illustrations, Shoberl filled his two Pacific volumes with imitative prints of Ludwig Choris's lithographs. In addition to these three European voyagers, Shoberl enlisted a certain Indigenous authority to deepen his readers' understanding of the Hawaiian, Marshall, and Caroline Islands. Here he offered details "according to the information given by Kadoo."[5]

Shoberl's informant "Kadoo" weighed in on topics ranging from Native political structures to the distinct cultural practices of island communities. Shoberl even cited an idea that Kotzebue had attributed to "Kadoo" in support of a "drift" theory of Hawaiian Island settlement—the idea that a Native group in the deep past had haphazardly "drifted" in the ocean's expanse until they found themselves "planted" ashore on the Hawaiian Archipelago. A skilled navigator, Kadu may have rejected this theory had it been presented to him.[6] Regardless, the presence of "Kadoo" as an Indigenous authority raises a curious question: How did a Woleaian man named Kadu, known to only a handful of fellow travelers on the *Rurik*, appear as a cultural authority in the pages of a popular English book that sought to explain the distant world to its readers? The most direct answer is that Frederic Shoberl had read about him in Kotzebue's and Chamisso's works, and he wanted to use Kadu as an expert source. However, a more complete answer is that Shoberl placed Kadu, Kotzebue, Chamisso, and

Choris in a public conversation about colonialism and the island Pacific—a conversation in which he, Shoberl, served as the arbiter. Shoberl viewed empire as a civilizing project guided by Christianity, and he exploited knowledgeable travelers in support of his mission. If only "in miniature," Shoberl's books offered a grand and celebratory account of imperialism's advance.

The impact of colonialism on Indigenous populations certainly interested the *Rurik*'s personnel. Their attention came as much from humanitarian concern as from ethnographic curiosity, although the two impulses intersected and reinforced each other at various times during and after the voyage. The personnel witnessed the effects of colonialism on distinct Indigenous populations, and they concluded that some groups (such as the Marshallese) prospered due to their isolation from Europeans, while others (such as the Aleut) suffered greatly due to colonial subjugation. Frederic Shoberl believed otherwise. He argued that "intercourse with Europeans" had "uplifted" Pacific "tribes" and "the atrocious cruelties of the ancient superstition have yielded to the beneficent influence of the Gospel of Christ!"[7] In one significant way these contrasting perspectives found common ground: the social environment—and especially the level of colonial rule—rather than biological or racial attributes, explained the condition of Indigenous communities. In the coming decades the concept of race would gain greater prominence in scientific explanations of human difference, but naturalists in the early 1800s primarily viewed Indigenous groups through the prism of their environment and social conditions rather than relying on racial determinants.[8]

Three imperial locations most intrigued the personnel of the *Rurik*. The Russian outposts in Alaska, especially the Russian American Company (RAC) settlement on Unalaska Island, represented the empire's ambition for expanded wealth and power in the North Pacific. Russia's colonial project relied on the forced dependence of Aleut labor—a fact well known to those aboard the *Rurik* due to their three visits to Unalaska Island and their own use of Aleut workers. The second site of colonialism was Alta California, where a waning Spanish empire clung to a coastal infrastructure of missions, pueblos, and presidios constructed by the compulsory labor of Native Californians since the 1770s. While the Russian empire pondered new possibilities for imperial expansion into Alta California, those on board the *Rurik* reported that colonialism had wrought havoc on the Native population.[9] A third imperial setting, the Kingdom of the Hawaiian Islands, stood in contrast to the other two by virtue of its Indigenous leadership. King Kamehameha consolidated his mostly benign rule across the island chain during the previous forty years, creating a trading entrepôt that touched many places around the Pacific. But the aging Kamehameha, recognized by Hawaiians as an *ali'i akua* or "god-king," had only a short time to live when the *Rurik* visited in 1816 and 1817. Signs of foreign incursion, introduced European pathogens, and population decline among the *kanaka maoli* were already too evident.

The reports and diaries produced by Kotzebue and the naturalists present their individual perspectives on colonialism in these settings. However, it was the artist Ludwig Choris's visual record—the focus of this chapter—that reached the broadest and most enduring audience. Reproductions of his watercolors and prints appeared in notable publications before and after his illustrated travelogue *Voyage pittoresque*. Choris knockoff images showed up in British, French, and Russian publications documenting the latest views of the Pacific during a time when new explorations set off for the Great Ocean. One of his watercolors—the first formal portrait of King Kamehameha—was reproduced and widely viewed by Pacific populations. Only a portion of Choris's works explicitly address colonial relations, but the large majority of his images depict Indigenous people, their social environments, and their material culture. Choris prized documentary authenticity above stylistic concerns because he considered it fundamental to his position as a voyage artist. He hoped that what he chose to illustrate—and how he rendered it—would influence the accumulated knowledge about distant lands and colonized people.

"SEND THE BAIDARA": UNALASKA ISLAND, ILIULIUK, AND THE ALEUTS

The Kotzebue expedition spent more time at Unalaska Island than any other place because of the need for ship repairs and the assistance made

available by RAC personnel. The expedition also spent more time with
Aleuts than any other Pacific islander population, because they served as
translators and guides during the two northern expeditions. Four Aleut
seamen would ultimately remain on the ship for its return to St. Petersburg,
where they were "handed over to the Russian-American Trading Company"
for language training.[10] In the late eighteenth and early nineteenth centuries, the Aleut perhaps best embodied the contradictions and ambitions of
Russia's imperial consolidation, which stretched from eastern Siberia,
across southern Alaska, and down the North American coastline. This
Indigenous group experienced the severity of Russian subjugation and
population decline, but at the same time, the Aleut secured a principal
position within Russian operations. Without Aleut labor, Russia's economic
and territorial ambitions in the North Pacific would have floundered mis-
erably. Intermarriage and sexual assault over previous generations had
created a sizeable and vital creole population.[11] Evidence of the Aleuts'
centrality to the Russian project personally greeted the *Rurik* when it arrived at Unalaska Island: Ivan Kuskov, the head of RAC operations on the
island, was married to an Aleut woman, and one of their creole sons would
serve as a RAC functionary in the 1820s.[12]

Similar to other North Pacific groups such as Tlingit, Chukchi, Yupik,
Eskimo, and Iñupiat, the Aleut showed a capacity to survive and adapt in
a forbidding northern environment over thousands of years. Their hundreds of villages stretched across large and small Aleutian Islands in a
spoon-shape band from *Sasignan* (Commander Islands) in the west to the
Qagaan (the Alaska Peninsula) in the east. They all spoke some version
of Unangam, but a shared linguistic tradition hardly prevented conflict
among the dispersed Aleut communities. Clashes with neighboring
groups frequently erupted, and these conflicts typically involved contests
over marine mammal resources, such as seals, sea otters, and other prized
species. Aleut origin stories frequently expressed their connection with
sea otters, while their tales "are obsessed with the ocean and its creatures,"
according to historian Ryan Jones.[13] Their communities exhibited a strati-
fied social order of high-ranking *toions*, skilled hunters, commoners, and
captive individuals.

The arrival of Russian hunters and traders in the mid-1700s represented a new group of outsiders to confront. Unlike the Aleuts' Indigenous adversaries, Russians arrived with powerful technologies, novel items to trade, and a desire to claim territory. By the late eighteenth century, historian Matthew Romaniello argues, the "new Russian plan" for the region included "outright conquest."[14] Aleut violent resistance included some victories over the Russian newcomers in the late 1700s, most notably in 1763, when Aleuts destroyed four Russian ships and killed almost two hundred men. Russians responded with blunt violence against all those who opposed them, frequently taking female and child captives to gain advantage over individual Aleut groups.[15] By 1800, Russian colonizers and the Aleut had forged fragile ties based on an ever-present threat of violence, a shared desire to survive, intermarriage, and the impact of Aleut depopulation. Aleut populations had dropped by more than 50 percent during the decades before the *Rurik* arrived, as a result of both violence and introduced pathogens.[16]

Despite the dire circumstances imposed by Russian colonization, Aleut communities maintained a pivotal role within Russian economic activity and its expansionist plans. They led the Russian hunt for marine mammals, and the RAC contracted out their labor to American ship captains who sailed down the California coast in search of sea otter colonies in the early 1800s.[17] When the RAC began its own territorial grab in northern California in 1812 with the founding of Fort Ross, Aleut hunters and creole workers were a central part of the effort. Russian communiqués between Alaska and St. Petersburg were littered with references to the need for Aleut participation in exploration and colonization. "Send the baidara [with the Aleut] and the surveyors," wrote the Russian Admiralty to explorer Vasilii Golovnin in 1817—a shorthand way of indicating the need for Aleut skills and their specialized seacraft.[18]

The *Rurik*'s naturalists and artist knew the general state of Aleut conditions due to information offered by Captain Kotzebue as well as their general knowledge of RAC activities in the North Pacific. When the ship first arrived in the small port of Iliuliuk on Unalaska Island, in September 1816, Choris understood that this had been a Russian-held settlement for

decades. He welcomed the feast of beef, cabbage, and potatoes offered by
Ivan Kuskov, and he especially enjoyed the "Russian steam bath" prepared
for the officers and crew. But Choris's attention quickly turned to the
Russian system of bonded peonage against which the Aleut seemed to

Habitans des îles Aléoutiennes.

Figure 3.1 *Habitans des îles Aléoutiennes.* The "inhabitants" of Iliuliuk village on Unalaska
Island spanned the entire Aleut social hierarchy, from the high-ranking *tukux* (Russians
called them *toions*, or chiefs) to the lowest-ranking *kalgas* (enslaved individuals). Choris
sketched some lower-rank Aleuts, but the man and woman he depicts in this lithograph
are clearly of higher rank, based on their clothing and attention to personal presentation.
Choris focuses the viewer's attention on the Aleut woman due to her enigmatic gaze and
composure. Her long, tightly braided hair and her Russian Orthodox cross necklace suggest
a high status in the "hybrid" Aleut-Russian community of Iliuliuk. She was most likely
creole born and married to a Russian officer or creole Aleut. Choris identifies the man's high
status by his juxtaposition to the woman and by his occupation: his headwear demonstrates
that he's a hunter of marine mammals. The traditional visor was shaped from one piece
of bent spruce wood and adorned with sea lion whiskers and ivory amulets. Worn while
paddling long distances to block the sun's glare, its utilitarian function should not obscure
the fact that it signified both wealth and social position. Courtesy Internet Archive.

hold little power. "They are all in debt up to their necks with the [Russian American] company," he noted.[19] Choris filled his sketchbook with drawings of their tools, ancestral decorations, seacraft, and hunting methods. He also completed portraits of Aleut men and women.

Other personnel on the *Rurik* agreed with Choris's assessment of the Aleuts' subjugated status. Chamisso initially claimed that he was not yet "competent to speak on the Aleutians and the Russian American Company," but he soon concluded that the Company had turned Aleuts into "wretched slaves" and predicted that they "will soon be extinct." He contrasted the Aleuts' servitude to the Chukchi's "independent" status and their celebration of "inborn freedom."[20] Even Captain Kotzebue, who led this Russian expedition, wrote about "a former time" when Aleuts "were still in possession of their liberty" and the present time "when slavery has nearly degraded them to the level of brutes."[21] What transpired between the "former" and present times was the entrenched colonial violence of the Russian American Company. Count Rumiantsev had championed the Company twenty years earlier, but even he believed it stood for little beyond dwindling profits in the fur trade.[22]

Kadu expressed his own thoughts regarding the Aleuts' condition to Chamisso and Choris, both of whom recorded his opinions in their diaries. Kadu observed and interacted with a sizeable group of Aleut who boarded the *Rurik* in the early summer of 1817, and a smaller group who remained on the ship after it departed from the North Pacific for the Hawaiian Islands. He recognized two different social classes of Aleuts: those who were bound to servitude in the Russian-controlled settlement, and those he intermingled with during his year on the ship. Of the former group, Kadu remarked on their "misery" and "poverty" as the Company tried to "squeeze the very marrow from the [Aleuts]" in a way that baffled the Woleian navigator.[23] Kadu noticed the other social class by their skills: they constructed and maintained *baidarka* canoes, paddled for days at a time on the open ocean, and successfully hunted even the most difficult prey—sea otters—through a collective effort. It was these unique skills that attracted Kadu to the Aleuts on board the *Rurik*: they possessed talents and knowledge that he lacked. Kadu's appreciation for Aleut skills resonated with Choris, who sketched their most important technology—their seacraft—and described the "rapidity" with which their *baidarkas* cut through the ocean swells.[24]

Choris produced drawings, watercolors, and a final lithograph of the Aleut seacraft. The *baidarka* features prominently in many images, including *Bateaux des îles Aléoutiennes*, which shows both the interior frame and exterior skin of the kayak. The precise craftsmanship, he suggests, explained the extraordinary functionality of the *baidarka*. "The Aleuts use them for long voyages," he wrote, paddling the "boats from Unalaska to Kodiak [Island] and even [the RAC headquarters at] Sitka. They do not go far from land; if a great storm comes up, they attach several boats side by side. Then they are able to defy the most furious waves."[25] Previous European

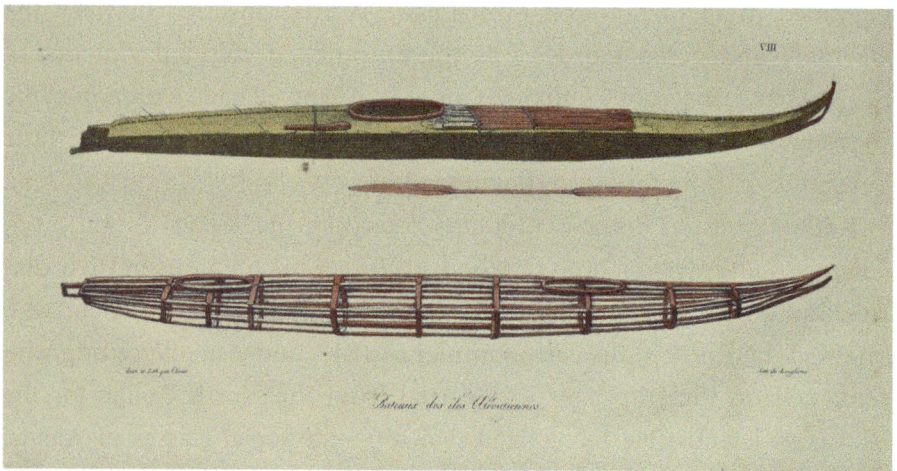

Figure 3.2 *Bateaux des îles Aléoutiennes.* Handcrafted by an Aleut craftsman from wood slats, whalebone, sealskin, and baleen over a period of many months, the *baidarkas* were assembled with an almost mystical precision. The Russian Orthodox priest Ivan Veniamnov, who lived among the Aleut in the 1820s, stated, "the Aleut baidarka is so perfected in its type that even a mathematician cannot add much, if anything, to perfect its seaworthiness.... [They are] so light that a seven-year-old child was able to move it from place to place without strain" (Veniaminov, 1984). Aleut craftsmen constructed three types: the single-hatch *iqakh* for hunting, the double-hatch *ulliukhtadak* for training of young hunters, and the triple-hatch *ulliukhtak* for transporting passengers. The outer skin was frequently dyed red and waterproofed with seal oil. As Choris's image shows, the hunting implements (throwing spears, harpoons, and darts) were secured in a pouch directly in front of the paddling hunter. For the Aleut, according to Chamisso, "the one-passenger baidare is what the horse is to the Cossack" (Chamisso, 1836). Courtesy Internet Archive.

artists, including John Webber and Friedrich von Kittlitz, had sketched the Aleuts' *baidarka*, but none had shown the level of craftsmanship and artistry as Choris did.

The *baidarka* also appeared in Choris's widely reprinted image of the Unalaska village of Iliuliuk, *Oululuk principal etablissem sur l'ile d'Ounalachka*. It offered a perspective in sharp contrast to the typical coastal "view" drawn by exploration artists in the late eighteenth and early nineteenth centuries. Rather than a coastal perspective with an imposing European vessel in the foreground—suggesting European technological and imperial superiority— Choris placed two Aleut paddlers in a double-hatched *baidarka* as the central focus of the image. The Russian settlement itself appears in the background, almost as an afterthought to the daily work conducted by the Native residents of Iliuliuk.

Choris seemed intent on separating his personal reaction to the Aleuts' subjugated status from his desire to document what he valued in their

Figure 3.3 *Oululuk principal établissem sur l'île d'Ounalachka.* Choris inverts the traditional European "view" of a Pacific island port in this image of Iliuliuk. The viewer's gaze is drawn to the Aleut paddlers in the foreground and only secondarily to the "principal village" in the background. Unlike other expedition artists' typical views of a Pacific island, Choris excludes a tall-masted European ship in the foreground. The village itself shows mixed structures of Russian buildings and Aleut *barabaras*, which featured a rounded earthen roof and subterranean living space for warmth. The tall Russian building on the far left suggests a Russian Orthodox church, although Ivan Veniaminov reported that a formal church was not established on Unalaska until 1824. Courtesy Internet Archive.

traditional culture. The former represented a condition imposed upon
them, while the latter revealed their ancestral knowledge and expertise.
Aleut maritime culture—whether their seacraft or apparel—became his
main subject matter. "When at sea," Choris wrote, Aleuts "place over their
eyes a type of visor in order to protect them from the blows of the waves."[26]
He sketched the visor with its detailed depictions of sea life, later producing it in lithographic form. The visor narrated a way of life for Aleuts: it

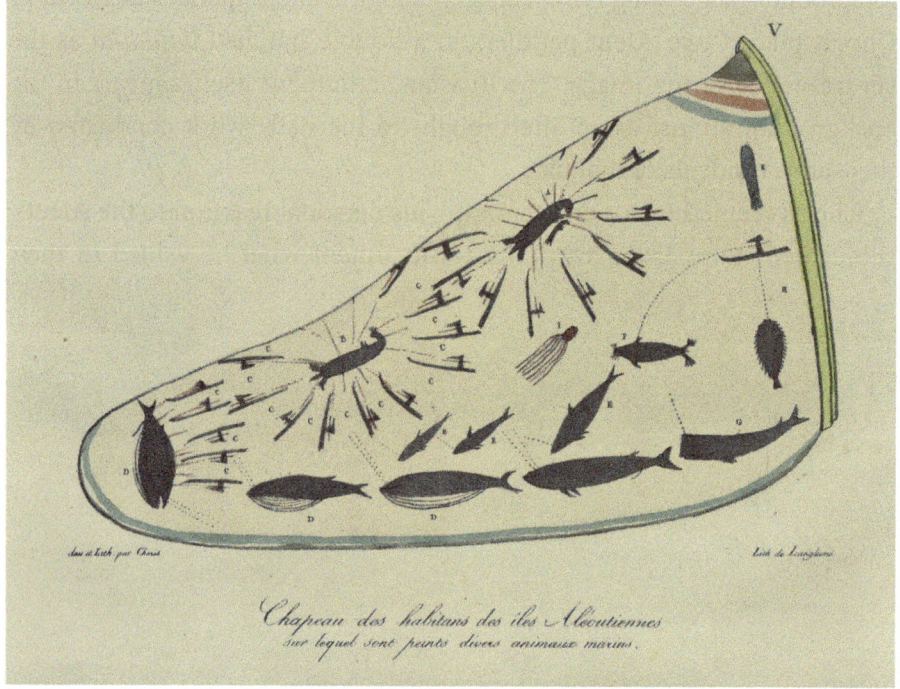

Chapeau des habitans des îles Aléoutiennes
sur lequel sont peints divers animaux marins.

Figure 3.4 *Chapeau des habitans des îles Aléoutiennes, sur lequel sont peints divers animaux marins.* Choris's caption identifies the object as a hat or visor used by the "inhabitants" of the Aleutian Islands, but this special headgear would be worn only by the skilled hunters who pursued their prey in the coastal waters and open ocean. The caption also refers to the "diverse" marine mammals of the hunt, images of which decorate the conical-shaped headgear in different colors. Aleuts gathered the paint pigments (black, white, yellow, red, and green) from sources on the Alaskan mainland as well as the neighboring islands. The white shading, for instance, may have come from the *Aigagin* volcano (known as *Makuschkin* to the Russians), which rises more than two thousand meters from Unalaska Island. The figures on this visor show the harpooning of a whale by many hunters as well as the strategy used by Aleuts to kill sea otters, which was a group effort of encircling the prey once it surfaced from the sea. Courtesy Internet Archive.

showed their means of hunting and the diversity of the marine life that sustained the people—whales, fish, octopus, and seals. "When they see [an otter]," he wrote, "they form a large circle around it, and, as the sea otter swims with much swiftness, it seeks to escape from the enclosure.... Then they kill it by throwing spears from all sides."[27] Choris documented this hunting strategy by reproducing what he saw on the visor.

With human subjects, Choris endeavored to create "the most accurate portraits that one could acquire" given the circumstances.[28] His subjects' faces rarely appear with smiles or welcoming gestures. Instead, their eyes and postures make them appear apprehensive about having their likeness drawn. But Choris's attention to human details was not replicated in the many reproductions and adaptations of his work. Some illustrators who copied his work inserted features that altered his sense of a people or place, as shown in Лодка Зунда Котцебу ("Boat from Kotzebue Sound"), published in the Russian edition of Kotzebue's voyage account. Here, an unnamed Russian artist used a Choris watercolor to create a sense of Iñupiat paddlers happily welcoming the *Rurik* to Kotzebue Sound.

Each member of the *Rurik* expedition offered an individual critique of the Russian colonial project in the North Pacific. In general, they found it depressing and repugnant, a reflection of an autocratic empire that nonetheless sought enterprise and European recognition following the Napoleonic Wars. Their views of the Russian colonial project contrasted with what they found valuable in the Indigenous cultures of the North Pacific. For instance, some of Chamisso's scholarship would draw extensively on Aleut knowledge. Choris, for his part, produced a visual record focused almost solely on the Native inhabitants: their gestures and expressions, tools and watercraft, and their habitations. It was not their mere presence he documented in this colonized setting, but also their attitudes, skills, and, in some instances, their stories. None of his work truly captured the Aleuts' complicated position in the Russian colonial system, especially the ways Aleuts were forced to accommodate themselves to a radically altered world as a means of survival. But Choris's visual record prioritized the original inhabitants, who for centuries had made these islands their homelands—it documents a place and culture during a period of startling transformation.

Figure 3.5 Лодка Зунда Котцебу ("Boat from Kotzebue Sound"). Unknown Russian illustrator, based on a Choris watercolor. This print by an illustrator appeared in the Russian edition of Kotzebue's three-volume account of the *Rurik*'s voyage. It is based on an unpublished watercolor that Choris likely loaned to Kotzebue. The print displays exaggerated coloring, generalized facial features on the individuals, and hazy background elements. "Boat from Kotzebue Sound" suggests how the Russian publisher presented this expedition to its Russian audience. Ten smiling "inhabitants" of Kotzebue Sound appear to welcome the captain and crew of the *Rurik* to their homeland with accommodating gestures. Rather than wary or threatening, they seem happy at the prospect of being *discovered* by the Russian expedition. Choris's own rendering of the "inhabitants" offers a strikingly different view of the reception offered by the Iñupiat of Kotzebue Sound. Courtesy of Otto von Kotzebue, *Journey to the Southern Ocean and the Bering Strait in Search for the North-Eastern Sea Passage*. Russian edition, 1821. Library of Congress. https://www.loc.gov/item/2018694172/.

A "SOJOURN IN SAN FRANCISCO"

One year into the voyage, the Kotzebue expedition spent a month-long "sojourn" in Alta California. Since its departure from Plymouth, England, the *Rurik* had crossed the Atlantic Ocean and sailed north through the entire Pacific into the newly named Kotzebue Sound, before turning south for

Unalaska Island. With the cold season closing in, Adelbert von Chamisso confessed, "[o]ur chief task now was to escape the northern winter." As for winter in general, he grumbled, "I cannot and will not praise it or honor it." Fortunately for him, the next six months would take the expedition to the tropical climate of the Hawaiian Islands, and then farther west to the Marshall Islands, where Kadu would join the voyage. But first came a visit to Alta California, Chamisso noted, "for the rest and relaxation of [the] crew and the provisioning of the *Rurik*."[29]

Captain Kotzebue had reasons to visit Alta California beyond rest and relaxation. For the previous fifteen years, this northernmost Spanish colony had loomed large in the strategic thinking of some Russian imperial planners. Diplomatic communiqués and RAC reports took particular interest in the region's natural abundance. Whereas Russia's northern settlements lacked basic provisions, wrote Nikolai Rezanov in 1806, "New California has an abundance of various kinds of grain and livestock." The Spanish "Californians" possessed so many livestock, according to one official on the eve of the *Rurik*'s voyage, that "herds run wild in the forests" and Spanish authorities had to "decree" that "10,000 to 30,000 head be slaughtered" and "buried" every year to prevent damage to crops.[30] By contrast, the RAC in Alaska produced few crops or livestock, which made the Company a chief advocate for expanding Russian operations in Alta California at this time.[31]

Apart from the supply shortage, Russian reports expressed broader concerns about the empire's stability in the North Pacific. One official noted the lack of international recognition for Russian claims to "the *entire expanse* of Northwest America and its islands," while another official cited a "shortage of manpower" in the form of Russian settlers and "capable Russian *promyshlenniks*" who could expand the fur trade down the American coastline. Foreign traders had intruded in "Russian waters," where they "carry on contraband trade in our possessions by furnishing dangerous weapons to the savages."[32] Another RAC report lamented the "gross" incursion by American and English privateers on the Northwest Coast fur trade. John Cabot Astor's Pacific Fur Company and Britain's Hudson's Bay Company were quickly building forts and solidifying their trade networks with Indigenous groups, while American vessels traded on the Northwest Coast with complete disregard for all parties.[33] Russian planners could not agree on the means to counter these competitors, and yet it was painfully clear that Spain, England, and the United States were outpacing Russian interests in the region.

Alta California seemed to offer new possibilities to the proponents of Russian expansionism. The amount of supplies shipped north to Alaska from Alta California increased in the early 1800s, especially after the establishment of the "Ross Settlement" (Fort Ross) on Bodega Bay in 1812. This Russian outpost represented the empire's most productive colonization effort to date, despite its relatively small population of imported RAC officials, creole workers, and Aleut hunters. The Russians forged a relative peace with the neighboring Kashia Pomo communities, traded for supplies, and intermingled (including intermarriage) with the Native American populations. Spanish authorities gave tacit consent to this Russian outpost. By the time of the *Rurik*'s visit to San Francisco—and with the Mexican War of Independence underway—one RAC official reported that Spanish officials "in Mexico" were "indifferent about the new [Ross] settlement." The Spanish focused their ire on American and English parties, "because of the aid they have given the [Mexican] insurgents, [which] leads them to feel that our proximity is a lesser evil."[34] Fort Ross served as the headquarters for the ongoing Russian hunt of marine mammals on the coast, especially the search for sea otters. "Everywhere sea otters are rare, except California," wrote RAC Governor Ferdinand von Wrangel. "There lies our only hope."[35] The species' rapid decline represented a diminishing hope.

In late September 1816, the *Rurik* headed south down this contested coastline toward San Francisco Bay. Kotzebue kept close to the shore and remained watchful of the rock formations that caused many shipwrecks. Chamisso, like previous travelers, spotted the high plumes of smoke caused by Native-lit fires. Captain Fedor Lütke provided the best description of the Indigenous fires as he approached Fort Ross on the *Kamchatka* in 1818:

When it was completely dark we had a very interesting spectacle: a certain extent of land near the [Fort Ross] settlement was all afire. The Indians who live in this area eat a wild plant which resembles rye.... When the kernels of the [rye] have been harvested, the straw which remains is generally burned. This procedure makes the next year's crop bigger and more flavorful. The fires continued throughout the night.[36]

Especially in the fall burning season, ship captains could follow the smoke all the way south down the coastline. Chamisso marveled at this sight and, arriving in San Francisco Bay on October 2, he remarked on Alta California's welcoming Mediterranean climate—the soft light, warm temperature, fragrant air, and gentle brown landforms. From this tranquil setting Chamisso produced a striking critique of Spain's "avaricious" colonial system.[37]

A strained set of diplomatic conversation commenced upon the *Rurik*'s arrival in San Francisco Bay. Given Spanish restrictions on the entry of foreign ships to its ports, the San Francisco Presidio Commandant Luís de Argüello balked at formally welcoming the unanticipated Russian visitors to his territory. Argüello immediately dispatched a letter to Governor Pablo Vicente de Solá in Monterey apprising him of the *Rurik*'s arrival and Kotzebue's request for "viveres, lena, y aguada" (provisions, firewood, and water). Kotzebue also desired a meeting with the Spanish Governor.[38] Governor de Solá arrived two days later, and he met with Kotzebue in the Presidio during the following week. With Chamisso translating between Spanish and German, the two officials discussed the status of Fort Ross and the rights of Russians to hunt marine mammals in California waters. Both sides agreed to consult their respective superiors in Mexico City and St. Petersburg, which proved to be the most convenient way of resolving nothing. Govenor de Solá allowed for the release of several Russian and Aleut prisoners currently held in Monterey on charges of illegal hunting, because he had no use for prisoners. He also released a Portuguese-English beachcomber and trader named John Elliot de Castro, who would accompany the expedition to Hawai'i and served as a translator for discussions with King Kamehameha (with whom he had previously worked). Overall, this meeting hardly constituted diplomacy, since neither side held the power to negotiate with authority, but its pretense seemed to justify the month-long stay of a Russian naval vessel in a territory held by a Spanish empire at war with its colony, Mexico, of which Alta California was the northernmost province. Govenor de Solá sent a report to Mexico City regarding these proceedings. Spanish officials, fighting for control of New Spain's heartland against insurgents, ignored de Solá's message.

Chamisso's report on Alta California served as the expedition's official statement and was included in Kotzebue's voyage account. He described the Spanish colony from personal observation, but he also drew information from numerous texts available to him at the time.[39] Regarding California's geographic setting, he referenced Miguel Venegas's well-known history *Noticia de la California* (1757) and the five-volume compendium on Pacific explorations authored by James Burney, a close confidant of the Royal Society President Joseph Banks—both of whom Chamisso met in London at the end of voyage. On the settlement and expansion of Alta California's Franciscan missions, Chamisso cited Gaspar de Portolá's diary from his expedition into Alta California, as well as assorted journals from the "[v]oyages of La Peyrouse, Vancouver, and Langsdorff." On California flora and fauna, he relied on the works of the naturalist Archibald Menzies and the botanist Carl Asmund Rudolphi, in addition to his own botanizing with Johann Eschscholtz. Chamisso also made a vague reference to a study of bears produced by "Lewis and Clark," neither of whom ever visited California, but both had many encounters with bears a decade earlier. Finally, for information on Indigenous California languages and cultures, he read French naturalist Robert de Lamanon and German linguist Johann Christoph Adelung. Chamisso, to say the least, did his homework with the available literature.

His personal reaction to Spanish colonization in California was far from measured. The Spanish military presence was feeble and in disarray, he stated, and "even the Presidio has not a single boat." The empire's restrictive commercial policy shifted potential profits to a flourishing "smuggling trade" with foreign vessels along the coast. Given the colony's natural bounty, "a little liberty would make California the granary and market of the northern coasts of these seas"—a sentiment echoed by other European and American visitors throughout the eight decades of Spanish and Mexican rule. The Franciscan missionaries sought to increase "the conversion of heathen nations" but proceeded in an "injudicious" and "ill-executed" manner. Chamisso described the "paternal anxiety of the missionaries" to convert Native groups while also likening their condition to slavery—"it would differ only in name." The Spanish colonial system resulted in un-productive work, malnutrition, and diseases introduced to the Indians, "who die in the missions in an alarming and increasing proportion." In Alta California, he concluded, "Spain here expands merely in order not to allow others to have the territory."[40] It was an apt summary of the Spanish empire's dysfunction and cruelty on the eve of Mexican independence.

Chamisso's report focused extensively on Native Californians. Their desperate condition and declining numbers, he believed, were due to co-lonial control and violence rather than Indigenous inferiority. Chamisso certainly offered derogatory statements about "mission Indians" as a group ("these tribes are far below those on the north coast and the interior of America"), but he also presented a rare level of specific observations about California Indian cultures, including traditional subsistence patterns, burning practices, the location of culture areas and individual "tribes," and the multiplicity of "quite different languages" spoken by groups "living near to each other." He provided tribal or village names for almost twenty distinct communities living in the area from San Francisco Bay to the Sacramento–San Joaquin Delta, and he expressed the need to "collect more satisfactory information respecting the natives of California and their languages." Chamisso's report was hardly comprehensive, since he visited only the Mission San Francisco area, but it nonetheless offered the most thoughtful account by a foreign visitor to date. For a visual ethnography of the Indigenous groups, he urged readers to consult Ludwig Choris's "ines-timable series of portraits" of the "native tribes."[41]

Choris sketched and painted from the moment he set foot on land. He stationed himself in the small "village" of adobe structures and huts surrounding Mission San Francisco de Asís that included, by his count, "fifteen hundred Indians."[42] From this central location he produced a set of intimate portraits and scenes documenting Indigenous countenances, activities, and cultural practices. While previous artists, most notably Gaspard Duché de Vancy and Jose Cardero, had depicted the domineering power of Franciscan missionaries and the seeming incarceration of mission Indians, Choris documented deeper dimensions of Indigenous life. He produced rough sketches of individuals, watercolors of scenes, finished drawings of group activities, and the hand-colored lithographs that appeared in *Voyage pittoresque*. Many of the images were reprinted in the coming decades as the iconic views of colonial California—and his lithograph of an Indigenous performance in front of Mission San Francisco appears today in many publications, including the best-selling American history textbook.[43]

This lithograph, *Danse des habitans de Californie à la mission de San Francisco*, captures a rare moment of Indigenous performance decidedly at odds with almost every existing depiction of Native Californians. Choris witnessed the dance on October 4, 1816, the day when Spaniards celebrated the annual Feast of Saint Francis. The performance took place outdoors following a lengthy Franciscan service inside Mission San Francisco. Choris's image combines Spanish and Indigenous visual elements, including the Christian cross, Franciscan priests, the mission buildings, and the Indigenous dancers. He identified the performers as members of the Olompoli and Sactan communities, although he was likely mistaken, because Mission San Francisco consolidated Native Californians from dozens of villages around San Francisco Bay. The dancers move to their own rhythm, seemingly unaware of the imposing mission structure and the two priests in the background. The final lithographic version of this scene built upon many sketches, watercolors, and group portraits, as well as Choris's firsthand observations from that day. In this way, *Danse des habitans* represents an entirely intentional work of visual ethnography. What story did Choris intend to tell with this lithograph? An initial watercolor of two dancers offers some clues.

Danse des habitans de Californie à la mission de S. Francisco.

Figure 3.6 *Danse des habitans de Californie à la mission de San Francisco.* In this lithograph Choris offered the viewer no simple interpretation of the scene and, by extension, of Spanish colonialism in Alta California. On the one hand, the Franciscans appear to have securely contained the Native population within the confines of the mission complex. On the far left, two priests guard the entrance to the church, suggesting their power to determine who may enter the holy structure. On the other hand, the artist depicts a large group of Indigenous individuals in the act of performing a ritual of their own, purposefully ignoring the watchful gaze of the two missionaries. To the extent that Franciscans desired to extinguish Native culture as part of the colonial process, "Dance of the Inhabitants" documents a partial failure of their efforts. Courtesy Internet Archive.

The watercolor, with a handwritten caption, *Costumes de danse de guerre des habitans de la Californie*, provides insight on Choris's creation of the final lithograph. Two male costumed figures appear in the upper-right quadrant, while the rest of the page contains faint pencil sketches of the dancing figures that recur in other versions. The size and unfinished quality of the watercolor suggests that Choris painted it as an experimental study to document certain details. He carefully depicted elaborate headdresses, body paint, and feather-adorned waist coverings of the two figures. He hand-colored the two figures for his own reference to use in later prints. The caption *Costumes de danse de guerre* ("War Dance Costumes") suggests a common stereotype of warlike Native Americans, despite Native Californians having remarkably little tradition of organized group warfare. He reconsidered the meaning of this dance a few years later, when he created the lithographic version for *Voyage pittoresque*. His written text describes Indigenous rituals associated with death and deceased ancestors rather than warfare. This represents one of the most revealing comments offered by Choris in *Voyage pittoresque*—a specific observation about Indigenous mourning not echoed by any previous European visitor to Alta California. He described a typical Sunday "divine service" in the mission attended by "Indians of both sexes" as well as "armed soldiers [who were] stationed at each corner of the church." When the service finished, he observed:

> the Indians *gather in the cemetery*, which is in front of the mission house, and dance. Half of the men adorn themselves with feathers and with girdles ornamented with feathers and with bits of shell that pass for money among them, or they paint their bodies with regular lines of black, red, and white. Some have half their bodies (from the head downward) daubed with black and the other half red, and the whole crossed with white lines. Others sift the down [feathers] from birds on their hair. The men commonly dance six or eight together, all making the same movements and all armed with spears.[44]

Apart from the sketch of the two dancers created at the time, Choris also painted a watercolor of the scene that served as the basis of the final lithograph. In this watercolor, *Danse des Californiens*, Choris firmly established the setting to evoke a colonial context (Spanish buildings) and religious mission (the towering cross and church), but the scene more closely reflects an Indigenous mourning ritual due to the absence of any Spanish authorities. It may have been what anthropologist Lee Panich describes as an "annual mourning ceremony" for all Native community members who had died in the previous year—and given the population decline associated with all Spanish missions, the Indians at Mission San Francisco had innumerable ancestors to commemorate.[45] In contrast to the earlier decades of

Figure 3.7 *Costumes de danse de guerre des habitans de la Californie.* This watercolor from a Choris sketchbook offers insight to his daily work process. The page includes faint pencil drawings of dancers who later appeared in his watercolor and lithograph of the mission, handwritten notes, and the figures of two individuals in dance costumes. Like other artists, Choris assembled his finished paintings from experimentation with color and form, using the materials he had on hand. The coloring would assist his memory when, years later, he produced the final lithographs. Courtesy of the Honeyman Collection, Bancroft Library, University of California, Berkeley.

Figure 3.8 *Danse des Californiens*. Watercolor, 1816. Choris produced this watercolor after viewing the dance on the day of the Feast of Saint Francis, October 4, 1816. Choris described "Sunday" dances as taking place in the cemetery, but he sets this one directly in front of the mission building. Music accompanying the dance included clapping, singing, and percussion-like stick instruments. Indigenous commemorations for the dead happened regularly due to the death rate; according to Chamisso, forty "Indians" had died in the previous month and more than three hundred died in the previous year. Choris attributed the high mortality rate to the recurrence of "severe fevers" (Chamisso, 1821). The figures in this watercolor, while similar to those in Choris's lithograph *Danse des habitans*, are unfocused and less physically robust. The most notable difference between the two depictions is the absence in this watercolor of the two Franciscan priests who surveille the performance. Courtesy of the Honeyman Collection, Bancroft Library, University of California, Berkeley.

Franciscan control, when missionaries sought to prevent most expressions of Indigenous culture, missionaries during this later period allowed such ceremonial dances to proceed if the cultural meaning of the event remained ambiguous.

The two different depictions—the watercolor featuring only Indigenous dancers and the final lithograph that prominently includes Spanish missionaries—raise questions about the artist's intent. Did he initially want to convey information primarily about Native California culture and ritual, but at some later point in time he felt it necessary to include a direct symbol of the missionaries' controlling hand? Are both images primarily representations of colonialism, as shown by the imposing Spanish struc-tures built by the ancestors of the people dancing before them? Choris may have initially wanted to highlight a greater level of Indian autonomy and cultural expression at Mission San Francisco, yet years later his memory of Spanish control resonated more strongly, and he felt the need to assert this perspective. One possible explanation offered by historian Ron Tyler is that Choris altered the final lithograph due to the assistance of an artist named Jean-Augustin Franquelin, who worked in the Paris studio where Choris produced the lithographs.[46] But artists—even those in training like Choris—rarely add key elements to an image without deliberate consider-ation of how the element would alter its meaning. Furthermore, Choris altered a second lithograph in a similar way that focused attention on the violence of Spanish colonial rule.

Choris sketched the San Francisco Presidio (military fort) during his time in Alta California, and he produced a watercolor of the same scene once the *Rurik* departed for the Hawaiian Islands. The watercolor depicts the gentle hills of the landscape sloping down to the bay, where the *Rurik* sits at anchor. The low and indistinct rectangular presidio hardly disrupts the graceful landscape, nor does Choris include in the scene any soldiers or Indigenous workers adjacent to the military building. Spanish colonial-ism, one might think, hardly intruded on this peaceful setting. Yet Choris entirely altered the presidio scene for the published lithograph. A mounted Spanish soldier drives forward a group of Native Californians in the foreground, while the presidio itself dominates the background. A few Indigenous workers rest around a fire, but an approaching Spanish soldier on horseback appears intent on disrupting their break. The lithograph de-picts colonial power at its height: mounted soldiers commanding forced labor through the use of violence.

In neither the Presidio nor the Mission scene does Choris offer a close-up view of individual Native Californians. Instead, he abstracts them as groups forced to experience the calamity of Spanish colonization. But he did produce many portraits of Native Californians, which share a common

Vue du Presidio s.ᵗ Francisco.

Figures 3.9a and 3.9b "The Presidio of San Francisco" and *Vue du Presidio San Francisco.*
These two images offer alternative meanings of the Spanish presidio. The untitled watercolor
(above) includes no human presence apart from the low-lying Presidio building, a fenced
pen for cattle, and the *Rurik* at anchor in San Francisco Bay. Spanish colonial rule, it would
seem, blended almost naturally into California's Mediterranean landscape. By contrast, the
control and violence practiced by Spanish soldiers dominate the lithograph that Choris
produced for *Voyage pittoresque.* With this lithograph he conveyed a clear message of
Spanish colonizers imposing their rule on the landscape and inhabitants alike. Courtesy of
the Bancroft Library; and Courtesy of Internet Archive.

feature: an impassive, almost stunned expression on the faces of the sub-jects. "I have never seen one laugh," he wrote. "I have never seen one look [at another] in the face. They look as though they were interested in noth-ing."[47] In this uncharitable and naïve comment, Choris failed to consider the possibility that Indigenous Californians carefully controlled their be-havior and emotions when in the presence of Europeans. Two generations of Spanish colonization had severely fragmented the lives of those who lived near the coastal Spanish settlements—a direct result of drastic popu-lation decline, forced labor, disruption of Native subsistence and repro-duction practices, and sexual and martial assault by soldiers. Not surpris-ingly, the Native people with whom Choris interacted had little interest in revealing their individual emotions or generational trauma. For example, the watercolor "Indians from New Albion" shows the facial features of a man and woman clothed in homespun Mission cloth. Both individuals appear in subsequent lithographs, indicating that this watercolor served as a study for other images. Choris focused on the man's long dark hair, lined forehead, and handsome face with deep-set eyes. A younger woman with beaded hair and ceremonial facial markings appears to his right, her eyes staring directly at the viewer. Both individuals seem resigned to the horrendous conditions they experience at Mission San Francisco, and yet Choris also captured an inner dignity that allowed them to survive the trauma of colonial rule.

Leaving Alta California at the end of October, the Kotzebue expedition could claim certain accomplishments for the month-long "sojourn." Johann Eschscholtz had gathered a large collection of flora, and Choris had amassed dozens of sketches and watercolors that he would rework in the coming months and years. Chamisso had assisted Kotzebue with his quasi-diplomatic discussions, and the naturalist also assembled an impressive amount of information on Native California groups. Chamisso could not help but contemplate the future of this colonized region and the Spaniards' impact on the Native inhabitants. He noted the "generous hospitality" of the Spanish authorities and the "unconstrained freedom, which we here enjoyed on Spanish ground." Yet he, like other European visitors to Alta California, viewed Spanish control of the region as transitory. "Spain's

Figure 3.10 "Indians from New Albion." Choris painted this watercolor of two Indigenous inhabitants of Mission San Francisco in October 1816. His accompanying text addressed work life at the mission, Indigenous servitude, and the crops produced by the Native inhabitants. The men "cultivate the land for the community" and produce "corn, wheat, beans, peas, and potatoes." Despite this apparent abundance, Choris remarked, "they usually begin to grow fretful and thin, and they constantly gaze with sadness at the mountains which they can see in the distance." Women worked in the fields and spun "a coarse cloth from sheep's wool" with the assistance of children. "I saw twenty looms that were constantly in operation." He reported that missionaries had created separate housing for unmarried women "to protect the women from mischief," by which he referred to sexual assault by the soldiers. The missionaries "watch over this establishment with the greatest vigilance" (Choris, 1913). Courtesy of Ajaloo Museum, Talinn.

claims to the territory of this coast were not esteemed any more highly by the Americans and English than they were by the Russians," Chamisso wrote.[48] International trade vessels from England, France, Russia, and the United States moved up and down the coastline in 1816 and 1817 despite Spanish trade restrictions. Most of those vessels were busily plundering the coastline for sea otter pelts, and like the *Rurik*, many of the vessels would sail for the Hawaiian Islands as their next destination in the Pacific Ocean.

A HAWAIIAN EMPIRE

After more than a year of voyaging, the members of the Kotzebue expedition had visited three different colonial settings. Brazil represented a profitable though horrific colony largely based on Portuguese colonists brutally subjugating a constant inflow of enslaved African laborers. Russian Alaska extended across the North Pacific with small settlements of RAC employees, a creole population, and conscripted Aleut laborers. Meanwhile, Alta California comprised the northernmost province of a Spanish empire under assault from within, where Franciscan missionaries and disgruntled soldiers would soon vie for the land and Indigenous laborers in what became Mexican California. Arriving at the Hawaiian Islands, the Kotzebue expedition encountered a different imperial setting: an Indigenous kingdom under the mostly benevolent rule of its founder, Kamehameha I.

The *Rurik* arrived at the twilight of Hawai'i's autonomous status and close to the end of Kamehameha's long life. For almost forty years Kamehameha had cautiously welcomed some benefits of foreign engagement, including international trade, the acquisition of European ships, and the respectful recognition of his rule. But he rejected any direct infringement by European or American powers. Kamehameha had constructed a commercial maritime system that stretched—if haltingly and somewhat unprofitably—east and west across the Pacific Ocean. Contact with visiting foreigners had proved devastating to the health of Hawaiians. Here and elsewhere in the Pacific, foreign intercourse introduced the microbes of the West, and since the time of Captain James Cook's arrival in 1778, the Indigenous population steadily declined as communicable diseases swept across the islands.[49]

Apart from introduced pathogens, an increased foreign influence was unmistakable at the time the *Rurik* arrived at Kealakekua Bay in November

1816, where Kamehameha was currently in residence. Trading and whaling vessels would soon fill Hawaiian harbors, while American missionaries began their own colonization of the islands' spiritual realm in the 1820s. Kotzebue had his own trepidation about arriving in Hawai'i, due to the actions one year earlier of "a certain Dr. Scheffer," a German surgeon in the employ of the Russian American Company, who attempted an ill-advised coup against Kamehameha from the island of Kauai. Unsure of how the King would welcome a ship flying the Russian flag, Kotzebue sent "our gentlemen on shore, to acquaint the King with the object of our visit."[50] The two naturalists and the artist went ashore with the translator they had freed in Alta California, John Elliot de Castro, who convinced Kamehameha of their peaceful intent. He welcomed the foreign "gentlemen," who then sent a message to the reluctant Kotzebue to join them for an audience with the King.

Like the expedition's visit to Alta California one month earlier, it would be Choris's visual representations that had the most widespread influence on foreign impressions of the island kingdom. During the previous forty years, expedition artists had depicted the Hawaiian Islands as an exotic tropical paradise populated by beautiful Natives. Choris sought a different sort of reportage, one attempting to honor and visually document the cultural traditions, cosmology, and the ruling class of Kānaka Maoli. The Hawaiian-crafted idols he sketched almost come alive when reproduced as lithographs, while his rendering of a Hawaiian temple presents the spiritual architecture as a central part of everyday life. The traditions of dance also remain vital, although Choris tended to eroticize the dancers—both male and female—for the wealthy patrons who might purchase his volume of lithographs. Two of Choris's most widely circulated images—a portrait of Kamehameha and a view of Honolulu harbor—document a period of historic change between the traditional past and the commercial colonialism of the coming years.

The island ruler consented to sit twice for a portrait on the day of the *Rurik's* arrival at Kealakekua Bay. According to Kotzebue, Kamehameha took considerable persuasion, because he did not cherish the idea of being "transferred to paper."[51] But Kotzebue was not present for the King's first sitting with Choris, which took place before the Captain came ashore.

Temple du Roi dans la baie Tiritatéa.

Figure 3.11 *Temple du Roi dans la baie Tiritatéa* (Kealakekua Bay). This *heiau* (temple) honored Kamehameha at the site where the expedition members first met the King in November 1816. While a strict *kapu* restricted who could enter the temple as well as behaviors surrounding it, Choris depicts it as a functioning part of social life at Kealakekua Bay. A woman and child walk in the foreground, and two men paddle a kayak closer to the temple. Hawaiian idols guard the entrance to the *heiau*, and Choris produced detailed renderings of idols in a second lithograph. During Kamehameha's reign the polytheistic religion of Hawaiians remained intact, but upon his death in 1819, Liholiho (Kamehameha II) began altering the *kapu* system, and American Protestant missionaries soon made inroads on Hawaiian spiritual beliefs. Courtesy Internet Archive.

Choris sketched Kamehameha in the morning and again in the afternoon, and because the artist knew that this opportunity was unprecedented, he produced various versions of the King's portrait with pencil and watercolors. The final lithograph is the only skilled portrait of Hawai'i's greatest ruler completed during his lifetime.

The portrait of Kamehameha that Choris included in *Voyage pittoresque* presents the viewer with a curious expression to decipher. Kamehameha's visage is serious, almost forlorn, as he gazes just beyond the viewer. The portrait possesses an ethereal quality due to the backdrop: Choris situates the King in front of a coastline, as if he hovers above the water, slightly removed from the land he rules. He is an islander, Choris suggests in the

Figure 3.12 *Cammeamea, Rei des îles Sandwich.* The King carefully considered his clothing before he sat for a portrait with Choris. He changed out of the simple robe he

portrait's composition, and he may in fact be the King of all islanders. But the look in Kamehameha's eyes seems to acknowledge Hawaiʻi's coming transition from autonomous kingdom to something else. With his own health failing, Kamehameha was not long for this world. He died in May 1819, a fact known to Choris at the time he produced the lithograph of the island monarch in his Paris studio. Given his many sketches of the King, Choris had options for how to depict Kamehameha. The lithograph of the King he ultimately published was an intentional piece of work.

A second lithograph also speaks to the transitional period of the Hawaiʻian Islands. *Port d'hanarourou* shows the port-village of Honolulu with signs of its emergence as the most active marketplace in the island Pacific. During the next two decades the port of Honolulu (and other Hawaiian bays) would fill with trading vessels and whaling ships. Every year thousands of sailors, officers, missionaries, and haole beachcombers would inundate Hawaiian communities for business, pleasure, and proselytizing. Choris's view predates this transformation, but the factors leading to it are evident in the scene, which includes trading vessels and European-style commercial houses. Furthermore, his perspective inverts the coastal view typically shown by voyage artists, who drew or painted the shoreline as a backdrop to the real subject matter: the imposing European ships in the foreground. Choris challenged this traditional view in the way he visually prioritized the Indigenous dwellings and community. Human activity fills the scene, with people moving about, a horseman herding cattle, and paddlers shuttling amid the foreign ships. For this moment in time, Choris suggests, Honolulu embodies a thriving hybrid society of Indigenous and introduced elements.

wore that day for the outfit of a European sailor, and the resulting artwork is known as his "red vest" portrait. According to Kotzebue, the King changed his clothing after learning that his likeness would be presented to Czar Alexander I. Choris sketched him in the red vest, and the King seemed pleased with the results. Choris, however, was not pleased, because he wanted to depict this island monarch in "native costume" (Choris, 1999). So he did. In a later version of the portrait that the King did not see, Choris disrobed Kamehameha and re-presented him in a traditional tapa robe, as shown in this lithograph. Courtesy Internet Archive.

Figure 3.13 *Port d'hanarourou.* Choris presented a decidedly hybrid scene in this view of Honolulu. Native Hawaiian dwellings dominate the foreground, while two European-style structures sit closer to the water's edge. The people are all Hawaiian, in various manners of relaxation, play, and work. The palm trees represent Hawai'i's native flora, but the fauna—cattle, goats, and a horse—are all exogenous species introduced in the late eighteenth century. European trade ships lay at anchor in the bay, and yet Choris balances those foreign vessels with Native seacraft moving from ship to shore. Hardly noticeable on the left side is the Hawaiian flag adopted in 1816, which derived from an ensign of the English East India Company and flies over the European-style trade houses. A preliminary sketch for this lithograph shows Choris's careful study of the Indigenous structures and palm trees swaying in the wind. Courtesy Internet Archive.

❖ ❖ ❖

The *Rurik* remained in the Hawaiian Islands for a month during the winter of 1816, and it returned the following winter for a longer stay. The lithographs of Hawai'i Choris produced in his Paris studio beginning in 1820 capture an exceptional moment in the history of the islands. He documents an Indigenous King in the waning days of his rule, but one who still possessed the power to enforce *kapu* laws established by his ancestors. Choris depicts a large group of islanders performing ritual dances that celebrate life, in stark contrast to the dance performance he witnessed in Alta California that memorialized the deadly cost of the mission system. He drew portraits of the Hawaiian elite and other scenes of daily life filled with commoners, revealing a ranked society that nonetheless possessed the resources and mores to honor the needs of all people. Within his drawings and lithographs Choris includes clear signs of colonial intrusions that indicated major changes to come. The European and American ships that dotted the harbors, the lusty foreign sailors who came ashore for entertainment, the introduced livestock that altered the landscape, the European-style storehouses that offered access to the market economy—Choris incorporated these and other symbols of an encroaching colonial system to offer a glimpse of the future. The first Protestant missionaries did not arrive until three years after Choris departed. In Hawai'i and throughout the island Pacific, Chamisso stated, the social impact "of rising Christianity" would be profoundly negative.[52]

In contrast to the incipient foreign influences in the Hawaiian Islands, Choris documented the firmly established nature of colonialism in his representations of Alta California and Russian Alaska. His images of Mission San Francisco and the Presidio spotlight the two institutions that led Spanish conquest in 1769. Fifty years later, Franciscan priests and soldiers continued to collaborate in controlling the Indigenous population. At Mission San Francisco, Choris observed, "armed soldiers" were always present. He also noted the invisible forces of Spanish imperialism: the "violent fevers" and other maladies that "carry off great numbers" from the "Indian tribes" in the missions. Beyond the mission system—in the interior of California—Spaniards "had encountered armed tribes everywhere and had been well received nowhere."[53] The artist had no opportunity to visit the interior of California, where Europeans were unwelcome and resisted. Choris's visual record documents both sides of the colonial system: the forced labor and violence of Spanish religious and military institutions, as well as evidence of resistance on the faces of those individuals caught in the maw of colonization. More than any expedition artist since the arrival of the Spaniards, Choris developed a body of work that reflected the human condition of Native Californians. He produced not a single portrait of California's colonial authorities.

The same was true for his work in Russian Alaska. For an artist ostensibly under Russian employ and sailing on a Russian vessel, Choris was scathing in his assessment of the Russian American Company's manner of colonial control. The RAC's outpost settlements were staffed by "men without education, whose...bad conduct have forced them to abandon their country," Choris observed. The Company "seems to favor the tendencies of the Russians who wish to run into debt," and the cycle of debt kept them confined to this North Pacific extension of the Russian empire.[54] Against this backdrop of corruption and dysfunction, Choris was drawn to the people forced to labor for the RAC's unstable colonial system. He spent a great deal of time with the group of Aleut workers who remained on the *Rurik* for its return to St. Petersburg. He carefully sketched their portraits and personal possessions. Choris listened to their stories and noted their strong beliefs about magic. He concluded that they were a superstitious people, and yet their superstitions were consistent with living in an extreme environment with Russian intruders who might not remain for long. When the time came for Choris to illustrate Russian colonialism in lithographic form, he produced images of Aleuts and neighboring groups, their material culture, the stories embedded in their artifacts, and the animals they hunted. These things mattered the most, he decided.

All Species of Knowledge: A Voyage of Discovery, Failure, and Natural History in the Pacific Ocean. David Igler, Oxford University Press. © Oxford University Press 2026. DOI: 10.1093/9780197777718.003.0004

Studying Species and Indigenous Knowledge

A profound knowledge of life is the least enviable of all species of knowledge, because it can only be acquired by trials that make us regret the loss of our ignorance.

—MARGUERITE GARDINER, *Countess of Blessington, 1839*

Beyond gathering new information on subjects like geography and ethnography, voyage naturalists devoted much of their attention to the study of species. They collected specimens for the sake of profit and status. They described, cataloged, and named species for the advancement of Linnaean science. Naturalists introduced exogenous plants and animals to new places, and they uprooted native samples in order to take them somewhere else. They discovered new variations of known types, and they asked questions of local residents, for whom those variations were anything but new. Naturalists tirelessly examined their samples for weeks on end while their floating laboratory moved on the ocean's swells. Upon returning home, they unpacked crates, sorted types, sent samples to benefactors and colleagues, and hurried to publish their findings. The study of species ordered the rhythm of their voyage as well as their subsequent professional careers.

Their fascination with species was owed in part to the shocking variety of things they encountered in different environments. On the smallest coral islands in Oceania, Johann Eschscholtz studied a multitude of tiny creatures above the waterline as well as the assortment of living coral (zoophytes) beneath the ocean's surface. He had never before seen such wonders, and he pondered the process by which they created their habitats. Months later and five thousand miles to the north, Adelbert von Chamisso watched whales circling the *Rurik*, mesmerized by the sight. One whale species appeared to grow no more than fifteen feet long, while another variety stretched almost the entire length of the *Rurik*. Who could teach him about the characteristics of these North Pacific leviathans? Kadu, who trained as a navigator rather than a naturalist, nonetheless shared with Eschscholtz and Chamisso a fascination for the flora, fauna, and other natural entities they collected on the expedition. For voyage naturalists and their fellow travelers, the diversity of species represented an almost daily encounter with the unexpected.

How did naturalists acquire information on new species? Why did European expeditions transport species around the globe? To what degree did the study of species contribute to imperial science? These questions speak to the transformation and "mobility" of natural history in the early nineteenth century.[1] The voyage of the *Rurik* represents just one discrete episode in the history of systematics (the study of species), and yet the work processes of the naturalists offer an especially close and revealing view of how they practiced natural history as a vocation. The most fundamental tasks included collecting and naming species, the intentional transplantation of flora and fauna from one place to another, and the gathering of knowledge directly from Indigenous people who possessed relevant expertise. Indigenous knowledge contributed to most European science conducted in the Pacific during this era. As the general practice of eighteenth-century natural history transitioned to the distinct disciplinary research of the nineteenth century, the study of different species and how they operated became the paramount endeavor of naturalists.

A LONG VIEW OF PACIFIC NATURALISTS AND THEIR SPECIES

To understand the *Rurik* naturalists' study of species, it is important to reflect on a much longer history of plants, animals, and humans moving

about the Pacific. In this context, the intentional and unintentional introduction of new species comprised a key component of the celebrated
"discovery" voyages of the late eighteenth century.[2] Tahiti provides an important example due to the arrival of multiple European expeditions in
the late 1760s. The Tahitian Islands received new species at an astonishing
pace, all for the "improvement" of the islands as well as for the benefit
of future provision-starved European voyagers. Introduced animals—
including cattle, donkeys, goats, guinea pigs, horses, rabbits, sheep, new
varieties of dogs and pigs, and a pregnant cat gifted to "Queen" Purea by
Samuel Wallis in 1767—found their way to Tahiti in the late 1700s. A similar variety of birds also arrived during this period, ranging from Australian
parrots to English turkeys and Spanish hens. Plants constituted the largest
number of introduced species.[3] Dozens of varieties of fruit, vegetables,
legumes, trees, and seeds found their way to Tahiti. The vast majority arrived as intentional imports for the benefit of Tahitians and European
visitors alike. Some species invaded and multiplied with evident impact,
while others existed as relatively harmless additions to Tahiti's natural
diversity. Tahitians, for their part, welcomed many of these introduced
species and, as historian Jennifer Newell observes, the islanders maintained "much more of a controlling hand [over the new introductions]
than the voyagers found comfortable."[4] However, the islanders could
not exert control over the viral and bacterial agents introduced through
the voyagers' bodies. Introduced pathogens severely sickened Tahitians,
and their population plummeted within two generations of the first
European visitors.[5]

New arrivals represented a fact of life across historical and geological
timescales in the Pacific. The Hawaiian Islands burst through the ocean's
surface as a result of volcanic action, with island after island expiring and
disappearing back under the Pacific swell during Deep Time. Species
arrived, evolved, and many, if not most of them, vanished long before
humans appeared.[6] But when the first human settlers from the Marquesas
Islands arrived in the Hawaiian Islands one thousand years ago, they ac-
celerated a pattern of disruption found throughout the island Pacific: the
extinction of certain species that formerly lived there. Birds were especially
hard hit in Hawai'i and elsewhere, according to historian Daniel Lewis,

who estimates "the global extinction of nearly 1,000 species of birds" because of human colonization.[7]

In exchange for the extinction of bird species and other life forms, the ancient settlers of Hawai'i introduced their own fauna and flora, including chickens, pigs, fowl, lizards, snails, and dozens of plant varieties—all stuff packed on the ancestors' double-hulled canoes for future sustenance. Whether intentionally or not, the ancestors also carried with them the Polynesian rat (*rattus exulans*), which over time played a significant role in island deforestation and the extinction of lowland birds.[8] The *Rurik* personnel was stunned by the prevalence of rats throughout the island Pacific, and they wondered "whence did they come?"[9] Some introduced species thrived alongside the human settlers, while endemic birds such as the Stumbling Moa-nalo (*Ptaiochen pau*) was swept into the dustbin of history. The Stumbling Moa-nalo had little chance of survival. It was a large, flightless, and likely tasty bird, certainly an attractive meal for the masses of new islanders, whose population rapidly grew and spread out across the Hawaiian Island chain. In the end, the human settlers prospered due to what they brought, what they found, and how they engineered the island landscape for human habitation.

Ancient Pacific settler populations transported their "portmanteau biota" (both flora and fauna) to survive, but they were also motivated by the human need to re-create a sense of home.[10] For later European explorers, the practice of introducing and transporting species reflected one element of larger imperial goals to civilize, colonize, and transform an unfamiliar landscape into a more productive environment. As naturalist George Forster mused in 1777, "I cannot help thinking that our late voyage would reflect immortal honour to our employers, if it had no other merit than stocking Taheitee with goats, the Friendly isles and New Hebrides with dogs, and New Zealand and New Caledonia with hogs."[11] The "employers," in this instance, refer most directly to the British Admiralty that funded Cook's second expedition to the Pacific, but in a more meaningful way Forster's employer was the British empire, writ large. The islanders themselves occasionally benefited from the new animals, but this hardly seemed to be Forster's intended message. Nor does Forster's comment suggest that Indigenous islanders had a strong desire for the "stocking" of their homes with alien species—species that were often quite destructive to native flora and fauna.

In many instances the transportation of species sought to advance both material and imperial goals. The most notorious episode in this regard involved Captain William Bligh's transplantation of a specific plant: *Artocarpus altilis*, better known as breadfruit (or *uru* in the Society Islands). The global and ecological dimensions of this event is frequently obscured by the high-seas drama of its disastrous first attempt.[12] In 1789, Captain William Bligh acquired the desired breadfruit cuttings in Tahiti, only to face the wrath and mutiny of his crew on the *Bounty*, led by First Mate Fletcher Christian. Captain Bligh and eighteen other officers and sailors were set adrift in a boat, while the mutineers sailed off on the *Bounty* to confront their various fates. For obvious reasons, the resulting human drama of mutiny, capture, shipwreck (of the *Pandora*), rescue, court-martial, acquittal, and public hangings became well-trod historical narrative, while the less sensational environmental story of transplanting breadfruit received less attention.

The British empire had many objectives with the breadfruit transportation. British plantation owners in the West Indies sought a bountiful source of calories for its enslaved African labor force, and the empire also desired the collecting of the world's flora and fauna for the benefit of science and commerce.[13] Coordinating this latter goal for the Crown and the Royal Society was naturalist Joseph Banks, who busily sent plant collectors "around the world to bring back a stream of new species" to London, "where they were transplanted, grown and studied," according to historian Anne Salmond. Banks had a particular fixation with breadfruit due to his many months in Tahiti with Captain James Cook in 1769. Breadfruit, he wrote at the time, "is procured [in Tahiti] with no more trouble than that of climbing a tree and bringing it down."[14] Surely, Banks believed, the British should transport this Tahitian staple crop to the enslaved laborers in Britain's tropical colonies. Imperial science would function as an organizing tool of nature's productions by shuttling what grew bountifully in one place to a different place in need of the crop. The act embodied pure "benevolence," according to Banks's colleague Bryan Edwards: "it is that of spreading abroad the bounties of creation by transplanting from one part of the globe to another such natural productions as are likely to prove beneficial to the interests of humanity."[15]

The actual transplantation of breadfruit from Tahiti proceeded with little trouble once the *Bounty* debacle had passed. When Bligh's new ship, the *Providence*, arrived in Matavai Bay in April 1792, his gardeners immediately set to the task of cutting and potting breadfruit samples, eventually making a full cargo comprising "780 large, & 3012 small Pots: 35 Tubs and 28 boxes of Bread Fruit."[16] Six months later the *Providence* arrived in the West Indies with its cargo of breadfruit cuttings ready for dispersal among the British slave colonies. At St. Vincent the crew offloaded more than five hundred potted breadfruit plants to the dock, where a long line of enslaved Africans gathered the plants for delivery to the island's botanical garden. The same process took place the following week at Point Royal Harbor, Jamaica, where Bligh placed a gardener in charge of overseeing the plants' proper dispersal among the island's counties. Breadfruit trees matured rapidly in the tropical Caribbean climate, but the enslaved beneficiaries cared little for the new addition to their diet.[17] Bligh and Banks nonetheless considered the transplantation a huge success. When Bligh died two decades later, his tombstone memorialized "the celebrated navigator who first transplanted the Bread fruit tree from Otaheite to the West Indies."[18] The tombstone omitted any reference to the sensational mutiny on the *Bounty*.

The way that naturalists collected and studied their discovered species sometimes amused the Indigenous people who witnessed the activity. In November 1769, a Maori youth named Horeta Te Taniwha watched from a safe distance as Joseph Banks and Daniel Solander botanized near the shore of Whitianga harbor, New Zealand. Banks noted the day's work in his journal: "we botanized with our usual good success, which could not be doubted in a country so totally new."[19] Decades later, observer Te Taniwha recalled the bizarre behavior of the naturalists: "They collected grasses from the cliffs, and kept knocking at the stones on the beach, and we said, 'Why are these acts done by these goblins?'"[20] Certainly this was a legitimate question, to which Banks may have answered that collecting new grasses and minerals was an essential way to understand nature's mysteries.

Naturalists agreed on the social and scientific value of collecting unrecognized species. But naming those species could spark controversy. Naturalist Archibald Menzies, who sailed with George Vancouver in the early 1790s, collected the first specimen of the tree that eventually became known as "Douglas-fir," on what became known as Vancouver Island. It took well over a century for the naturalist community to agree on a scientific name of the towering evergreen conifer: *Pseudotsuga-menziesii* (for Archibald Menzies). In the intervening decades, a dozen different botanists assigned different names and descriptions to the tree, which already had a name established by the coastal Salish communities. They called it *lá:yelhp*.[21]

These episodes in the long history of transporting species and naturalists' activities share some common elements. Voyage naturalists studied and classified species due to personal and professional ambitions, which included the desire to name and claim their findings, to relocate and map some of the world's biota, and to provide support for imperial objectives, including science. Like other voyagers before them, naturalists also transported species to meet the human need for sustenance and to re-create familiar landscapes. The study of nature, all the way down to the level of tiny species, represented some of the most heralded achievements of European voyages of discovery. Russian voyages were no different in this regard. The *Rurik* produced more research on species than any previous or subsequent Russian endeavor.

COLLECTING SPECIES AND CONSIDERING ORIGINS

Johann Eschscholtz disappeared during the daytime of the expedition's monthlong stopover in Alta California in October 1816. He strolled the bayside marshes and trekked across the wind-swept sand dunes fronting the Pacific Ocean. He walked the modest hills immediately west of the mission complex, and he climbed the higher peaks to the south of the pueblo Yerba Buena. Everywhere he gathered plant samples. By his own count he acquired hundreds of native plants, more than any previous naturalist to visit the area. At some point in his wanderings, Eschsholtz found a small patch of golden-orange wildflowers, slowly fading in the cool autumn. He picked one and carefully added the specimen to the "collecting bag" that always hung from his shoulder.[22] The Spaniards called this beautiful flower *copa del oro*. Native Californians had dozens of names for the cup-shaped flower due to its abundance throughout the region. Scottish naturalist Archibald Menzies collected it in 1792, but he mistook it for an English Mainline.

Eschscholtz showed his sample to Adelbert von Chamisso, who was so delighted by his partner's discovery that he named it *Eschscholzia californica*. Chamisso included the new botanical name and a print of the flower in his 1820 essay on plant species for the journal *Horae physicae Berolinenses*.[23] Eschscholtz's specific specimen traveled all the way to Russia, where today it resides as part of the founding collection of the Herberium of St. Petersburg University. *Eschscholzia californica*, also known as the "California poppy," was named the state flower in 1903. This species, one of thousands collected by Eschscholtz and Chamisso during the voyage, had been found, picked, named, typed, systematized, cited, and transported abroad. The two naturalists agreed that the flower appeared perfectly situated in its natural habitat of California's sunbaked gentle hills, and in the coming decades Californians would put it to commercial and cultural use as a symbol of natural splendor and tourism in the Golden State.

Sailing out of San Francisco Bay with their California poppy specimen, Chamisso and Eschscholtz scrutinized the flower's parts with the naked eye, and they also peered through a rudimentary microscope they reserved for tiny life-forms. Neither of them, it should be noted, joined the expedition with extensive training in botany, but this was the case for many if not most voyage naturalists. They learned along the way by virtue of their own close study of samples, interactions with local inhabitants, and constant consultation with their small shipboard library. Alta California, Chamisso wrote, "offers the botanist much that is new…and most species are still

Figure 4.1 *Eschscholzia californica Ch.* This first published illustration of the California poppy is still reproduced today for botanical books and posters. Drawn by Chamisso, it was engraved by the well-known botanical illustrator "Prof. F[riedrich] Guimpel," who taught at the Berlin Academy of Arts. On the engraving Chamisso identified six different parts of the flower, ranging from the sepal (outer leaves) to the pistol (which contains the stigma, style, and ovary). In an 1820 article, published in *Horae physicae Berolinenses*, Chamisso noted that he named the flower "in honor…of all the labors in the journey of the most skillful, the most learned, the most friendly Eschscholtz" (Chamisso, 1820). Johann Eschscholtz collected the specimen in the vicinity of Mission San Francisco de Asis in October 1816. Engraving by Friedrich Guimpel, based on a drawing by Adelbert von Chamisso, 1820.

undescribed."[24] Eschscholtz had gathered hundreds of specimens, and as the *Rurik* sailed for the Hawaiian Islands, the two naturalists set out to describe many of the flowering plants, including lilac (*Ceanothus*), monkeyflower (*Mimulus*), primrose (*Oenothera*), goldenrod (*Solidago*), aster (*Compositae*), buckthorn (*Rhamnus*), willow (*Salix*), and buckeye (*Aesculus*). They knew few of these species by name and could sometimes only guess at the genus or order, but this lack of knowledge hardly diminished their enthusiasm, nor did it hinder their process of studying seeds, flowers, and other specimens that could "enrich our gardens."[25]

Chamisso and Eschscholtz carefully labeled each specimen with relevant details of where, when, and under what conditions they acquired it. Throughout the voyage they might compare a specimen to a similar one collected months earlier on a distant shoreline in order to view related plants from different locations. Their various collections grew larger as the voyage neared its end. A few parts of their collections had simply vanished by the time they unloaded the ship in St. Petersburg. For instance, upon his arrival in Berlin, Chamisso regretted "the complete loss of an invaluable crate of Californian birds," but he still had in his possession almost five hundred animal specimens for Berlin's Zoological Museum and far more plants for the Royal Herbarium.[26] Eschscholz's plant collection included thousands of samples from the expedition.

Processing the collections and naming new species occupied the two naturalists for years to come. They regularly exchanged letters between Berlin and Dorpat, where Eschscholtz lived, and they occasionally jostled each other's memory of a certain species' characteristics and where it had been located. In 1820, Eschscholtz enthusiastically wrote to Chamisso: "I'm pleased with the possibility of increasing the family of *Hippuris* with a new species," referring to a small plant commonly known today as a "mare's tail." Eschscholtz had found the specimen on Unalaska Island, where he botanized extensively during their second visit, but he could not remember if Chamisso had accompanied him on the day he collected this exact sample. He attempted to jog Chamisso's memory of the precise location: "Did you really never see [this *Hippuris*] near a little sedge which we found very high up in the mountains in Unalaska in wet places? It grew in a valley; I found it beside a big aster; it was in one specimen."[27]

The specificity of Eschscholtz's recollection is stunning. He recounted a moment in time from years earlier, and he recalled taking the single specimen "near a little sedge" and "beside a big aster." His memory suggested the way these two naturalists shared an appreciation for the precision of botanizing. Remembering exactly where they collected the sample was as important as the fact that they had found it. Even if the scientific field of biogeography was far off in the future, these naturalists understood the relationship among place, climate, and biota. In the end, Eschscholtz decided his specimen was a variant of what Linnaeus had named *Hippuris vulgaris*, and he called his species *Hippuris eschscholtzii Cham* to celebrate their joint discovery, even if Chamisso could not recall the day.[28] Eschscholtz might have learned more about the *Hippuris* sample if he had been accompanied that day by Aleut guides, who occasionally joined him for botanizing jaunts in the North Pacific. It was a plant with toxic elements, according to an Aleut informant, and perfect for poisoning an enemy if ingested.[29]

While Chamisso failed to remember harvesting Eschscholtz's *Hippuris* "very high up" a mountain on Unalaska Island, he faithfully documented their regular botanizing in his "Remarks and Opinions of the Naturalist of the Expedition." This report follows the entire voyage in the narrative style of a Humboldtian scientist, and it includes the study of species in particular places ("here we found about eight species of fern"), comparisons with other locales ("the vegetation here is considerably higher than in the interior of St. Lawrence Bay"), and a wide-angle perspective that Chamisso utilized to "cast a look over the waters of the Great Ocean."[30] Like any daily journal, Chamisso's account could be scattershot. One day he estimated the northern range of sea otters, sea lions, and "sea-bears" (polar bears) based on information from the *Rurik*'s Aleut guides, while days later he and Eschscholtz studied their collection of beetles from the Aleutian islands ("Dr. Eschscholtz counted sixteen kinds, many of which are not hitherto described").[31] As Chamisso assembled his different collections, he also educated himself by reading the works of notable naturalists, including Leopold von Buch, Georg Wilhelm Steller, Peter Simon Pallas, Carl Heinrich Merck, and, of course, Alexander von Humboldt. Chamisso acknowledged and referenced these naturalists who came before him, because he recognized the limits of his own knowledge.

Like Chamisso, Eschscholtz collected and studied the species readily available in each locale. In Chile he collected and described 318 "kinds of autumnal plants" that he sorted by classification. Across Oceania he studied and carefully mapped many species of living coral. Eschscholtz collected forty-nine distinct samples of minerals throughout the voyage, and in the Philippines, he described more than a dozen types of butterflies and three new species of sea turtles.[32] His number of collected species was thoroughly impressive, but perhaps more significant was the breadth of his collections, which represented a large swath of the natural world.

Eschscholtz also studied species to advance larger theories of natural origins. For instance, his observation of different types of coral led him to consider the "origins" of the "low [coral] islands of the South Sea." As the amount of living coral increased on the ocean floor in one location, he suggested, they "approach the surface of the sea" and gather shells and larger coral to form structures above sea level. Over time the "seeds of trees and plants cast upon it by waves" contribute organic matter, and lizards and insects become the island's "first inhabitants" by piggybacking on driftwood. "At a much later period," Eschscholtz concluded, "man also appears, builds his hut on the fruitful soil formed by the corruption of the leaves of the trees, and calls himself lord and proprietor of this new creation."[33] This somewhat playful origin story of a coral island roughly approximates the process described in 1842 by Charles Darwin, who referenced Eschscholtz's ideas.[34] However, the point is not that Eschscholtz arrived first to Darwin's theory, but instead that his holistic and speculative view of island origins reflected the close observational method of naturalists in this era. His story also relied on the reader's imagination to connect the underwater assembly of zoophytes to the eventual arrival of human settlers.

Throughout the voyage Chamisso and Eschscholtz collected, classified, and named species to fulfill their roles as naturalists. This is what naturalists did, and they quickly grew into their roles. Yet they were also motivated by two larger concerns similar to those of previous voyage naturalists. The first was linked to their professional future: the accumulation of significant natural artifacts that could sustain their research for years to come, gain them access to professional societies and institutions, and provide them with permanent appointments. Chamisso and Eschscholtz each proved successful with their professional pursuits. The second motivation to collect, classify, and name species responded to the personal and imperial ambition of the *Rurik*'s sponsors, Count Nicolai Rumiantsez and Adam von Krusenstern. The empire, Rumiantsev believed, desired discoveries and natural collections for the sake of science, national pride, and possibly commercial profits. He viewed the naturalists as the vehicle for his imperial goals. As historian of science Londa Schiebinger writes, "Europe's naturalists not only collected the stuff of nature but lay their own peculiar grid of reason over nature so that nomenclatures and taxonomies... served as 'tools of empire.' "[35] To this end the *Rurik*'s two sponsors monitored the expedition's progress and publicized the naturalists' work to claim its scientific findings. Rumiantsev wanted European nations to respect the Russian empire for its "scientific knowledge advancement," and he wanted personal recognition for his sponsorship of the *Rurik*. During the voyage he informed a Russian admiral about his appreciation for the scientific work of navigators and naturalists: "through their activities the Fatherland would increase both its honor and advantage."[36] The "Fatherland" may have been far from Eschscholtz's mind as he cut a sample of *Hippuris* on Unalaska Island or studied zoophytes in the shallow waters of a coral island, but he certainly understood the relationship between his personal employment on the *Rurik* and the larger ambitions of a wealthy sponsor like Count Rumiantsev.

TRANSPORTING AND INTRODUCING SPECIES

The desire to improve a new place through the introduction of a cherished staple crop is uniquely human. Kadu expressed this desire when the *Rurik* arrived at Unalaska Island in late April 1817. Since departing the Marshall

Islands a month earlier, he had undergone persistent questioning from his new shipmates, and he had survived the great storm that left the *Rurik* barely seaworthy. Arriving at Unalaska meant temporary safety on mostly dry land, yet he also encountered an island unlike any in his previous experience. It was barren of trees and still frigid in springtime. It appeared bleak to all of the *Rurik's* personnel, but to Kadu, whose life experience was limited to tropical island environments, it seemed especially miserable. By all accounts, including those written by Kotzebue, Chamisso, and Choris, Kadu reacted as strongly to the Aleuts' condition as to the island environment itself. He pitied the Aleuts' subterranean domiciles, Kotzebue noted, and he "did not like the air" they breathed, because it was so different from the fragrant tropical air to which he was accustomed. Kadu "point[ed] to the misery of the inhabitants" who appeared impoverished and oppressed, Chamisso wrote.[37] In Kadu's eyes, something was fundamentally wrong with these islanders' social condition and their environment.

Drawing from his own life experience in the Caroline and Marshall Islands, Kadu arrived at a solution. He "surveyed this desolate earth, devoid of all trees," Chamisso noted, and concluded that the island suffered from a lack of useful plants, tropical trees, and, more specifically, coconut palms. Kadu "hurried busily to request that we sow some coconuts, which we had on board and to which he would add some of his own."[38] The fact that Kadu traveled with his own supply of coconuts suggests something significant about his association with the tropical fruit: when traveling, bring coconuts. European voyagers prepared for travel in a similar fashion. They stocked their ships with brandy, sauerkraut, dried meat, and a menagerie of animals—all items they deemed necessary for their survival. Kadu not only traveled with the coconuts, but he also knew what to do with them. In the days ahead he went about the business of soaking his coconuts, placing them pointed side down in the best soil, and tending his small garden. One can only imagine what the Aleut thought of the odd-looking fruit, its taste, and Kadu's determined planting. Chamisso acknowledged Kadu's good intention but described the effort as "completely superfluous."[39]

Kadu, like the naturalists with whom he traveled, acted upon instinct, intention, and experience when it came to transplanting species. In fact, he had reason to hope that coconuts might successfully propagate on an island four thousand miles from his homeland, because he had already observed the *Rurik*'s officers' determined efforts to plant various biota on Pacific islands. Upon arriving at Unalaska, he immediately noticed the few cattle previously brought to the island by Russians from a land thousands of miles away—Alta California. Kadu appeared fascinated by the way these large and ungainly beasts could accustom themselves to an island environment where they did not appear to belong. If cattle could survive on Unalaska Island, surely his own island staple could find a way to propagate there.

Something specific to the coconut palm also spurred him to action. Apart from breadfruit, no plant in the Caroline Islands held more meaning and uses than the coconut palm. Carolinians like Kadu—as well as other Pacific Island groups—turned the tree's husks, fronds, trunk, roots, and fruit into many of life's necessities, including tools, rope, clothing, receptacles, and food. The coconut itself offered various edible forms, from milk and meat to the production of copra—the dried white flesh from which they extracted coconut oil. Men and women used copra as a general body oil, as Ludwig Choris witnessed in the Marshall Islands. While sitting outside a Marshallese hut, Choris voyeuristically gazed upon a woman who "covered her hair and body with a lot of coconut oil." Men, according to Kadu, also rubbed coconut oil on their body prior to some ceremonies to properly prepare their spirit.[40] The coconut palm was more than sustenance for islanders, it nurtured the entire body and soul. With this knowledge in mind, Choris included a detailed lithograph of a coconut palm in his volume.

Given the significance Kadu attached to coconuts, his resolve to sow the plant on Unalaska Island was hardly surprising. He hoped to accomplish exactly what his ancestors had done long ago with their imported plants to the Caroline Islands, and he clearly knew the method of sowing coconuts in the soil. If he had reason to believe that Unalaska's climate would reject

Fruit du Cocotier.

Figure 4.2 *Fruit du Cocotier.* The personnel and crew of the *Rurik* enjoyed coconuts everywhere they stopped in Oceania. For Pacific islanders, this staple crop had significance well beyond basic sustenance. Different parts of the coconut tree (*Cocos nucifera*) provided essential uses for various implements and clothing. The tree symbolized life and friendship for the Marshallese people, which may explain Kadu's efforts to plant coconut trees on the island of Unalaska. When the *Rurik* departed from the Marshall Island of Wotho, the *iroij* Lagediak "brought [Captain Kotzebue] a final gift: young coconut trees, which he wanted to see planted in Russia, as he had heard, there were no coconut trees there" (Chamisso, 1836). Courtesy Internet Archive.

his offering, he kept those doubts to himself. Kadu might have hoped for a successful transplantation for personal reasons: he was, after all, a foreign transplant from the Caroline Islands to the Marshalls, and he understood the ways that something new might benefit an established community. The new species could even bring power to those who nurtured them. Chamisso had referred to Kadu as their Indigenous "scientific authority," but the naturalist certainly doubted a successful outcome with Kadu's coconut transplantation.[41]

The *Rurik*'s collection of species had steadily increased as it circled the Pacific in the first two years of the voyage. The naturalists added new species for study, while Captain Kotzebue also accumulated foodstuffs to eat along the way and sometimes to introduce at different locales. In Chile they acquired a pig who they named Shafekha, after a member of the crew. In California the *Rurik* took on a load of watermelons, grapes, and some goats. Somewhere along the route they acquired cats and dogs. Pigs came onboard the ship at the Hawaiian Islands, as did bushels of yams. The Russian settlement of Unalaska did not have much to offer in terms of desirable native foodstuffs, but it supplied the ship with dried beef and in return received a pig, coconuts, and bananas. This biota-exchange aspect of the *Rurik* kept the personnel well provisioned throughout the voyage, and yet they also accumulated plants and animals for the expressed purpose of introducing them to new places. The Marshall Islands, which Kotzebue heralded as his great discovery and Chamisso called the "First Province of the Great Ocean," seemed in desperate need of new foods.[42]

It took the personnel of the *Rurik* less than a week to begin introducing species to the Marshall Islands. On January 9, 1816, "Mr. Kotzebue set [a few goats] on [one] island, where they at first served to terrorize the islanders." The "bloated body" of a goat was found on the beach two days later, which suggests the residents may not have appreciated the new animals.[43] They also introduced a cock and hens, and they sowed "a few roots and plants" before departing for the next island in the Ratak chain. At the Wotje Atoll they met the *iroij* Lagediak, who, according to Chamisso, "understood very well our intention of introducing species of useful plants still unknown here for the good of the people." With Lagediak and other Radakians looking on, the naturalists and crewmembers cleared some ground and went about the work of planting yam roots and watermelon seeds. "We distributed seeds, for which there was a pleasing demand, and in the next few days we had the pleasure of seeing several private gardens develop according to our model," Chamisso noted. Unfortunately, by the time of the *Rurik*'s departure, rats had "pulled most of the seeds out of the ground," but Chamisso still claimed success for the project.[44] They left behind some cats to deal with the rats.

Following his first meeting with the Marshall islanders, Lieutenant Gleb Shishmaref penned a short report about the ritual exchange of food items. According to Shishmaref, Chamisso and a contingent of sailors joined him for the landing on "Goat Island" just days after arriving in the Marshall Islands. The Europeans' appearance "drove [the inhabitants] into the woods," but he was able to approach a group headed by an "elderly man [who] held something white in his hand, on leaves, which he seemed to [offer] me."[45] The older man taught Shishmaref the word *aidara*, or "friend," and he invited the newcomers to sit in his hut, where they exchanged gifts. Chamisso presented watermelon seeds as a gift, and he demonstrated how to plant them. In return, the Radakians showed how to turn the proffered white substance (on leaves) into an edible paste. They called the food "mogomuk," a dried and ground root to which they added water.[46] Neither the planting of seeds nor the process of grinding roots was novel to either party—they each understood the basic mechanics of food production. What resonated about this initial meeting was the way each group ritualistically offered what they believed to be a new and important food item to demonstrate their generosity and peaceful intent. The exchange of food also symbolized the transfer of knowledge between their distinct cultures—one from continental Europe, the other from the island Pacific.

Following this initial encounter, the personnel of the *Rurik* introduced their seeds, plant cuttings, and animals to many islands in the Ratak chain. Their motivation in presenting "all branches of food," as Chamisso noted, coupled a desire to uplift the condition of Radakians with a larger goal of improving the environment of the place they claimed to have discovered.[47] These islands did not previously have yams; now they had yams. The Marshallese did not previously have goats; with the *Rurik*'s arrival they could tend a goat population if they chose to do so. Neither these nor other additions to the islands' flora and fauna prospered in the years ahead, although Kotzebue would claim otherwise.[48] The Radakians, like most Pacific islanders, preferred to process and consume their own traditional foods—a decision hardly anticipated by the *Rurik*'s personnel, because they could not imagine a world without European domesticated animals and extensive agriculture. They believed such advancements fit within a larger mission, the "building blocks of civilization," argues historian Carol Harrison. Yet this colonialist logic embodied a "fantasy of mutually

beneficial discovery" and a belief in their power to uplift Natives by altering the newly discovered lands.[49]

To a certain extent Kadu fell into a similar colonialist worldview with
his attempt to transplant coconut palms from the Marshall Islands to
Unalaska Island. He hoped to raise the condition of Aleuts by improving
their environment with his favorite tree and fruit. Like European explorers
and naturalists, he hoped his generous effort would take root and benefit
the deprived islanders. However, there were notable differences between
Kadu's logic and the mindset of his fellow travelers. Kadu's worldview was
not shaped by long-held attitudes about "civilization" or European philosophies that viewed empirical science as a means of knowing and ultimately
controlling the natural world. Furthermore, while Kadu came from a
ranked society and understood its rationale, he was properly mystified by
the treatment of the lowest-ranking Aleuts and their complete lack of personal freedoms. He may have understood that introducing a single plant
species to Unalaska Island would hold few benefits for most Indigenous
islanders due to the way Russians had already shattered their traditional
world, even if his chosen species symbolized the warmth and freedoms of
his own world. But he also understood that new biotic species could grant
additional power to the individuals who nurtured them. This belief may
explain Kadu's actions when he left the expedition upon its return to the
Marshall Islands: he located some of the fledgling gardens created by the
naturalists, dug up the plants, and transported them to Aur for propaga-
tion under his own protection.[50]

ACQUIRING INDIGENOUS KNOWLEDGE OF SPECIES

Kadu's parting from the voyage in the Marshall Islands saddened Adelbert
von Chamisso, who believed the two men had formed a strong bond due
to his fondness for the islander's "humane spirit."[51] From the Marshall
Islands the *Rurik* sailed for Guam, the Philippines, and into the Indian
Ocean en route to Cape Town. A group of four Aleut hunters remained on
board the ship for the expedition's return to St. Petersburg, where they

would undergo training with the Russian American Company. Their presence on the ship gave Chamisso a unique opportunity to gather further information on the diverse species in the North Pacific.

The whales of the northern ocean especially fascinated Chamisso. Whales surrounded the ship on many occasions in the Arctic and Chukchi Seas and, according to Chamisso, the *Rurik* "ran over two whales of the species *Kuliomoch*" on the way to Unalaska Island on July 20, 1817.[52] He described how the Aleut hunters on board the vessel struck one of the two whales with spears, but the creature did not "pay much attention" to the brief assault.[53] Chamisso desperately wanted to describe the different whale species of the North Pacific, but he lacked the relevant knowledge and experience. Fortunately for him, he had the opportunity to converse with Aleut whale hunters over the course of a two-month stay at Unalaska Island, and then he interviewed the four Aleut who remained on the ship for its return to St. Petersburg. They, more than anyone else alive at the time, knew the types and behaviors of northern whales. Once home in Berlin, Chamisso published the first comprehensive description of North Pacific whales in the journal *Nova Acta Academiae Caesarae Leopoldino-Carolinae Germanicae naturae Curiosorum*.[54] His article, titled "Cetaceorum maris Kamtschatici imagines, ab Aleutis e lingo fictas" (or "Models of Whales from the Kamchatkan Seas, Made from Wood by the Aleuts"), was based almost entirely on his informants' specialized knowledge. He used their own *Unangam Tunuu* words for whale types, and for his intended audience, he wrote the article in Europe's scientific language of Latin.

Some Indigenous groups in the North Pacific hunted whales for sustenance.[55] These groups included the Yup'ik, Chukchi, and Iñupiat in the far north, and the Nuu-chah-nulth and Makah on the west coast of the Americas—all of whom consumed and utilized whale parts and maintained deep cultural ties to the species. Other groups, such as the Tlingit, did not hunt whales for their own cultural reasons. Aleut and Alutiiq groups took a midway position, with some communities committed to whaling and others shunning the hunt. The practice had "heterogeneous roots and its development was extremely complex," according to anthropologist Lydia Black, who argues that Aleut whale hunting waxed and waned over long periods of time.[56] Spread across dozens of islands, Aleut people "did not consider whale killing an unambiguous good," according to historian Ryan Tucker Jones. Some Aleut "associated killing whales with killing humans" due to specific spiritual beliefs.[57] Still, what remains clear from the *Rurik*'s experience was that the four Aleut on the ship did hunt whales, they possessed extensive knowledge of marine mammals in general, and they had specialized information about the varieties of North Pacific whales.

Their sharing of knowledge with Chamisso reflected a complex relationship with the Russian American Company. Their association with the Company likely went back a couple generations, and their hunting and linguistic skills made them highly valued RAC assets. Some, if not all of them, had mixed parentage and complicated obligations entailed by their creole identity, while they also possessed lineages rooted in "whaling families."[58] They may have understood their knowledge of whales as proprietary in some circumstances, but they also seemed to view the inquisitive Chamisso as a safe repository for their expertise. He desired facts about the types, attributes, and behaviors of whales. He listened closely and grew animated when they spoke, and he encouraged them to share their personal knowledge. Chamisso appeared especially fascinated by the Aleuts' many uses of whale parts as well as their ancestral method of hunting the massive creatures—typically, they used spears dipped in aconite poison.[59] Furthermore, the intelligence they provided to Chamisso seemed innocuous, because they could not imagine the circumstances—just one generation in the future—of the world's whaling fleet commencing a wholesale slaughter in the North Pacific.

Chamisso's attraction to North Pacific whale species drew upon the sublime and the scientific. Many Pacific naturalists studied certain species for commercial reasons, such as earlier reports on sea otters, Hawaiian sandalwood, and *beche de mer*—all natural products with high value and thriving specialty markets in China. The commercial value of whales held little attraction for Chamisso (beyond his sarcastic proposal to "domesticate the whale" for the purpose of transportation).[60] Instead, he was drawn to the majesty of the creatures and the way they unabashedly approached the ship in large groups. One morning, he wrote in his diary, "[c]ountless whales frolicked around our ship and shot jets of water high into the air in all directions within our range of view."[61] The magnificent sight thrilled the young naturalist and inspired him to ponder the sublime nature of the world's largest mammal. Chamisso experienced this wonder on an emotional level, and he wanted to translate his fascination with whales into significant scholarly findings. For this task he needed information from the Aleut experts who possessed generations of inherited knowledge.

Despite its publication in a scientific journal, Chamisso's article reflected his personal style of writing natural history. It contained elements of travelogue, references to known experts, descriptive asides and digressions, and exceedingly detailed coverage of the subject at hand. He called that subject "the Balaenology of that [Northern] Ocean." A talented writer who understood the elements of a good story, Chamisso centered his article on the physical setting and the characters, both the human and the cetacean characters. He described the location as "Unalaska in the Aleut territory," a clear affirmation of the Indigenous homeland where "Russians" appeared only lately and inconsequentially in terms of the cetological knowledge desired by Chamisso. His Aleut "teachers," on the other hand, offered thorough descriptions of whale varieties, uses, attributes, and behaviors.[62] Since Chamisso spoke neither *Unangam Tunuu* nor Russian (which many Aleut learned by necessity), he relied on Ludwig Choris as the translator between himself and the Aleut informants. When the translated descriptions failed to convey nuanced Aleut meanings, "we made sure the Aleut, by their art, would carve some wooden models of the Cetaceans that were known to them."[63]

The Aleut carvings demonstrated specific attributes of the different species, and Chamisso used the models as templates for his own hand-drawn illustrations of the different whale types. Eight separate illustrations appear in his article, and most of them contain multiple views of the same whale type—from the side, top, bottom, and, in one case, a straight-on view of the head. Chamisso's drawings offer two layers of evidence to his published findings. First, they support his written descriptions of each species' physical attributes, such as shape, size, and coloring. Second, they testify

Figure 4.3 Wood-carved models of North Pacific whales. Adelbert von Chamisso urged his Aleut hunter-informants to carve models of the whales "known to them" so he could better understand their verbal descriptions. "Moreover," he wrote, "the Aleut would paint these carved images with colors" for greater clarity. Chamisso's subsequent drawings of the different whale species derived from these models as well as from details offered by the Aleut. While Indigenous individuals occasionally produced physical artifacts such as maps or drawings for naturalists and explorers, these carved whale models represent a unique example of detailed knowledge transfer on species from Native experts to a European naturalist. Courtesy of Museum für Naturkunde Berlin, photograph by Carola Radke.

to the source of this new knowledge, which all derived from the Aleut individuals who carved the models. Chamisso even utilized one Aleut carving to correct a previous classification of a fin whale by the Prussian zoologist Peter Simon Pallas: the models, he wrote, "certify that he [Pallas] had committed a mistake regarding such a name."[64] In the long history of naturalists' activities and publications, there exist few clearer examples of knowledge acquisition directly from Indigenous people than Chamisso's "whaleology."

To describe the different species, Chamisso provided Aleut names, Russian translations, as well as some designations previously given by Pallas. The descriptions ranged from the *Kuliomoch* (right whale), "the fattest

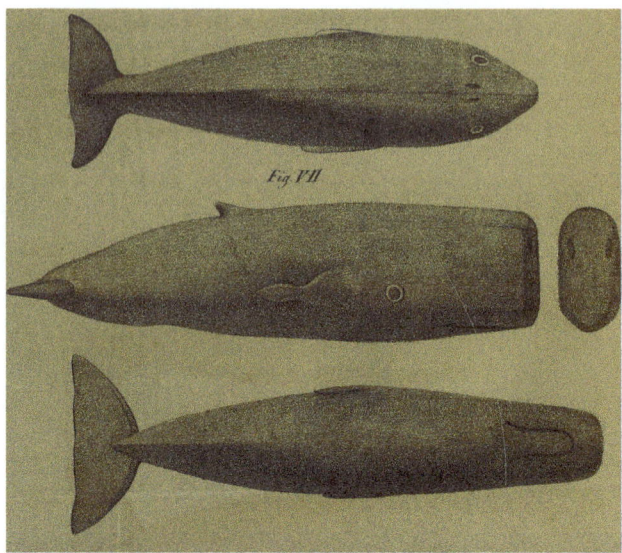

Figure 4.4 *Agidagich*, or *Physeter Linnaeus* (Sperm whale). The sperm whale, classified by Carl Linnaeus in *Systema Naturae* (1758) as *Physeter Linnaeus*, was also called *Agidagich* by the Aleut. Chamisso's drawings included the Latin attribution "Ad. De Chamisso del," an abbreviation for "delineavit," or "he drew it." Chamisso based his eight whale drawings (each whale from multiple perspectives) on the wood models carved by his informants. While Chamisso may have not seen a sperm whale, he correctly described the long jaw with large teeth as well as the head "similar to one of a pig" (Chamisso, 1824). Drawing by Chamisso, Courtesy of Internet Archive.

whale among all," Chamisso stated, but "only the stronger fins are eaten by the Aleut," down in size to the *Tschikagluch* (bay whale), which contained "valuable bones" for the "edges of spears [with] which the sea otter is hunted."[65] The specific whale names allowed Chamisso to compare the species' characteristics (fins, bones, size, and so on), but it was the actual uses of the different whales that his Aleut informants most desired to convey. The "tongue skin" of the *Abugulich* (rorqual whale) was used to make "feminine undergarments," while the oil rendered from the *Agidagich* (sperm whale) could serve as both a purgative and "use in lamps." The *Mangidach* (humpback whale), though smaller than some varieties, provided an excellent source of food for Aleuts, who considered it "savory and healthy." Similarly, the fat of the *Aliomoch* (gray whale) "is quite tender," and it possessed a relatively small "bony head," which may explain why Captain Kotzebue brought an *Aliomoch* skull all the way home to St. Petersburg.[66]

The Aleut names for whales recorded by Chamisso did not survive into modern usage, as early nineteenth-century "whaleology" transitioned into the scientific field of cetology. Nor did his groundbreaking systematic on the species receive praise from the next generation of whale specialists. Late nineteenth-century researcher Joel Asaph Allen harshly criticized Chamisso's reliance on Indigenous informants. Chamisso's descriptions, he contended, "are of interest as showing the proficiency of savages in carving natural objects in wood, but as diagnoses of actual species they are not entitled to recognition, and the barbarous names by which they are specifically designated may well drop from the system as indeterminable synonyms."[67] Allen objected most vehemently to Chamisso's methodology. Chamisso's reliance on Aleut whalers' knowledge made it a "barbarous piece of work," Allen concluded.[68] Chamisso might have responded that it was the Aleut who knew more about North Pacific whales than anyone else in the world at the time, and his article had faithfully assembled their specialized knowledge for European scientists. Furthermore, the truly "barbarous" work ensued two decades later, when the American whaling fleet turned its attention to the oil-rich Arctic hunting grounds.

The significance of Chamisso's article for today's audience resides in its Indigenous research methodology: the presentation of Aleut knowledge of different species, and the voices of those Aleut whalers who informed the naturalist. He listened carefully to their voices. Chamisso described how "an Aleut says the names" of a specific whale type and its attributes, and he weighed the value of this information "due to the scarcity of some greater knowledge" held by Europeans. He listened as the whale names were translated by the Russian-speaking Choris, and he sought further details from the Aleut experts to deepen his understanding of specific whale species. The Aleut informants articulated the important distinctions between "younger" and "adult" whales (which often possessed different Aleut names), because the age and size of the whale mattered for Aleut uses. European and American whalers, by contrast, only considered the size of the whale in relation to the number of barrels its rendered oil would fill.[69]

(Whalers considered a fifty-barrel whale a great success.) The knowledge Chamisso offered did not merely hint at an Indigenous presence or voice in the deep background, nor did he claim the knowledge as his own discovery.[70] Instead, he credits Aleut knowledge in the article's title, with its many illustrations of Aleut-carved whales, and through the detailed information they presented about the species of the North Pacific. Chamisso, who operated with a high level of humility, offered the knowledge and voices of Aleut whaling experts to an audience of scientific readers who could debate the merits of his unorthodox methodology.

Modern-day marine biologists, botanists, geologists, and other specialized researchers of the natural world have good reason to marvel at the methods and conclusions of nineteenth-century naturalists like Chamisso and Eschscholtz. How could these relatively untrained predecessors study and classify whales, coral samples, butterflies, sea turtles, and numerous other intriguing parts of nature—all concurrently, and with so little expertise, time, or technology? How could they conduct seemingly legitimate experiments and dissections on a small worktable in the sailing vessel? Eschscholtz described the challenges they faced in conducting their research: "It is understood that a naturalist as a gatherer of a collection during a sea voyage can do little in comparison with a traveler on dry land, especially if the aim of the ship is to hastily cross a large expanse [of ocean]."[71] Voyage naturalists frequently complained of the limited time they were allowed "on dry land" by the ship captain, but Eschscholtz seemed to offer a more nuanced point rather than a complaint against Captain Kotzebue. A long sea voyage, he suggested, introduced the naturalist to so many different orders of nature given the diversity of environments and species they encountered. Furthermore, Eschscholtz and Chamisso were not "gathering" for the purpose of selling specimens to wealthy benefactors, even if Count Rumiantsev would claim some of their artifacts for his own collection. Instead, they primarily collected samples to understand the natural world according to the ongoing study and organization of species. This project, they suspected, was a very long-term endeavor.

In the eighteenth and early nineteenth centuries, naturalists had identified less than a fraction of 1 percent of the world's species. To the extent that researchers like Carl Linnaeus, Adelbert von Chamisso, or Charles Darwin understood this fact, it seemed to represent more of a great opportunity than an insurmountable task. The opportunity included the addition of new species to the Linnaean system as well as the more difficult challenge of presenting new theories about species, such as the mechanism by which species evolved. "To determine species is not easy," Chamisso stated to a critic of his salp study in 1820. "[T]he subject is difficult [and] I am inexperienced, but I reject reproach for carelessness. I did not work in a [disorganized] manner but did that which was within my competence."[72] Eschscholtz faced the challenge of ordering species with his own tremendous zeal. Writing to "my dear" Chamisso in 1820, he spilled forth with enthusiasm for their individual and joint projects. He encouraged Chamisso to write up the "Flora of the Environs of the Kamchatka Sea," and he joked about placing "cetaceans to a more honorable place, far ahead of the horned cattle" in his recently published work that attempted to revise the Linnaean order. Eschscholtz offered Chamisso detailed comparisons, distinctions, and classifications for their plants collected in Radak, Chile, Unalaska, and a half dozen other locations. If Eschscholtz felt intimidated by the task of seeking order in the complexity of the natural world, he certainly did not express it. "I have to think up many new names and this amuses me greatly," he told Chamisso in reference to his study of butterflies. The names he chose for the new butterflies referenced his European companions on the *Rurik* as well as many of the islanders they met, including Kadu, Rarik, Kamehameha, and someone named Kraimoku. He concluded the letter to Chamisso with one final name: Richard. He had given the name to his first child, born two weeks earlier. "Mother and son are doing very well," he noted, "I await similar news from you in your next letter."[73]

All Species of Knowledge: A Voyage of Discovery, Failure, and Natural History in the Pacific Ocean. David Igler, Oxford University Press. © Oxford University Press 2026. DOI: 10.1093/9780197777718.003.0005

The Afterlife of a Voyage

Networks and Claiming Discoveries

A sense of anticipation filled the *Rurik* as it sailed east through the Baltic Sea toward the final destination—a stately dock on the Neva River below Count Nikolai Rumiantsev's St. Petersburg palace. After three years of circling the globe and subsisting daily on shipboard provisions, the personnel feasted on fresh foods, French wines, and ample liquor purchased during a weeklong stop in Portsmouth, England. Captain Kotzebue expected a hearty welcome in St. Petersburg from the expedition's patron, Rumiantsev, and the promoter, Adam von Krusenstern. Surely, Captain Kotzebue assumed, his many discoveries and accomplishments would overshadow the expedition's failure to locate a northern passage. He had already laid the groundwork for a positive reception when he took the opportunity to visit London as the *Rurik* lay at anchor in Portsmouth. In London he met with Sir John Barrow, the Second Secretary to the Admiralty, who also served as the most enthusiastic booster for maritime exploration, and Arctic expeditions in particular. Barrow did not disappoint. Soon after their London meeting, Barrow published a "personal conversation with Lieutenant Kotzebue" in which he praised his command and noted a few extraordinary discoveries.[1] Arriving in St. Petersburg on August 3, 1818, Kotzebue had reports to complete and plans to discuss with his Russian patrons. The voyage of the *Rurik* had come to an end.

The afterlife of the voyage had just begun. The most successful and celebrated exploratory voyages sustained long afterlives—a process initiated by the offloading of crates, the initial announcement of accomplishments, and the dispersal of all personnel. Networks of associates would coordinate how best to disseminate information and research findings gathered from the expedition. Naval promotions might be decided, and in some instances, court-martials took place to judge the actions taken by officers and crewmembers. Common sailors—unemployed and desperate for work—cast about for a new ship with a reputable captain. Voyage artists, naturalists, and officers hoped to capitalize on the unique experiences they had endured. Ideally, they wanted to parlay their acquired knowledge, collections, and skills into a secure career. They had acquired a unique professional standing shared by only a handful of their contemporaries: they had circumnavigated the globe and witnessed things that other people could only read about. Surely, they could market their accomplishments for permanent employment, if not a touch of fame.

For a small ship populated by a relatively unknown cohort of participants, the *Rurik* generated a particularly successful afterlife that reverberated far wider than most voyages of discovery. In purely material terms, thousands of pages (translated into five European languages) would appear in print; visual renderings of distant places and peoples circulated throughout the public sphere for decades; its reports would encourage new Arctic explorations; and several participants established substantial careers in the sciences and the arts. None of these outcomes resulted through happenstance. The *Rurik* was a highly managed expedition from its inception, and it benefited from a transnational network of individuals and shared resources rather than reliance on the Russian state, which viewed Count Rumiantsev's success with envy if not distaste.[2] The personnel of the *Rurik* had a great deal of work to develop from the moment they unpacked the ship in St. Petersburg. The things they carried home included physical items of use to science, but they also returned with novel findings generated by what they witnessed and intriguing stories drawn from distant seas. The first member of the expedition to present his findings was Kadu.

MARSHALL ISLANDS, 1817

The *Rurik* returned to the Marshall Islands at the end of October 1817, nine months before it arrived in St. Petersburg. Kadu had initially expressed his desire to remain on the *Rurik* until the expedition's end, but upon reaching the Wotje Atoll in the Ratak chain, he informed his fellow travelers that he would stay there. Kadu's decision surprised Captain Kotzebue, while Ludwig Choris thought Kadu should be encouraged to reconsider, because "he would [be] a very useful man for our current voyage" during the months ahead.[3] Chamisso, who believed he knew Kadu better than the others, seemed to grasp the essential issue: "Kadu, I say, from the moment he had caught sight of and recognized the reefs of [Wotje]...was a complete Radakian among the Radakians." Kadu had arrived home, or at least to his adopted home in the Marshall Islands. On the island of Aur he would seek a new status in the social hierarchy. He had much to offer his friends and relations, and even more to offer the high-ranking *iroijs*. Chamisso attempted to understand Kadu's decision, even if he presented it in an infantilizing manner. "He brought [the Radakians] presents, stories, fairy tales, joy and exulted with them in rapturous pleasure," Chamisso wrote.[4] The naturalist failed to recognize how this description mirrored his own gifting rituals and storytelling when he arrived home in Berlin. The "presents" and "stories" that Kadu and Chamisso chose to circulate may have differed in evident ways, but their objectives were strikingly similar.

The material possessions Kadu brought home ranged from European tools to natural artifacts. He had collected scraps of iron on the *Rurik*, and he procured other pieces of metal in Unalaska and Hawai'i. Kotzebue gave him gardening tools and many sharpened blades that Kadu gifted to elders over the coming weeks and months. Kadu kept an iron lance for himself, which was similar to the weapons Kotzebue had presented to the *iroij* Lamari and Tigedien one year earlier. Kadu possessed a collection of rocks and shells unknown to the Marshallese—all samples gathered on distant beaches and hillsides, each with its own story only Kadu could tell. (Chamisso and Eschscholtz had also amassed collections of rocks and shells, and they would create stories about these specimens in the language of scientific classification.) Kadu also arrived with pigs and bark cloth from Hawai'i, cats and goats from the ship, woven mats and sail material, European-style clothing, and an assortment of "presents" and "useful things" given to him by members of the expedition.[5] In material terms, he was a wealthy man by Marshallese standards. He followed Marshallese tradition by giving away many of his possessions. This gifting was both customary and transactional, as he had much to gain through his generosity.

The process of distributing his gifts involved careful consideration. At Wotje he gave some iron to the *iroij* Lagediack, but Kadu reserved the bulk of his material possessions for dispersal at his home atoll of Aur, where he arrived weeks later. There, he offered small gifts to relations and friends and more significant gifts to patrons such as the *iroij* Tigedien, who had offered Kadu protection when he had washed ashore years earlier. The hierarchy of power among Ratak *iroijs* had consolidated further during Kadu's yearlong absence, with Lamari exerting greater control over resources, fighting men and women, and lower-ranking *iroijs*.[6] Lamari would receive most of the iron and forged weapons—this was all but necessary—and he would soon put them to use against adversaries. Apart from his material possessions, Kadu had other things of significance for his Marshallese community.

Kadu, recognized by his peers as an oceanic explorer who survived a yearlong voyage on a foreign vessel, had knowledge and experiences held by no other member of Ratak society. He was singularly unique in his exposure to the world beyond the Marshall Islands. Kadu began relaying his stories as soon as *iroij* Lagediack greeted him on Wotje Atoll. Kotzebue described the scene: the islanders "formed a circle round [Kadu], in the middle of which he was obliged to sit, and immediately words flowed from his lips, his eyes sparkled, and the faces of the audience strongly expressed the sensations which his long narrative had excited."[7] Kadu's narration went on so long that Kotzebue felt compelled to interrupt, which he did. In the days and weeks ahead, Kadu recounted his experiences to many audiences, and within these stories lay the intelligence he had gathered—much of it highly pertinent to Radakian systems of knowledge and the islands' future.

Kadu's account must have begun with the voyage itself. Ratak navigators knew the seas and islands encompassing the Marshall Islands and, to some degree, the existence of neighboring seas. Kadu informed those navigators about sailing north for an entire month without encountering any land as the nights grew shorter and the sunniest days remained bitterly cold. Sleet, snow, and ice—elements unknown to his listeners—required endless explanation, and even then, these natural phenomena may have seemed inconceivable. He certainly narrated the great storm that battered the *Rurik* near the Aleutian Islands, because his audience could relate to fierce storms and lost navigators of their own, and he likely described the impenetrable wall of ice that prevented the ship from traveling north of the Bering Strait. Some listeners may have pondered the meaning of this barrier, and they may have asked Kadu if other walls of ice surrounded the great ocean. A fellow navigator may have asked how the ship found its way back to their island chain in such a vast ocean, and Kadu would have described the captain's metal instruments that allowed for close reckoning. The many details Kadu had to offer about the voyage provided new intelligence about geography, the natural environment, and the immense ocean surrounding the Marshall Islands.

If Kadu's report about the ocean struck some listeners as unreal, his stories of other island societies may have been more relatable. Radakians had their own stories about the peculiar ways of neighboring groups, especially the people of the nearby Ralik chain, but also of island groups in adjacent seas, to say nothing of the *dri-belle* foreigners they had met from the *Rurik*. Kadu could now describe groups of island people who represented different realms of humanity. At Unalaska, he witnessed Aleut villagers who lived in subterranean dwellings and existed in a state of servitude to their Russian rulers, while other Aleut worked independently with these foreigners and possessed realms of knowledge about ocean creatures like whales and seals. These northern people grew no coconut palms or breadfruit, Kadu may have added to his listeners' astonishment. Imagine their poverty!

But a very different group of islanders grew extensive groves of coconut palms, and they lived near the Ratak chain. Kadu spent five weeks on the big island of Hawai'i, where the islanders "looked at him with great astonishment," and he certainly returned their friendly gazes. Chamisso reported that Kadu had "disappeared among the natives" almost as soon as the *Rurik* next anchored at O'ahu.[8] There, on an island not entirely dissimilar from the Marshalls, Kadu witnessed throngs of people far too numerous to count and island natural resources that spoke of wealth and health. On Oʻahu more people surrounded him than he had ever seen in his life; far more people than his home island in the Carolines or his adopted home in the Marshall Islands, and again, more people than he had witnessed anywhere during his travels on the *Rurik*. Despite the ongoing population decline, the people who gathered around him in Honolulu outnumbered any village he had ever visited, and to some extent, Kadu must have been awestruck by the island civilization produced by the Hawaiians.

Kadu could also describe an elite class of Hawaiian rulers similar to the *iroijs* of the Ratak chain, and he met the absolute ruler of them all, King Kamehameha. He could not help being impressed by Kamehameha, the one man who the *Rurik*'s officers identified as "more powerful than ourselves." Chamisso remarked that the King "showed [Kadu] some attention and had [Kadu] tell him" about their voyage. Chamisso added that "this mighty [ruler] was a man of [Kadu's] race and his color"—although one can only guess the extent to which Kadu shared this conception of racial markers.[9] Kamehameha queried Kadu "about the [Marshall] islands that he had left" in order to sail on the *Rurik*.[10] In that exchange, Kamehameha sought information from Kadu about other island groups, and months later Kadu would convey information about the Hawaiian ruler to his Marshallese listeners. His account of the Hawaiian kingdom represented vital intelligence about a prodigious island society not too far away. Kadu may have asked Ludwig Choris to show his portrait of Kamehameha to the people of Wotje—something that Choris did elsewhere for the remainder of the voyage.

The person most interested in Kadu's impression of Kamehameha was also the person who could determine his new status in Radakian society. *Iroij* Lamari held increasing power in the Ratak chain—a process he initiated before the first arrival of the *Rurik* and continued after Kadu's return. In a show of strength, Lamari's forces attacked the islands of Mili in 1817 and Majuro in 1818. The clashes involved men and women in physical fighting and ritual warfare. Lamari claimed victories, if only limited casualties resulted from these clashes. His concentration of power represented a heightened form of leadership and violence in the Ratak chain. According to Chamisso, some portion of Lamari's confidence derived from the iron weapons supplied by Kotzebue.[11] Lamari had to be curious about the strategies of other island rulers, such as Kamehameha, who possessed European-style ships and commanded a population far larger than his own. What did Kadu have to say about Kamehameha's rule? How had the Hawaiian king expanded his control over an island chain? How could this island chain support such an unbelievably large population? The exact nature of Lamari's inquiries is unknown, but Kadu's life in the coming years suggests he adequately answered the questions and gained the respect of the powerful *iroij*.

The sparse details on Kadu's life after the *Rurik* derive from information provided to Captain Kotzebue and Johann Eschscholtz upon their return to the Marshall Islands in 1824 on the *Predpriatie* (Enterprise). They never saw Kadu in person during their visit, but they heard about him from the people they met. In a letter to Chamisso after his return to Estonia, Eschscholtz informed his friend: "Kadu was not [at Wotje]; he had moved to Aur with all the plants and animals. We did not find even vestiges of the plants and animals that [we left] there [years earlier]."[12] Kotzebue confirmed these details, adding that "Kadu was well and residing on the Aur group of islands with their chief Lamari," who had "forcibly carried to Aur all the animals, plants, tools, pieces of iron,—in short, whatever we had left on [Wotje]." Lamari had placed Kadu in charge of managing the introduced plants and animals. According to Lagediak, Kadu married the daughter of an *iroij* and had given "half of his treasures" to Lamari, who in return "had raised [Kadu] to the dignity of a *Tamon-ellip*, or great commander." Finally, Kotzebue's source described Kadu's valor in a battle under Lamari's command against the islanders of the Majuro Atoll. "Kadu had especially distinguished himself," Kotzebue wrote. "He was armed with a sabre and lance, and wore a white shirt, and wide trowsers, which formidable attire was completed by a red cap on his head."[13] Chamisso, who had long since parted company with Kotzebue, received this account "with a doubtful heart." Kadu, he claimed, "abhorred the shedding of blood," and he thought Kotzebue's informants on Wotje had their own motivations for describing Kadu's actions in this way. "So the friends said," Chamisso bitterly concluded.[14] Even years later, Chamisso clung to his memory of peaceful Ratak islanders, and he wanted to maintain this romantic impression, due in part to the relationship he believed he had formed with Kadu.[15] Kotzebue concluded his report on Kadu's life with a general assessment of the expedition's impact on Marshallese islanders. Kotzebue stated that the "crew of the *Rurik*" had left the people of Ratak with "a favourable opinion of white people."[16] Curiously, this statement was the only instance of Kotzebue using the term "white people."

Kadu had certainly formed his own thoughts about white people on the voyage, and one related incident suggests he shared his opinions with his Marshallese audience. In 1824, the same year Kotzebue returned to Wotje Atoll on his next voyage, a group of mutineers from the American whaling vessel *Globe* sought refuge at Mili, the southernmost atoll of the Ratak chain, less than one hundred miles south of the island where Kadu lived. Nine sailors made it ashore at Mili when a small faction of reluctant mutineers recaptured the *Globe* and sailed to Valparaiso, where an American consul took them into custody. Acting on the information provided by these individuals, the commander of the U.S. naval ship *Dolphin* sailed for the Mili Atoll and arrived in late 1825. The people of Mili denied any knowledge of Europeans in their midst, but Lieutenant Hiram Paulding of the *Dolphin* refused to believe them. Searching the island with an armed guard, he found two survivors, Cyrus Hussey and William Lay, both of whom claimed no active part in the mutiny. Based on their statements and the self-published *Narrative of the Mutiny* authored by Hussey and Lay, Lieutenant Paulding wrote his own account of the mutineers' arrival at Mili Atoll, the conflict that led to the deaths of seven sailors, and his search for survivors.[17] The Lieutenant's narrative is convoluted in style and colonialist in message, but he made two points clear: first, he had heroically "rescued" the two "captives" from "all their enemies" at Mili; and second, the islanders had brutally attacked the nine *Globe* sailors, whose existence they initially denied to Paulding. They only tolerated the presence of white foreigners who served a purpose, and in the case of their captives Hussey and Lay, the purpose was forced labor as dictated by a Mili elder.[18]

Knowledge of the *Globe's* arrival surely spread from Mili to the neighboring Aur Atoll, where Kadu had lived since 1817. He would know something about the foreign vessel, the killing of seven foreigners, and the continued presence of two mutineers. What did he make of the arrival of a foreign ship not long after his journey on the *Rurik*? It seems inconceivable that high-ranking *iroijs* would not consult Kadu on the matter of these foreigners. The information Kadu brought home about Europeans had circulated across the Ratak chain for years. Kotzebue confirmed this fact during his second visit to the Marshall Islands.[19] What Kadu's audiences gleaned from his experiences seemed to confirm their thoughts about the presence of outsiders: they posed a threat, and, at the very least, they would consume valuable island resources for their survival. Kadu, who may have appreciated his time spent with the personnel of the *Rurik*, appears to have counseled against welcoming any "white people" to their islands. Chamisso echoed this belief in his second voyage account, directly addressing Kadu: "May [God] keep Europeans away for a while from your bleak reefs."[20]

Unlike the personnel of the *Rurik*, who published their findings in articles and books, Kadu relayed his accumulated knowledge through oral stories to an interested Marshallese audience. Since he left no writing of his own, his voice and experiences could have easily vanished from the historical archive. But this did not happen. Kadu's voice—though filtered through European interlocutors—appears in the works subsequently published by the *Rurik* personnel, and his perspectives also appeared in other publications. In 1824, Frederic Shoberl's mass circulation "miniature" book on the island Pacific enlisted "Kadoo" as an expert. Kadu unknowingly assumed a similar role in Jules Dumont d'Urville's highly regarded 1834 narrative, *Voyage Pittoresque Autour du Monde*, in which the explorer records Kadu's knowledge of the Caroline and Marshall Islands.[21] Decades later, German ethnographers cited Kadu as a firsthand source in their studies of the Caroline Islands due to their close reading of Chamisso's reports. In these and other historical records, Kadu's perspective survives to the present day, offering a vital "glimpse into a different world" rarely accorded to Indigenous islanders who lived in the early 1800s.[22]

THE KRUSENSTERN-RUMIANTSEV NETWORK

The personnel of the *Rurik* employed a different set of practices than did Kadu to share their experiences, claim their discoveries, and acquire new status. They circulated their studies via the printed word and through far-reaching professional networks across national borders. Like Kadu's method, the afterlife of the "Rurikians" involved telling stories: narratives about ice and land, species and elements, colonized and independent Indigenous communities, and the quest for Arctic discoveries. These stories took many forms, including lithographs, a doctoral dissertation, letters, government reports, scientific journal articles, books, compelling rumors, and American newspaper articles thrice removed from the original source. The *Rurik* personnel utilized their professional contacts as well as a network of institutions to advance their work. Upon the expedition's return, the web of connections already established by Adam von Krusenstern and Nikolai Rumiantsev prior to the voyage was available to promote the expedition's accomplishments.

How extensive was this network, and who did it involve? The two principal planners, Krusenstern and Rumiantsev, operated at the center of the system and remained in contact with the returned voyagers as they developed their collections, publications, and careers. Rumiantsev regularly communicated with a "core group" of fifty associates across Europe and a larger group of people involved with "research issues," according to scholar Alexandra Bekasova.[23] Maritime and naval contacts represented a vital group of associates for Rumiantsev and Krusenstern. Rumiantsev maintained tense relations with Russian government officials, who expressed jealousy of the public attention to the *Rurik* voyage, while Krusenstern nurtured his connections with the British Admiralty, and Second Secretary John Barrow in particular. Barrow and Krusenstern worked closely with the successful London publisher John Murray, whose book list centered on exploration. In France, they sought publicity through Conrad Malte-Brun, the founder of the popular exploration journal *Les Annales des Voyages*. In the scientific world, their network extended to some of the most esteemed naturalists, including Alexander von Humboldt, Georges Cuvier, Sir Joseph Banks, and many others who lent different forms of support to the returned voyagers. The *Rurik*'s personnel also benefited from the timing of their return, which coincided with a veritable "mania" for Arctic exploration, especially in Britain, where the government renewed its offer of £20,000 for the first explorer to "find out and sail through" a northern passage. In 1818 Captains John Ross and Edward Parry responded to the government's proposal. They failed to find the Northern Passage during a brief one-year expedition into the North Atlantic.[24]

Krusenstern sought maximum publicity for the *Rurik*'s return, even though he knew the final verdict on Kotzebue's captaincy would include the failure to achieve its main objective. He regularly corresponded with Second Secretary John Barrow in the year before the *Rurik*'s arrival, with Barrow noting "some ridiculous stories... circulat[ing] in this great town [London]" about Kotzebue's discovery of a passage. Krusenstern responded with a request for Barrow to receive Captain Kotzebue when the *Rurik* arrived in England.[25] Barrow agreed to a meeting with Kotzebue, because he was the one captain who had recently experienced the open seas north of the Bering Strait. Barrow wanted to hear Kotzebue's experiences for his own knowledge, and also to include the information in his 427-page tome, *A Chronological History of Voyages into the Arctic Regions*, which he was completing for the publisher John Murray. Murray's company dominated London's book market for exploration and travel, which itself constituted about 20 percent of British book sales. Murray's periodical, *The Quarterly Review*, boasted a sizeable share of London's highly competitive literary trade, and Barrow's essay for the *Quarterly* (titled "On the Polar Ice and Northern Passage into the Pacific") sold over twelve thousand copies in a single day.[26] If Kotzebue desired immediate recognition for his discoveries—and he certainly did—then Barrow and Murray were the best individuals to circulate his news. It was with this in mind that Kotzebue traveled to London as soon as the *Rurik* docked at Portsmouth in June 1818.

The results of their meeting appeared in Barrow's *A Chronological History of Voyages into the Arctic Regions* (1818), published by Murray's company. The book served double duty: it painstakingly surveyed Arctic expeditions dating back to the fifteenth century, and it announced a new "spirit of discovery" once "the European world [felt] the blessings of peace" following the Napoleonic Wars. Kotzebue, who, Barrow reminded his readers, was the "son of the celebrated writer of the same name," offered two important findings. The first was not the discovery of an actual northern passage, but, instead, a newly named bay (Kotzebue Sound) above the Bering Strait from which future attempts could be made.[27] Barrow accepted Kotzebue's excuse of ill health for his failed effort to reach the Northern Passage during his second attempt—an allowance he would not grant Kotzebue four years later when he savagely reviewed the Captain's three-volume voyage account.[28] By that time a fierce rivalry between British and Russian Arctic exploration had reached a peak, and Barrow desired nothing less than complete victory for Britain.

A second finding of the Kotzebue expedition publicized by Barrow might have struck readers as a curious oddity, and yet it gained trans-Atlantic circulation in the press. At Kotzebue Sound, Barrow reported, the naturalists and captain found "an extensive perpendicular cliff" composed of chalk and "covered with plants." To the "astonishment of the travellers," this cliff "was actually a mountain of solid ice, down the sides of which the water was trickling by the heat of the sun." Mammoth tusks lay at the foot of the cliff, while higher up an "offensive smell of animal matter" emanated from the ice and a thawing mammoth carcass.[29] Barrow got the story mostly correct, but he emphasized the wrong natural element as frozen solid.

Johann Eschscholtz had discovered and recognized the geologically unique character of this rocky prominence, which encouraged Kotzebue to name the adjoining bay for the naturalist (Eschscholtz Bay). Rather than a mere "mountain of solid ice," as Barrow described it, Eschscholtz identified an enormous earthen embankment that later scientists would call the Yedoma phenomenon, or permafrost, with "perennially frozen soil containing large bodies of ground ice and the remnants of mammoths."[30] Ludwig Choris captured this strange scene with sketches, a watercolor, and at least two lithographs that circulated widely in the coming years. Barrow reported this story of the land-bounded "iceberg" to the London press, and then it crossed the Atlantic Ocean on the maritime wire service of the day.[31] In 1815 American newspapers had reported on the departure and initial progress of the *Rurik* (due to Rumiantsev's publicity efforts), and now, in the fall of 1818, many American newspapers republished a condensed version of Barrow's iceberg story. The *Portland Gazette* described how the *Rurik* personnel "fell in with an Iceberg" covered with "deposits of earthly matter" and "part of the remains of [a] mammoth in a

Figure 5.1 The Icebergs of Kotzebue Sound. In contrast to Choris's watercolor and lithograph (Figures 1.4 and 1.5) of the earthen "iceberg" discovered by Johann Eschscholtz, this engraving by John Heaviside Clarke was produced in London for the English edition of Kotzebue's *A Voyage of Discovery* (1821). Clark based his version on drawings Choris gave to Kotzebue and Rumiantsev following the voyage. The engraving contains far less detail than Choris's final lithograph, and Clark also placed an Indigenous man in the foreground. Clark captured the immense size of the permafrost earthen glacier. According to Chamisso's rough measurement, "[t]he length of the profile, in which the ice is exposed to sight, may be about [the length of] a musket-shot" (Chamisso, 1821). Engraving by John Heaviside Clark, from original by Ludwig Choris. Courtesy of Cambridge University Press, www.cambridge.org/9781108057578.

state of putrefaction."³² Newspapers in Portland, Maine; Providence, Rhode Island; Edwardsville, Illinois; and many other locales reprinted the article almost verbatim. The key elements of the story remained the same: a ship in the Arctic, a land-based iceberg, a strange deposit "of earthly matter," and a putrefying mammoth. Readers could almost smell the ancient creature slowly thawing in the Arctic wilderness.

As popular science of the day, the components of the story struck the right chord on both sides of the Atlantic. It evoked heroic maritime explorers who battled the elements for the sake of discovery; a natural phenomenon that appeared in one guise (a wall of ice) but was something different (frozen earth); and the remains of an extinct beast with actual rotting flesh. The mammoth's "state of putrefaction" caught readers' attention because it suggested a creature from antiquity nearly coming back to life as it emerged from the ice. For an American audience, the location of the discovery in North America supported their own quest for the ancient origins and natural grandeur of their continent—a point Thomas Jefferson had taken great pains to convey to European naturalists.³³ The reprinted newspaper articles were short, little more than blurbs describing a strange finding. Yet the chain of connections and communications that led to this popular story revealed a trans-Atlantic flow of information that attracted learned naturalists and lay readers alike.³⁴ That chain of connections led from the wealthy patron Rumiantsev to the Anglophile Krusenstern, to the returning Captain Kotzebue, who convened in London with the Arctic booster Barrow, and finally to the publisher Murray, whose books and periodicals gained circulation on both sides of the Atlantic. Furthermore, this piece of popular science moved through the network simultaneous to the *Rurik* completing its voyage from London to St. Petersburg. Later generations of earth scientists would reflect on its significance as one of the first accounts of permafrost.³⁵

Upon the ship's arrival in St. Petersburg, Krusenstern and Rumiantsev had many decisions to make about the *Rurik*'s collections and the announcement of discoveries. As the funder of the expedition, Count Rumiantsev could have claimed possession of all research material, because voyage organizers often demanded the submission of personal journals and collections to control the publication of reports. Rumiantsev refused to stake this claim. Instead, he desired the speedy dissemination of news about the *Rurik*'s voyage to buttress his own reputation as Russia's most enlightened patron of science. Despite the obvious failure to discover a northern passage, Rumiantsev had much to celebrate and publicize, including the first circumnavigation since the Napoleonic Wars, numerous island discoveries in the Pacific, a glimpse of what could be a route to the northern ocean, and the survival of an expedition that demonstrated Russia's potential in the European world. In other words, the voyage had overall been a success rather than a failure.

Russian bureaucrats had little interest in cooperating with Rumiantsev or advancing his reputation. The Russian American Company accepted his assistance in planning minor explorations north of the Aleutian Islands, and the company politely heard his proposal for "an overland expedition by dog sled to map the unexplored Arctic shore of America"—a proposal Rumiantsev shared with John Barrow with hopes of British collaboration. But the company directors remained wary of Rumiantsev due to his ongoing publicity campaign for the *Rurik* and his close ties with foreigners like Barrow. In Russia, one RAC official concluded, "[Rumiantsev] steals their fame by introducing the discoveries to the foreign public."[36] Whatever the RAC or the Russian government officials might have to offer foreign powers, sharing information was not a typical part of their system, nor did the state view collaborative ventures with other nations in a positive light.[37]

Russia's naval officials were equally wary of Rumiantsev, as they planned not one, but two polar expeditions after the *Rurik*'s successful return. One voyage would go north to the Arctic, while a second vessel in the Pacific would search for land in the Antarctic Ocean. Rumiantsev and Krusenstern recommended Kotzebue to lead the Arctic expedition, and they agreed with the choice of Fabian Gottlieb von Bellingshausen for the Antarctic expedition, a choice likely made by French-born Russian Naval Minister Jean-Baptiste Prevost de Sansac, Marquis de Traversay. Instead of Kotzebue, the Navy appointed his former *Rurik* lieutenant, Gleb Shishmaref, to lead the Arctic voyage. Shishmaref had certainly expressed his disappointment to the Russian naval command that Kotzebue had turned the *Rurik* around when it faced a wall of ice in 1817. Krusenstern blamed internal politics for the sidelining of Kotzebue: "[Russian Admiral Gavriil] Sarychev, who hates me and Kotzebue, probably had a role in this appointment [of Shishmaref]." Krusenstern referred to Sarychev as a "blockhead."[38] Palace intrigue aside, it seems clear that Count Rumiantsev's funding of the *Rurik* and his coordination of publicity in Europe had forced the Russian government from its state of lethargy in the area of exploration. The "disturbing" success of Rumiantzev's voyage encouraged the Russian Navy to assert itself in the competition for polar discoveries.[39]

The effectiveness of the Krusenstern-Rumiantsev network contrasted with the dysfunction of a corrupt Russian government in this post-Napoleonic era. The early-modern Russian state was "an empire learning to function," according to historian Erika Monahan. It lacked scientific expertise and a willingness to openly engage with Europe.[40] By contrast, Krusenstern and Rumiantsev sought recognition in western European scientific communities, in which oceanic exploration played a major part. The advancement of scientific endeavors—including the failure of many projects—relied on the circulation of knowledge and the open critique of ideas. Rumiantsev and Krusenstern operated in this world for their own personal ambitions, and they believed their professional reputations would grow alongside the scientific publications of the individuals who sailed on the *Rurik*. The two naturalists had publications nearly ready to go as soon as the *Rurik* docked in St. Petersburg.

DISSEMINATING THE EXPEDITION'S NATURAL HISTORY: CHAMISSO AND ESCHSCHOLTZ

Kadu left the ship at the Wotje Atoll carrying a few armloads of goods and a mind shaped by his experiences. Adelbert von Chamisso left the *Rurik* in St. Petersburg with similar material and intellectual baggage. The voyage had sharpened his thinking and developed his skills as a naturalist, as demonstrated in his personal writings, correspondence, and the range of his research subjects. Chamisso's demeanor throughout the voyage had swung between romantic exuberance and critical inquiry, the natural sciences and the arts. He was the "Janus character of his day," an impulsive actor with diverse interests and desires, according to historian Gerhard Kortum.[41] He had longed for his Marshallese acquaintances to tattoo his body, to no avail. He had carefully studied North Pacific whales with his Aleut informants, and then, in a bizarre passage, he considered the domestication of a whale—and if so, by which means—for the sake of oceanic locomotion. Chamisso had carefully dissected a poem by Goethe on the Brazilian coast and messily dismembered countless creatures pulled from the sea. He proudly claimed to have "shak[en] hands with three of the outstanding men" of the era, one of whom was the ruler of the Hawaiian Islands, Kamehameha.[42] Once safely home, he corresponded with an assortment of individuals, including scholars who commended and critiqued his theories. Years later, Chamisso expressed only one regret from his time on the *Rurik*: his pillaging of human skulls from two burial sites in the North Pacific.

Chamisso began planning for a decade of productive work during the return voyage. The success of his research agenda would rely on professional mentors as well as the dissemination of his scholarly ideas in learned circles. Most immediately, however, he needed to secure employment in his chosen city, Berlin. To one degree or another, these goals were dependent on maintaining control of approximately twenty crates containing his collections—"well-caulked and well-packed crates," he noted in a letter to Martin Lichtenstein, his Berlin academic mentor and patron.[43] Planning ahead during the *Rurik*'s stop in Portsmouth, Chamisso wrote to Lichtenstein requesting his aid in arranging travel documents from St. Petersburg to Berlin.[44] Lichtenstein was most eager to see Chamisso and to unpack those crates, and the two worked on his travel plans from Russia as soon as the naturalist arrived in St. Petersburg. Chamisso offered certain prize artifacts to Rumiantsev, who in return insisted that Chamisso begin publishing his research and promoting the expedition's many discoveries. "All the books and instruments that had been provided for me at the cost of the expedition were demanded back from me," Chamisso explained later. But, he added, "I remained in possession of what I had collected."[45]

It took Chamisso two months to remove himself from Russia, and in the meantime, he reported on his voyage experience in a lengthy letter published in Europe's most popular exploration periodical, *Journals des Voyages*.[46] The intended audience was twofold: Count Rumiantsev, from whom he was still seeking control of his collections; and the large European readership of this journal. To those readers, Chamisso announced a wide-ranging research agenda. He outlined a comprehensive "article" on the voyage that ultimately became his four-hundred-page "Remarks and Opinions of the Naturalist of the Expedition." He discussed the quasi-discovery of the Marshall Islands and his "worry" that "repeated visits of Europeans" would cause considerable harm to the islanders. Chamisso introduced readers to Kadu, a "man devoted to the spirit of our mission," he wrote, "to whom we owe our most important information." He made general observations of Indigenous languages and the process by which ancient Pacific groups "expanded across the surface of the sea against the course of the prevailing winds." He hinted at his forthcoming theory on the "alternative generation" transformation of salps—those small sea creatures he and Eschscholtz found worthy of study more than two years earlier. In support of his theory about salps, he enlisted the esteemed French scientist Georges Cuvier, whom he met in London. Cuvier wanted to know more about the shape-shifting salps and thought it should be Chamisso's "first publication." Chamisso concluded his letter with a misleading plea to Rumiantsev about his collections. "The expedition...did not make any natural history collections," he stated. "[H]ere and there we gathered a few remains of birds," and in the "interest to science" they should remain "in the hands of the person who collected them."[47] Rumiantsev agreed with him, and Chamisso arrived in Berlin in the fall of 1818 with his twenty crates of artifacts and specimens.

Publishing this letter in *Journals des Voyages* might seem unusual even for a compulsive writer and correspondent like Chamisso. Literary scholar Monika Sproll argues that naturalists like Chamisso used letters—both private correspondence and published posts—to establish and shape their identities as intellectuals.[48] Chamisso certainly felt the need to represent himself as a serious researcher due to his sparse formal training in natural history. But it was also significant that he utilized a mainstream exploration periodical to gain maximum publicity for the expedition. Rumiantsev and Krusenstern had employed this method during the voyage, and it kept the *Rurik*'s progress in the public's mind. Chamisso had his future employment in mind. His mentor Martin Lichtenstein read the letter in *Journals des Voyages*, and upon Chamisso's arrival in Berlin, Lichtenstein had arranged for the donation of the twenty specimen crates to the university's Zoological Museum. Chamisso needed a steady job—not simply a vague role as an "instrument in the vast realm of science," as he had once described himself to Rumiantsev.[49] With Lichtenstein's recommendation, the Royal Herbarium at the university offered him employment with an adequate annual salary of six hundred Reichsthaler.

During the next decade Chamisso did not produce a focused body of work that defined him in one area of the natural sciences. Instead, his research and publications scattered in different directions—zoology, marine biology, botany, linguistic, and poetry—and he openly celebrated his collaboration with individuals from the voyage, including Johann Eschscholtz, Kadu, and his Aleut informants. For instance, what was arguably his most significant scientific discovery—the alternation of generations in salps—came soon after his return to Berlin, and he gave credit to Eschscholtz for their shared observations after collecting salps in five different locations in the Atlantic and Pacific Oceans. Eschscholtz described in a letter to his advisor Carl Ledebour how they observed multiple life cycles of salps from their samples on the ship. "[They have] a great number of offspring...which do not resemble their mother," he wrote. They "grow [and attain] the size of their mother, and bear one offspring. It resembles the first animal, its grandmother." Eschscholtz told his mentor it was Chamisso who "worked out the diagnosis" and "drew up a detailed description of the transparent tissues and the organs of reproduction."[50] They agreed that Chamisso would write up and publish their discovery. Chamisso outlined his initial thinking on salps in his letter published in *Journals des Voyages* (1818), submitted his dissertation "De Salpa" to Berlin University in 1819 (for which he received his doctorate), and published a truncated version of his findings in the scientific journal *Isis* in 1820.[51]

Naturalists had classified different types of salps since the 1750s. Chamisso and Eschscholtz gathered information on these types by reading Louis Bosc, Peter Simon Pallas, Georges Cuvier, and Jean-Baptiste Lamarck. But their theory that salps took on alternating forms between generations was "something completely new in zoology," according to researchers Matthias Glaubrecht and Wolfgang Dohle.[52] Chamisso's major finding did not immediately convince other naturalists who included salps in their studies. Throughout the 1820s and 1830s they rejected Chamisso's observation of alternating generations. Not until the 1840s did biologist Michael Sars, zoologist August David Krohn, and biologist Thomas Henry Huxley independently confirm the "alternating" theory later called "metagenesis." Huxley, known as "Darwin's Bulldog" for his strident defense of Darwin's theory, commented that naturalists had foolishly rejected Chamisso's observations, because it was "so strange, and so utterly unlike anything then known to occur in the whole province of zoology."[53] Huxley would offer similar support for Darwin's theory of evolution by natural selection ten years later.

Chamisso's study of salps offers two insights into his practice of natural history during the afterlife of the voyage. First, while he could gain fulfillment by working with his specimen collections and contributing to Linnaean taxonomy, he truly thrived on explaining the "fascinating enigmas of nature," as he commented after collecting his first salp.[54] The mysteries, the variations, and the operations of species revealed the beautiful strangeness of the natural world—a natural world he personally encountered throughout the voyage. Second, Chamisso had little interest in scholarly quarrels. He published his study with its radical discovery, and he felt confident that the theory would ultimately hold up to scrutiny despite scientific contemporaries roundly rejecting it. Then Chamisso moved on. He had a new family to support, many other areas of research to develop, and a healthy disdain for academic politics.[55]

He led a frenetic work life throughout the 1820s and nurtured transnational relationships to facilitate his research. Chamisso's publications appeared in English, Russian, German, French, and Latin. He corresponded with his voyage patrons Rumiantsev and Krusenstern, who continued to publicize the research of the naturalists. Chamisso exchanged detailed letters with Choris and Eschscholtz in which they critiqued each other's work. He visited Choris in Paris and received Eschscholtz in Berlin. He published dozens of works in the fields of zoology, botany, and geography, while his prose and poetry filled volumes.[56] The range of this scholarly output shows a prosperous trans-European identity in the sciences and the arts, one that continues to this day, especially in Germany.[57]

Despite his extensive networks and public recognition across Europe, Chamisso remained fixated on his pivotal life experience with the *Rurik*. He especially valued the information he gathered from Indigenous people. Their knowledge and ways of conceptualizing the world appear at the center of Chamisso's numerous investigations and publications. His study of North Pacific whales synthesized the information he attained from his Aleut shipmates. His publication of the first Hawaiian vocabulary in 1837 and his linguistic analysis of Micronesian dialects were completely dependent on islanders sharing their languages with the naturalist. Chamisso's late-in-life retelling of the *Rurik* expedition, *Reise um die Welt* ("Voyage Around the World"), focused extensively on his interactions with Indigenous people.[58] Chamisso partially attributed the sweeping overview he authored about the Pacific Ocean, "A View of the Great Ocean," to "our friend and instructor Kadu."[59] It might be difficult to establish Kadu's actual contribution to this forty-page essay due to its synoptic approach to Pacific geography, ancient voyaging, nature, linguistics, and island populations. But at the time Chamisso began drafting this essay—most likely as the *Rurik* sailed closer to Europe—Kadu lingered on Chamisso's mind. He certainly romanticized and exploited their friendship for years to come in his writing—he casts Kadu as his partner, devoted companion, and even muse. But unlike many naturalists who sailed on Pacific expeditions, Chamisso truly valued and properly credited the knowledge he gained from Indigenous people.

Until his death from typhoid fever in 1831, Johann Eschscholtz maintained a lively correspondence with Chamisso. In the immediate aftermath of the voyage, they shared their thoughts about professional employment, admission to academic societies, progress on initial publications, and how to best reach scientific and lay readers across Europe. They reminded each other of certain experiences in the Pacific, with Chamisso calling the voyagers "Rurikians" and Eschscholtz addressing his fellow naturalist as "my dear Rarik"—a nickname Chamisso acquired in a ritual exchange of names with the Radakian *iroij* Rarik. They confidentially referred to the voyage as a Russian "military cruise," a joke they would never share with their patrons Krusenstern or Rumiantsev.[60] They applauded each other's scholarly successes. Eschscholtz congratulated Chamisso on the publication of his salp research (he referred to the research as "your worms") and relayed Krusenstern's suggestion that the two naturalists share credit for this significant discovery. Eschscholtz disagreed with Krusenstern's advice and instead offered Chamisso his assistance: "I still have several final salps and *Lepas aurita* (barnacles), the rest turned into a putrid slime, phew!"[61] His other collections remained in good order, and Eschscholtz began working on those specimens as soon as he arrived home to Dorpat (Tartu), Estonia. With the assistance of both Krusenstern and Rumiantsev, he attained an appointment at Dorpat University in 1819 and membership in the Moscow Society of Natural Scientists in 1821. From the three-year expedition he acquired a trove of research material, firsthand observations of diverse species in their environments, a secure job, and a wide network of individuals to help launch his professional life.

The idea of announcing a grand discovery such as a northern passage mattered little to Eschscholtz. In fact, he seemed to downplay the notion of discovery as an individual achievement. For Eschscholtz, natural history—of which geographic findings formed only one part—was a cumulative process, a long and piecemeal scientific project of revealing the natural world for ongoing study. He disregarded personal credit for the supposed discovery of permafrost announced so publicly in London by John Barrow, because frozen land and ice did not especially interest him as a subject of research to pursue. Similarly, he viewed the salp study as Chamisso's project rather than his own. He took the long view of science, and this mindset placed him in the genealogy of innovative naturalists—stretching from

Carl Linnaeus's founding of systematics to the later theories of Charles Darwin and Alfred Wallace.

Eschscholtz believed the new era following the maelstrom of the Napoleonic Wars called for fresh thinking about the ordering of the animal kingdom. He had trained in adherence to the Linnaean system of classifying species, and he had read Compte de Buffon's critique of the system for its rigidity and belief in a conceivable natural order. French naturalist Buffon had argued in *Histoire Naturelle*: "It is in the succession, in the renewal, and in the continuance of species that Nature reveals herself as completely inconceivable."[62] Eschscholtz wanted to re-conceive it. These predecessors were eighteenth-century naturalists, and the nineteenth century had already introduced the ideas of Georges Cuvier and Alexander von Humboldt regarding species in relation to their environments. Eschscholtz was more akin to a naturalist-in-training by comparison to these figures, but like Humboldt, he had spent years on an expedition closely observing species ranging from tiny salps to massive elephant seals. He developed ideas of his own about the arrangement of species in the natural world, and once the *Rurik* began its return journey from the Pacific, he spent all of his time ordering his thoughts on this matter. Within a year of arriving home, and with the financial assistance of Count Rumiantsev, Eschscholtz published a short treatise. *Ideas About the Correlation of Vertebrate Animals* ("Ideen zur Aneinanderreihung der rückgrathigen Thiere").[63]

The word *Ideas* in the title indicated the speculative nature of the publication. Eschscholtz invoked ideas from scientists and philosophers going back to Aristotle, and he adopted telling examples from across the animal kingdom, including the flying lemur, sloth, and armadillo, due to their unique attributes. He debated openly with the ghost of Linnaeus, who "chose the structure of teeth as a basis of classification; but really don't toothless animals and those possessed of strong teeth fall into the same order (Balaena, Delphinus)?" Countering Linnaeus, Eschscholtz argued that "a zoological system cannot be built on external characteristics."[64] He understood internal anatomy better than other sciences, and as he admitted to Chamisso, "I have an aversion to hunting down external resemblances!"[65] Instead, he ordered vertebrate animals by their internal structure rather than outward appearance. For instance, did the animal have a spine, or more than one stomach? He devised a "ladder of creatures" descending from mammals to birds, amphibians to fish, while he made a special insertion of *monotremata* (the platypus and its kin) between the amphibians and the fish.[66] *Homo sapiens*, of course, stood on the top of this ladder above other mammals. To his credit, Eschscholtz showed no interest (here or elsewhere) in ranking humans by culture, anatomy, or race. Other scientists were in the process of advancing those theories, especially in terms of race.[67]

Eschscholtz's *Ideas* offered a glimpse of what he had pondered throughout the voyage. It quickly appeared in print, and according to Eschscholtz's only biographer, it "did not have particular success." The editor of the scientific journal *Isis*, Lawrence Oken, reviewed the book and found it confusing, but he nonetheless encouraged Eschscholtz to continue his work.[68] The naturalist needed no encouragement, because he firmly believed that comparative anatomy across species offered the best hope for new thinking about the animal kingdom. Chamisso cheered on Eschscholtz's endeavor. Eschscholtz had sent him six copies of "my *Ideas*" in September 1819, and within months Chamisso was preparing to lecture on the book in Berlin. "I hope," Eschscholtz confessed to his friend, "you won't say that these are the ravings of a mad man."[69] Clearly, Eschscholtz realized the preliminary nature of how he ordered vertebrate animals. Not yet thirty years old, Eschscholtz believed he had many decades to refine his ideas for public and scholarly readers.

In the *Rurik*'s afterlife Eschscholtz organized his areas of study and meticulously read the existing literature on different subjects. He explained this process to other researchers in one of his most notable publications, the first monographic study of jellyfish (or acelephs, *Scyphozoan medusas*). "I needed to study all the earlier-described examples in order to correctly differentiate the families.... [During the *Rurik* expedition] I found so many acelephs that were new to systematics that I decided to

combine all, so that old and new formed one whole." Eschscholtz stated
that the project's only "reward" was the "hard work" of "bringing order"
to this class of animals, rather than any specific discovery or remunera-
tion. He concluded: "Let [continuous study] be the guiding thread for
future naturalist-voyagers around the globe."[70] It was only at sea that he
had been able to observe the jellyfish, he wrote to his mentor Karl
Ledebour in 1817 from the *Rurik*: "I saw how quietly the medusa swims
on the surface of the sea; around and on her were many little fish.
Suddenly I noticed how the medusa turns onto her back and then over
again. Then I caught a medusa with a net."[71] Eschscholtz insisted that
research scientists needed to get out into the world to observe species in
their natural environments.

He took the next available opportunity to travel the globe, joining
Kotzebue's second circumnavigation on the *Predpriatie* (1823–1826),
during which he collected over two thousand specimens ranging from
mammals to zoophytes.[72] But before he departed, Eschscholtz published
more than a dozen scientific studies based on his *Rurik* research, including the first edition of his ambitious *Zoologischer Atlas*. Eschscholtz
also shared his collections with fellow researchers, especially fellow en-
tomologists. He sent extensive samples of bugs and insects to Finnish
entomologist Carl Gustaf Mannerheim, French entomologist Pierre
Francois Dejean, and German entomologist Johann Gotthelf Fischer
von Waldheim. He asked Chamisso to connect him with Berlin's "insect
hunters" to "carry on an exchange."[73] His collection had particular needs:
he wanted Prussian carob beetles to complement his Livonian and
Siberian varieties, he told Chamisso. Eschscholtz's various activities—
his collaborations, publications, correspondence, and generative ideas
about species in general—indicate that he anticipated a very long and
productive afterlife to the *Rurik* expedition, one that would have taken
him well into the era of Darwinian science. He was only thirty-eight
years old when he contracted and died from typhoid fever in 1831. At
the time he was completing a new edition of his lavishly illustrated
Zoologischer Atlas, which included a few images drawn by his traveling
companion Ludwig Choris.[74]

LUDWIG CHORIS AND THE TECHNOLOGY OF
REPRESENTING NATURE

During the return voyage to Europe, Chamisso spent long days and nights pondering the mystery of salps, while Eschscholtz developed his ideas on a new systematic for vertebrate animals. Similarly, Ludwig Choris had countless hours on the ship to practice his craft, sketching in pencil and painting in watercolor. On clear nights he slept on the deck close to the four Aleut men who were traveling to St. Petersburg at the request of the Russian American Company. The RAC's Main Administration had asked the governor for "bright young" Aleuts to come to St. Petersburg, but it also warned against sending anyone not already "vaccinated against smallpox,"

Figures 5.2a and 5.2b Watercolor portraits of Aleut men. Choris produced many sketches and watercolor portraits of the four Aleut men who accompanied the voyage on its return to Russia. The man on the right wears the upper-body cloak of a hunter, while the man on the left wears two pendants provided by the Russian American Company. Likely these men had worked for the Company since childhood, given their decision to travel to Russia for further training. These two individuals also appear in the group portrait "Habitans des iles Aleutéoutiennes," included in *Voyage pittoresque*. Courtesy of Louis Choris Paintings and Sketches, Yale Collection of Western Americana, Beinecke Rare Book and Manuscript Library.

because several unvaccinated Aleut had previously died in St. Petersburg.[75] On the return voyage, Choris drew and painted many iterations of the four Aleut men. These watercolor portraits hint at a companionable working relationship between the artist and his subjects.

Choris had only recently turned twenty-three years old when the *Rurik* arrived back in St. Petersburg. This was exceedingly young for a voyage artist. For that matter, Choris was young in comparison to most people who had completed a three-year circumnavigation of the globe. He had developed an ambitious plan to publish a comprehensive stand-alone

Figure 5.3 Frontispiece and title page of *Voyage pittoresque*. Choris dedicated *Voyage pittoresque* to the expedition's sponsor, Count Rumiantsev, noting his former title "Chancellor of the Empire." Despite his network of collaborators and supporters in Paris, Choris appreciated Rumiantsev's patronage, and this dedication reflected his dependent relationship with the Count. By contrast, Choris dedicated his second volume of lithographs, *Vues et parsages des régions équinoxiales, recueillis dans un voyage autour du monde* (Paris, 1826), to the naturalist-explorer he most admired, Alexander von Humboldt. Courtesy of William S. Reese, New Haven, CT.

"portfolio" of the entire voyage, unlike almost anything previously produced by a voyage artist.[76] To do so, Choris knew he needed training
among fellow artists and the patronage of scientists and scholars. He
would go to Paris, but not before gaining the support of Count Rumiantsev
and letters of introduction from Chamisso and Krusenstern. He presented
the Count with some of his illustrations from the voyage, but he took his
sketchbooks and watercolor paintings with him, just as Chamisso and
Eschscholtz had done with their collections. Choris would dedicate to his
patron Rumiantsev the completed volume of lithographs titled *Voyage
pittoresque autour du monde*.

This volume, initially published in serial form, contained studies of
Pacific landscapes, people, and colonial settlements still reproduced today.
As such, it extended the afterlife of the voyage in duration and impact in a
way surpassed only by some of the most celebrated voyage accounts, scientific theories, and masterful landscape paintings. When Choris arrived
in Paris in 1819, he possessed neither the skills nor the professional community to produce this work. Nor did he understand the way that lithography—a new and revolutionary technique for making high-quality
prints—would quickly transform the practice of visual representation. By
relocating to Paris, Choris fell into an intellectual and artistic world of
creative possibilities he could have hardly imagined.

In Paris he found mentors and collaborators who nurtured his craft,
and who in turn appreciated their proximity to a charismatic young
man recently returned from the farthest reaches of the globe.[77] His
endorsements from Chamisso and Krusenstern opened doors to leading
scientists, including ethnologist Julius Klaproth, zoologist Georges Cuvier,
botanist Karl-Sigimund Kunth, and neuroanatomist Franz Joseph Gall—to
whom he presented an Aleut skull for his phrenological collection.[78]
Alexander von Humboldt viewed some of his initial illustrations in Paris
and encouraged him to include "text about the voyage" to accompany the
images, because Kotzebue's written account had yet to appear.[79] Choris
studied painting with Jean-Baptiste Regnault and François Gérard at the
Académie Royale des Beaux-Arts. Gérard introduced Choris to painter
Alexis Nicolas Noël, who in 1818 produced a travel book of lithographs

titled *Voyage Pittoresque en France et en Allemagne*. This volume certainly offered a model for Choris's own visual travelogue. In the literary world, Choris gained the patronage of publishers Firmin Didot, Jean-Baptiste Benoît Eyriès, and Conrad Malte-Brun; the latter two served as co-editors of *Nouvelles annales des voyages*, a leading periodical of exploration. Eyriès would edit Choris's *Voyage pittoresque*, and Didot would publish it. Choris was welcomed into the newly formed Paris Société de géographie, which also extended an honorary membership to Count Rumiantsev for his patronage of the sciences. Simply put, Paris offered the young artist a moveable feast of talent and opportunities.

Most of all, Parisian artists introduced Choris to lithography. Developed in Germany in the early 1800s, lithography was an inexpensive and easily adaptable method of drawing (rather than carving) on stone with a wax crayon, allowing for rapid and highly detailed reproduction.[80] Franco-German artist Godefroy Engelmann studied lithography in Munich in 1815 before bringing it to Paris the next year for a special examination by the Académie Royale des Beaux-Arts, which endorsed its qualities to printers and painters. The manual *Notice sur la lithographie* (1818), written by Paris illustrator Claude Mairet, spread the gospel of lithography throughout France, and by 1819 books about this artistic form appeared in England, Germany, Belgium, and Italy. Printers throughout France quickly followed the lead of their Parisian colleagues. "Before long there was not a town in France without its lithographic press, where the printing was as good as in the capital," according to the first historian of lithography, Elizabeth Robins Pennell.[81] Lithography held numerous benefits in a world of expanding print culture, in particular the high level of finely lined illustrations. For the visual representation of nature, science, travel, and exploration, lithography produced images with "the quality of appearing true or real," writes scholar Michael Twyman.[82]

Choris studied lithographic techniques as he continued to train in painting and illustration. His Paris mentor Jean-Baptiste Regnault had been among the artists who assessed the quality of lithography for the Académie Royale des Beaux-Arts in 1816, and Choris also began working with the lithographers Jean Victor Adam and Jean-Henri Marlet. The successful printing house of Joseph Langlumé produced Choris's initial lithographs and experimented with full-color versions, which the artist completed by hand.[83] Experimentation and innovation was the key to "mark-making" on stone. An 1818 instructional volume described more than twenty different instruments for making marks, including a metal *porte-crayon*, steel pen, small brush, swan quill, and other tools. Each instrument, used in different ways, built up the tone of the image in a systematic fashion. Cross-hatching and the careful tapering of lines produced the minute detail associated with the finest lithographs.[84] Specialists in coloring or other parts of the craft were often required, and Choris sought their assistance when necessary.

The attention paid to Choris's work by artists and publishers had less to do with his talent and more with his singular experience of circumnavigating the globe. He had a unique story to tell, and he now sought to visually represent it in a comprehensive volume. The format Choris decided upon was an initial serial run (called a *livraison*) of different segments of the voyage priced between 7 and 15 francs, depending on whether the lithographs were colored or uncolored. Choris issued the book-length compendium of the entire expedition in 1822, priced between 160 and 320 francs.[85] He may have modeled this serial-to-book strategy on two successful lithographic volumes, Louis Forbin's *Voyage dans le Levant* (1819) and Baron Taylor's *Voyages Pittoresques et Romantiques dans l'Ancienne France* (1820). Taylor's work, supported by the government and depicting the charms of "old" France, grew to twenty volumes by 1878. "In scale as well as in subject matter," Michael Twyman argues, Taylor's "*Voyages pittoresque* was a product of romanticism."[86]

Choris's work contained some romantic elements, but as Chamisso observed, his objective was the "real and very lifelike portraits of particular individuals" and natural history.[87] His artistic process progressed from sketch to watercolor to final lithograph, and during the intermediate step he experimented with composition and color, as seen in his paintings of a Aleut baidarka, a Chukchi home, and a group of sea lions on St. Georges Island. Those lithographs with a touch of romanticism—for instance, the

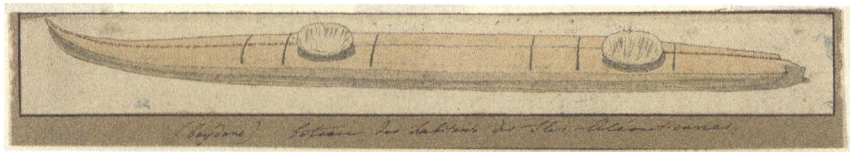

domestic scene of a Radakian home—stand in contrast to Choris's focus on practical objects and natural landscapes. Two of Choris's most widely reproduced lithographic landscapes, the *Port d'hanarourou* (see Figure 3.13) and *Vue des Glaces dans le Golfe de Kotzebue* (see Figure 1.4b), serve the dual purpose of showing an exotic landscape and also focusing close attention on the most unique human or environmental features.

At least half of the lithographs published in *Voyage pittoresque* are images of Indigenous people in individual or group settings. Voyage artists were typically instructed to give considerable attention to the physiognomy of human subjects, but Choris placed special emphasis on their social activities. The group illustrations generally situate people in their specific environment: Hawaiians dancing against a backdrop of coconut palms, or Chukchis sitting within their domicile, or Native Californians in forced labor for the Spanish presidio soldiers. Their distinguishing human characteristics, Choris seems to suggest, were rooted in their locations, cultures, and activities. While some of his portraits give attention to facial features, such as a person's profile or three-quarters view, Choris did not favor this approach to portraiture that would become common in mid-nineteenth century studies of race. "Profiles," he exclaimed to Chamisso in 1821, "do not think that I take pleasure in drawing them!—I have not—[and] be assured that I will not make too many of them." Historian Marie-Theres Federhofer argues that Choris paid particular attention to depicting culturally specific Indigenous symbols associated with the body—such as tattoos, piercing, and jewelry—rather than marking a person's racial background.[88] His portrait of Kadu, for instance, is set in profile to show

Figures 5.4a, 5.4b, 5.4c Watercolors of an Aleut baidarka, Chukchi home, and sea lions. Choris produced watercolor paintings from his initial sketches, and he often used the watercolors to experiment with color, composition, and subject matter. The largest collection of his watercolors, held by Yale University's Beinecke Library, includes many scenes from Aleut, Chukchi, and Iñupiat territory. Each of these watercolors contributed to specific lithographs published in *Voyage pittoresque*, as seen in Figures 1.6, 2.6, and 3.2. Courtesy of Louis Choris Paintings and Sketches, Yale Collection of Western Americana, Beinecke Rare Book and Manuscript Library.

the outline of his face, but Choris seems most interested in documenting Kadu's body art and ornamentation.

Choris took creative license in manipulating the final form of some lithographs. Two portraits from the Hawaiian Islands stand out in this way. *Femme des iles Sandwich* seems deliberately erotic in nature. It displays a young woman confidently returning the viewer's gaze as she disrobes the top half of her body. Her facial expression is both enigmatic and regal in the way she challenges the viewer to observe her confident pose. Partial nudity was not uncommon in Choris's portraits, and like other voyage artists, he typically presented nude figures from a distance rather than up close, and usually in a group setting. By contrast, this image was unique in the way Choris depicted youthful beauty and invited the viewers' gaze upon her body. Choris produced the final lithograph by drawing elements from two of his watercolors ("Femmes des iles Sandwich") that bore little resemblance to the resulting image.[89] The visual symbols within the lithograph—the band of lightened hair, the earrings, and especially the whale tooth pendant on the necklace—indicate the woman's elite if not royal status. Choris imbues her with a goddess-like aura; while decidedly human, her appearance and posture seem to transcend time. The lithograph's composition mimics classical sculpture, and specifically, *Aphrodite of Knidos* by the Greek sculptor Praxiteles, who rendered the goddess Aphrodite in nude form for the first time. Choris could not have viewed *Aphrodite of Knidos*, because it no longer existed. But a famous Roman copy of the Greek statue did exist, and Choris needed to look no further than the Louvre, where *Venus de Milo* was first displayed in early 1821. He surely visited the Louvre to see the arrival of this sensational Roman statue, and he would have taken note of Venus's ethereal expression and revealed torso—elements central to his *Femme des iles Sandwich* lithograph. Those who purchased *Voyage pittoresque* may have also recognized Choris's allusion to the sculpture of Venus in this lithograph.

Choris did not write about the *Femme* lithograph, but he commented extensively on the second unique Hawaiian portrait. As the first artist to sketch a portrait of the Hawaiian King Kamehameha, Choris, like his colleague Chamisso, understood he was in the presence of a great figure,

Figure 5.5 *Femme des îles Sandwich*. Apart from the woman's striking appearance—a "goddess-like figure" according to scholar Ron Tyler—this portrait shows the level of detail possible in the new artistic process of lithography (Tyler, 2017). The crayon drawing on stone allowed for the careful shading of body tone and facial expression, as well as the texture of hair and clothing. The folds of the tapa robe show the depth of texture now feasible with lithography, while the careful hand-coloring stands out especially in the bleached band of hair, piercing eyes, red earrings, whale tooth pendant, and green robe. The richness of detail allowed lithography to dominate the French printing business in the decade following Choris's publication. Courtesy Internet Archive.

a conqueror of the Hawaiian Island chain, and a leader who had dealt with European voyagers since the time of Captain James Cook. Choris made his request to draw the king on the morning of their arrival before Captain Kotzebue had come ashore. The idea of a portrait "pleased his majesty very much," and the artist liked the king's clothing, as he was dressed in a traditional tapa robe. Choris described what happened next in his journal.

Figure 5.6 Watercolor of *Femmes des îles Sandwich*. These two watercolors served as templates for the "Femme" lithograph (Fig. 5.5). The woman on the left displays the appearance of a Hawaiian elite, with a bleached band of hair, a necklace with a whale-tooth pendant, and a European blouse on top of a tapa wrap. The woman on the right bears none of these symbols of the elite class. In a subsequent etching and aquatint, published in the Russian edition of Kotzebue's voyage account, Choris combined these two images and portrayed the woman of rank in partial nudity. In the process, writes scholar Jean Charlot, "the woman acquires a gentle dignity" (Charlot, 1958). Choris seemingly exploits this dignity with the final lithographic form of the image, in which the woman's nudity becomes the central focus. Courtesy of Collection of the Honolulu Museum of Art. Gift of the Honolulu Art Society, 1944 (12157ab).

[Kamehameha] gestured to me to go for a walk and ordered one of his people next to him to accompany me. After a short while he called for me. They brought me to his house which is very big. I found him sitting on a beautiful big European chair and leaning on to a table. He was already dressed in sailor's clothes.... A white shirt, a red vest, a big silken scarf, [and] blue sailors pants made up his outfit. I asked him to please be so kind as to put on a native costume. But he wanted it that way. When I drew him, his majesty often forgot [to hold still] and rolled his eyes or moved his mouth. But he remembered immediately [when I reminded him]. He took on a rather frosty disposition after that.[90]

Kamehameha allowed a second portrait in the afternoon, and from these two sittings Choris produced a set of sketches and at least one watercolor. Copies of Choris's portrait rapidly proliferated from these drawings— some produced by Choris, others created by sketch artists, painters, and engravers in Canton, Boston, Paris, and elsewhere. This portrait's immediate reproduction reads something like a mystery novel, according to art historian Jean Charlot, who attempted to trace the many versions and the slight alterations of the work.[91] But one aspect remains certain: as a visual representation of Pacific islanders' nobility, Choris's portrait of Kamehameha circulated far and wide to viewers eager to glimpse the most celebrated Indigenous ruler.

Choris drew a few versions of the portrait while still on the island of Hawai'i, and he left behind a couple of sketches when the *Rurik* departed for O'ahu. At O'ahu, Kotzebue observed, "when it became known on shore that we had [Kamehameha] on paper we were visited daily by a great number of people to see him."[92] A trader visiting Hawai'i brought a copy of Choris's portrait to Canton for reproduction, and versions of that work had arrived in Manila by the time the *Rurik* docked there in 1817. American John Jones traveled from Manila to Boston with an oil painting version, and he presented it to the Boston Athenaeum in June 1818. The *Rurik* had not yet completed its voyage at this time, nor did Choris produce this painting (he did not paint with oils). Copies traveled around the island Pacific for years to come on trade vessels. The portrait circulated in Europe following the *Rurik*'s return and was published in volumes such as Frederic Shoberl's *The World in Miniature* and Jules Dumont d'Urville's *Voyage Pittoresque Autor du Monde*, among other books. Significantly, except for Choris's own 1822 volume of lithographs, all other publications published the version of Kamehameha in his red vest and sailor's pants. The four different translations of Kotzebue's voyage account—in English, Dutch, German, and Russian—each used the "red vest" portrait of the

King. Reproduced by different illustrators, they are all variations on a theme: a dark-skinned ruler in a sailor's suit "with his hair groomed to a fault."[93]

Choris kept for his own use the sketches and watercolor of Kamehameha dressed in the tapa robe, and he used this image for the lithograph in *Voyage pittoresque*. One could argue that Choris objectified and even ex-oticized the King as distinctly Native by presenting him in a simple tapa robe. Given the fact that Kamehameha maintained an extensive European

Figure 5.7 "Tamaah-maah, King of the Sandwich Islands." This engraving by John Heaviside Clark appeared in the Russian, Dutch, German, and English editions of Kotzebue's voyage account. In contrast to the lithograph (see Fig. 3.10) published in *Voyage pittoresque*, which presents Kamehameha in traditional clothing, here the King is dressed in a sailor's red vest and white shirt, an outfit he intentionally changed into for the portrait sitting with the artist. Kotzebue used this version of the King's portrait, because it was the only one Choris made available to him. Courtesy of The Huntington Library, San Marino.

wardrobe resulting from decades of explorers' gifts, Choris could have visually re-dressed him in European finery to appear more statesmanlike. But an alternative explanation for the tapa robe seems more likely: Choris desired to represent the King as he first appeared to him, in traditional attire and without pretense. Despite his royal status, Kamehameha possessed a gracious humility recognized by all visitors to the Hawaiian Islands.[94] The artist noted in his journal the way he offered protection to the *Rurik* personnel during their time on Hawai'i and further assistance when they sailed for O'ahu.[95] For Choris, the tapa robe and the King's forlorn expression convey a modesty rare among rulers—Indigenous or otherwise.

For a volume focused in large part on the many Pacific groups encountered by the expedition, *Voyage pittoresque* offers a rare visual reportage. No similar Pacific voyage book existed at the time. Almost half of the lithographs depict Indigenous people from Radak, Hawai'i, Alaska, California, the Philippines, and elsewhere, either in portrait form or, more typically, in landscape or domestic settings. Choris attempted to situate the inhabitants in specific environments and in relationship to the *Rurik* visitors— they might appear distant and hostile, welcoming and gracious, or simply unaware of the artist's gaze. In the end, Choris's images convey only a limited understanding of the people. He knew that his European perspective and the brief time he spent with his subjects resulted in something incomplete if not misleading.[96] Arguably, his illustrations of Indigenous material artifacts may be the closest he got to accurately documenting their cultures. The material culture, and especially the images of Indigenous watercraft utilized by groups, reveals his desire to record the most important technology of the communities visited by the *Rurik*. He rendered other material culture—the tusk carvings, weapons, clothing, and habitations— with tremendous detail, and he placed it prominently throughout *Voyage pittoresque*. He intended each lithograph to tell a story, and, intentional or not, some of those stories contained the "indirect voice" of the Indigenous subjects.[97]

Count Rumiantsev and Krusenstern had certainly hoped to broadcast an immediate announcement upon the *Rurik*'s return: the discovery of a northern passage and possibly the actual navigation of that passage. Such was not to be the case. Instead, the afterlife of the voyage contained a wide assortment of findings that stretched years into the future and appeared in various genres: newspaper and journal articles, scientific treatises, artistic illustrations, published voyage accounts, and travel stories communicated by the personnel to interested parties. Count Rumiantsev and Adam von Krusenstern facilitated the circulation of some of this work by securing professional placements for the personnel and utilizing their personal networks. The personnel of the *Rurik* made their own decisions about the experiences they shared and the knowledge they sought to disseminate.

The circulation of knowledge, at its core, involves the sharing of stories drawn from observations of the natural world and the human experience. The *Rurik* sailed with talented storytellers who further developed their craft during the voyage. Chamisso began the expedition one year after publishing his fairy-tale novella *Peter Schlemihl's Remarkable Story*, in which he narrated the strange discoveries made by a globe-trotting traveler-turned-naturalist. Chamisso's own experiences during the voyage were as fantastical as his fictional protagonist's: he observed tiny sea creatures that shape-shifted between generations; he gloried in the sublime sight of North Pacific whales and his extended conversations with Aleut hunters; he studied Indigenous languages in many locales; and he theorized a global perspective on the Pacific Ocean in its entirety. Once home, he conveyed this acquired knowledge in scientific journals, books, and theses.

Johann Eschscholtz developed his own set of observations and theories. A prolific collector of flora and fauna, he attempted to re-categorize all known species as his personal contribution to the ongoing science of speciation. In this way, Eschscholtz represents a transitional thinker between Linnaean and Darwinian science. He observed things closely: he sighted a massive wall of ice in Kotzebue Sound and then looked closer to reveal its surprising earthen composition. He found a new *Hippuris* specimen high atop Unalaska Island, and years later he badgered Chamisso to recollect that exact moment in time to corroborate his discovery. It was just one among hundreds of specimens he named, categorized, and wrote about. Like Chamisso, the stories Eschscholtz told of the natural world all appeared in textual form—a monograph, newspapers, personal correspondence, and the journal *Linnaea*.

The printed word, or more precisely the published text, might seem to define the method of producing and circulating knowledge. Except when it does not. Arguably, Kadu returned to the Ratak Islands with more useful knowledge than any other traveler on the *Rurik*. He neither wrote nor published a single word. But from the moment he stepped ashore at Wotje Atoll, he began transmitting the knowledge he acquired during the voyage to the islanders who surrounded him. Kotzebue belittled Kadu's initial presentation as a "long narrative" told to an "excited" audience, and yet the captain's impatience may have reflected a fear that none of his own stories of discovery would generate the level of interest received by Kadu. Nor could Kotzebue's written account of the voyage quite match the impact of Ludwig Choris's visual representations of the Pacific. The artist's images— grand landscapes, portraits, scenes of colonized places, marine mammals, and Indigenous material culture—were reproduced and transmitted in various forms at the time and for decades to come. Their power lies in the stories they tell and the way those stories transcend a specific voyage of discovery. Choris's work offers a visual embodiment of natural history as a field of study. Following his death in 1828, Alexander von Humboldt claimed that Choris's two lithographic volumes represented a stirring "final testimony" to "natural history."[98]

What Humboldt and others referred to as natural history splintered in the years to come. The holistic study of humans and nature fragmented into increasingly specialized areas of research. Some future voyages of discovery included a scientific corps representing these new specializations. The United States Exploring Expedition (1838–1842) carried two botanists, a geologist/mineralogist, conchologist, philologist, two artists, and two naturalists—one of whom specialized in ornithology, the other seemed most interested in the racial theory of polygenesis. Humboldt appreciated the scientific advancements resulting from specialization, but he continued to praise the holistic approach of natural history. Humboldt particularly loved beautiful prose, as he told Chamisso in 1836 after receiving a copy of his memoir of the *Rurik* voyage. At the time, Humboldt was in court with the King and Crown Prince of Prussia, to whom he read Chamisso's words out loud. He wrote to Chamisso: "It is rare that a poet like you...can write such spontaneous, simple and free prose....[The *Rurik*] voyage around the world may be old by now, but your personal stamp has given it the charm of a new world drama."[99] Humboldt praised Chamisso's contributions to natural history, but what he seemed to appreciate most of all was the naturalist's ability to present natural history as a story of adventure, observation, spontaneity, and self-discovery. Chamisso, suffering from late-stage tuberculosis, still hoped to return to the Sandwich Islands to complete his Hawaiian dictionary. He had a brief interview with Humboldt on the matter, which ended with Chamisso hacking blood into his handkerchief. He never made the voyage to Hawai'i.

All Species of Knowledge: A Voyage of Discovery, Failure, and Natural History in the Pacific Ocean. David Igler, Oxford University Press. © Oxford University Press 2026. DOI: 10.1093/9780197777718.003.0006

Conclusion

Failures, Discoveries, and Legacies in Natural History

In 1821 the Thanet Book Society purchased the most recent exploration narrative, bearing the cumbersome title *A Voyage of Discovery, Into the South Sea and Beering's Straits, for the Purpose of Exploring a North-East Passage Undertaken in the Years 1815–1818, at the Expense of His Highness the Chancellor of the Empire, Count Romanzoff, in the Ship Rurick, Under the Command of the Lieutenant in the Russian Imperial Navy, Otto von Kotzebue.* The leather-bound volumes arrived in Thanet, a remote hamlet on England's southeastern coast, at which point the book society members added their names to the request form. They could borrow the three-volume set for a period of twenty-one days. Mr. Freeman had first dibs, beginning on September 11, 1821, followed by Mr. Clarke, Mr. Swinford, Mrs. Denne, and so on. In the era before free lending libraries, book societies in England followed this procedure for the circulation of new literature. What the Thanet Book Society borrowers took away from Captain Kotzebue's voyage narrative is anyone's guess. But the fact that they read it—or at least had the opportunity to read it—is documented on the request form affixed to the inside cover of the first edition, owned today by the Huntington Library.

The London publisher of the volumes, Longman & Company, sold hundreds of copies in the first year to a market of readers desiring stories of travel and exploration. The members of the Thanet Book Society could meet a man named Kadu, visit with the King of the Hawaiian Islands, and visualize the seemingly endless field of ice that impeded the *Rurik's* northward advance in the summer of 1817. These and many other episodes spoke to a British reading public that desired adventurous stories and encounters with exotic people and places—all from the safety of their own homes.[1] However, one critic from the British Admiralty had much to say about Otto von Kotzebue's narration of the three-year voyage around the world, including some very pointed remarks regarding the Captain's failure to push farther north of the Bering Strait in 1817.

Secretary of the Admiralty John Barrow had previously applauded Kotzebue's accomplishments when the two men met in London in June 1818. Barrow immediately publicized a few of the expedition's key discoveries, including the widely circulated report of the peculiar "iceberg" composed of earthen matter and a gradually thawing carcass of a prehistoric mammoth. Barrow had trumpeted a new "spirit of discovery" following the "long [and] protracted war" that had "suspended all attempts at northern discovery."[2] Kotzebue's voyage, he wrote in 1818, represented the advance guard of Arctic discovery for ambitious European nations. For personal and professional reasons, Kotzebue happily accepted this praise from England's main promoter of northern exploration.

Four years later, John Barrow reached a different conclusion about the expedition when he reviewed Kotzebue's *A Voyage of Discovery* for the popular London journal *The Quarterly Review*. His appraisal exceeded twenty pages of tightly packed criticism of the Russian voyage and especially the actions of Captain Kotzebue. The Russian government, he wrote, approached exploration with "anxiety" in comparison to Britain's "ambitious" plans for new discoveries. He recounted how Kotzebue's expedition received "a cool reception in [Russian] imperial circles... for the failure of a private enterprize" funded by a man scorned in those circles, Count Rumiantsev.[3] Barrow questioned some of the newly named islands that "our navigator" enthusiastically "considered as a new discovery," and he even claimed that the "undoubted discovery" of Kotzebue Sound "was before known" by the inestimable James Cook, who humbly refrained from naming it forty years earlier. Barrow called one of Kotzebue's announced discoveries "sheer nonsense," and he underscored a particular decision made by the Captain as "a great error in judgment."[4] Barrow commended Adelbert von Chamisso's contributions to the voyage—both what he wrote for inclusion in Kotzebue's account and his research publications since returning to Berlin. Barrow also applauded the general knowledge they "learned from" the "extraordinary character" of Kadu. But Kotzebue, Barrow observed, not only failed to find the Northern Passage—he failed twice. During the first summer of exploration, Barrow remarked, the Captain should have "pushed forward, without a moment's loss of time, along the shore to the extreme north" of the Chukchi Sea. Instead, the Captain had dawdled for more than a week in the large bay he christened with his own family name. And then, during the second season's attempt at Arctic exploration, Kotzebue faltered in front of the "firm ice," which had not yet broken for the summer. "Here," Barrow concluded, Kotzebue "made up his mind, if that had not already been done, to lay aside all further attempt at discovery, and return to the more agreeable groups of coral islands." This "abrupt abandonment" of the mission "was hardly justified," Barrow sniffed. "It would not be tolerated in England."[5]

Barrow had publicly praised Kotzebue's efforts in 1818, while four years later he denigrated the Captain's narrative as well as his character. The shift in judgment is not difficult to explain. In 1818 Barrow sought to convince the Admiralty to pursue Arctic exploration at any cost. Kotzebue's safe return and novel findings justified his case. By 1822, England had fully joined the renewed competition for Arctic exploration, but the nation's lack of success in discovering a viable passage put advocates like Barrow on the defensive. He criticized Kotzebue due to his own insecurity as well as his belief that the British empire must reign supreme in the competition for Arctic discoveries. Indeed, Barrow argued, Britain had gained a tremendous amount of useful knowledge from its pursuit of oceanic exploration. Yet promoters like Barrow also disregarded the origins of some of that useful knowledge, especially the intelligence about a possible passage that came from Indigenous people. Barrow knew that, too.

In this regard Barrow himself had failed to act upon the most intriguing piece of information he reported from his 1818 interview with Kotzebue. In London they had discussed the conditions of the Chukchi Sea above the Bering Strait, including the broad inlet of Kotzebue Sound on the North American coast. According to Barrow, it was here that Kotzebue "found the current setting strongly to the north-east" and learned of an opening "through which there was a passage into the great sea." Any waterway headed "north-east" from Kotzebue Sound might terminate in the Beaufort Sea—directly above North America, with possible connecting routes to the Atlantic Ocean. Kotzebue had told Barrow of the source for this key intelligence: the "Indians" who "peopled" the region. In 1818 Barrow wrote:

> From these Indians Lieutenant Kotzebue learned, that…it required nine days rowing with one of their boats to reach this sea. This, Kotzebue thinks, must be the Great Northern Ocean, and that the whole of the land to the northward of the inlet must either be an island or an archipelago of islands.[6]

If Barrow's account of Kotzebue's information was accurate, and if both men gave even partial credence to the intelligence gathered from the Captain's Iñupiat informants, then they possessed a remarkable clue to one possible route of a northern passage.

Neither man followed up on the intelligence, which suggests that their exchange may have represented little beyond wishful speculation. But their failure to act is not the point. Instead, what the two men appeared to readily accept was the validity of Indigenous knowledge. Kotzebue had "learned" of this route from the "Indians," who supposedly knew the length of the "passage" and its likely terminus: "the great sea." Traversing the route would require Indigenous guides and paddlers: "nine days rowing with one of their boats."[7] In other words, they would need the intelligence, the skills, and even the technology possessed by the Iñupiat community. But Kotzebue and Barrow did not track this reasoning to its logical conclusion in 1818, which would have entailed advocating strongly for Indigenous participation in any future attempt. Nor did Barrow refer to this strategy four years later, when he declared Kotzebue's "enterprize" a "failure."[8]

Failure provides a consistent touchstone in the history of exploration as well as the practice of natural history. Even the most celebrated explorers failed in ways that proved costly to their voyages and sometimes deadly to themselves. In 1779 James Cook overstayed his welcome on the island of Hawai'i, demanding too much generosity and resources from his hosts. He paid with his life—and the lives of four other crewmembers—on the rocky shoreline of Kealakekua Bay. This was hardly the first instance in which Cook failed to comprehend the social customs of the people he encountered. Australian Aboriginal elder and storyteller Hobbles Danaiyarri confirmed this point about Cook. Danaiyarri blamed Cook's lack of proper etiquette for initiating the centuries of violent dispossession in his homeland. "He [Cook] should have come up and [said] 'hello,' you know, 'hello'. . . because it's aboriginal land," Danaiyarri stated. Cook not only failed to offer a humble greeting, but he also failed to ask whose "country" he had entered or query about "one bit of [their] story."⁹ Cook's lack of regard—*whose country is this?*—served as prelude to the legal assertion *terra nullius* (vacant land), which rationalized many imperial claims to Indigenous homelands around the globe.¹⁰

Failure aptly describes well over a century of exploration and colonization in the western hemisphere prior to the 1620s, argues historian Peter Mancall. The "Age of Failure" included bungled settlements, shipwrecks, pirate-infested seas, cannibalism, ill-plotted expeditions, and, of course, numerous disastrous efforts to locate the Northern Passage. "[D]espite the problems experienced by other European nations," Mancall writes, "the English legacy of failure was the most notable."¹¹ The English "learned" from their failures in the mid-1600s, Mancall contends, and some of their most successful new practices came from observing Indigenous settlement sites and agricultural methods. However, the eventual "success" of colonization came at the horrendous cost of introduced diseases, Indigenous land dispossession, and racial slavery.¹²

Failure presents new opportunities for those willing to learn from their errors. Failure allows the reconsideration of objectives, methods, and paradigms. Failure is central to the scientific process and humanistic endeavors alike, for the simple reason that researchers fail most of the time, until they don't. More to the point, the interstitial space between success and failure contains a range of creative possibilities for developing new knowledge. In maritime terms, to merely survive and return from a three-year voyage might amount to success, and yet such a metric seems unfair to some of the most celebrated navigators, including Vitus Bering, Ferdinand Magellan, Jean-Francios Galaup comte de Laperouse, and James Cook, all of whom died during their final voyages. Success might mean a new and thrilling discovery in geography, ethnography, or linguistics, but such findings were hardly new to the people who lived in the discovered place or embodied the discovered people. John Marra, who sailed aboard the *Resolution* on Cook's second voyage, may have best articulated the ambiguity of "proving" a new discovery. He titled his 1775 account *Journal of the Resolution's Voyage…by which the Non-Existence of an undiscovered Continent…is demonstrably proved.*[13] Marra published his journal anonymously due to the naval stricture against releasing an account of the voyage before Cook's own publication, who had his own story to tell about *not* discovering the Southern Continent. Kotzebue, it would seem, was in good company.

The hundreds of "voyages of discovery" that cast off in the eighteenth and nineteenth centuries typically carried specific instructions of what should be discovered as well as the means by which that discovery should occur. Only a few of these voyages could honestly claim to have achieved the stated goal. Yet many expeditions included curious individuals who viewed the voyage as a rare occasion to gather knowledge and develop new ways of thinking: a young midshipman who committed every notable observation to his daily journal, a naturalist who went rogue in the Southwest Pacific and began theorizing how species evolve, and an Indigenous navigator who seized the opportunity to explore the unknown seas of the great ocean.[14] For them, discovery was a process as much as an outcome, and the process demanded long periods of deliberate observation.

The *Rurik's* failure to locate a northern passage required an explanation. Otto von Kotzebue responded to the failure by citing his many notable findings. The most significant of these was his detailed survey of the Marshall Islands and description of the Marshall islanders. This chain of coral islands contained no desirable resources and therefore avoided colonization for decades, while the islanders resisted contact and inter-course with outsiders who appeared on their shores. But Kotzebue's dis-covery was less about the islands' value and more about announcing their existence to European readers fascinated by remote and exotic locales. The captain claimed other notable findings, such as the large bay north of the Bering Strait surely of use to future expeditions. He penned a lengthy report on his diplomatic meeting with the king of the Hawaiian Islands. Kotzebue also publicized some of the work conducted by his personnel, whose studies he supported throughout the voyage. The Captain explained his lack of discovering a northern passage in the context of these other achievements.

Apart from Captain Kotzebue, the personnel of the *Rurik* embraced their own notions of discovery and success. Once on board, Chamisso, Eschscholtz, and Choris almost immediately discovered how to work col-laboratively in the ship's close confines. Together they pulled sea creatures from the ocean, eagerly dissected animals as a team, and documented their prize findings. They followed their own specialized lines of research and provided one another with a healthy forum for discussion. For in-stance, Chamisso's shipboard investigation of salp metagenesis certainly benefited from Eschscholtz's constant input, while Choris's visual render-ings of Indigenous seacraft reflected their shared appraisal of the technol-ogy employed by the people they encountered. Even the organizers of the voyage, Rumiantsev and Krusenstern, recognized the chance to pursue knowledge and accomplishments in the face of probable failure. Did either of them seriously believe the *Rurik* would locate a northern passage when so many others had failed? Not likely. But their gambit had multiple pay-offs: they launched the first expedition following a prolonged European war, announced new discoveries in the face of Russian bureaucratic obsti-nacy, and supported the intellectual endeavors of the spirited young per-sonnel who brought home surprising ideas to share with the world. In these and other ways, Kotzebue's failure to find a northern passage was perhaps the least interesting result of the *Rurik*'s pursuit of natural history.

Kadu may have embodied the pursuit of natural history more than anyone on the ship. In a transitional era for European science marked by increasing specialization, commercial objectives, and racial thought, Kadu sought a holistic knowledge of the world around him. Prior to joining the voyage, he had already traveled more extensively than almost any Caroline or Marshall islander, and he would go on to expand his geographic understanding of the seas far beyond his home islands. His voyage represented a diverse natural history venture, combining ethnography, collecting, experimentation, intelligence gathering, and sharing of knowledge. He was also a subject of his shipmates' natural history. As Kadu observed and deciphered his surroundings, his traveling companions observed him. He was scrutinized and narrated as a source of information, and he did the same to the strange men who desired his company. When Kadu returned home he circulated his findings in the form of oral testimony rather than published reports. His natural history of distant seas, stark islands, new marine creatures, and Hawaiian abundance likely astonished his listeners. It also contained immediate warnings for his peers and elders about the people with whom he had traveled. Could his Marshallese audience imagine the forces to come, including Christian missionaries and colonial incursions, not to mention the world-shattering atomic technology unleashed on "Eschscholtz Atoll," renamed Bikini Atoll, in 1946?[15]

Whose interests did Kadu's new knowledge serve? It would be misguided to imagine it benefited all Marshallese islanders, even if the information he relayed spread widely among the population. Kadu generously shared his findings, but he also used his gathered knowledge and new material possessions to enhance his status in Radakian society. Once viewed as a curious newcomer due to his origins in the Caroline Islands, he earned a more privileged status from the powerful Marshallese *iroijs* following the voyage. Kadu's new knowledge and possessions may have especially served the interests of *iroij* Lamari, who was actively extending his authority among Ratak leaders and carrying out campaigns against rivals in the Ralik chain of islands. Kadu's knowledge—in addition to the iron weapons acquired from the *Rurik*—buttressed Lamari's growing power.

The legacies of the others on board the *Rurik* might have ended with their early deaths and their published research. However, from a different vantage point their legacies resonate into the twenty-first century because of the broad questions they asked and their ambition to discover meaning in natural history. As the preeminent scientist E. O. Wilson remarked, "the naturalist's journey...will go on forever" due to a shared sensibility across the centuries.[16] While only Adelbert von Chamisso is widely known to contemporary scholars, the others each embody specific approaches to the natural world still evident today.

Chamisso's popularity peaked in the mid-nineteenth century as a writer of prose and a natural historian. One hundred years later, European and especially German scholars rediscovered his work as a poet, romanticist, and world-traveling naturalist. Publications about Chamisso's work peaked in the late 1980s and then leveled off until the early 2000s, at which point a new generation of scholars began reexamining his natural-history collections and contributions to nineteenth-century science.[17] Researchers explored his theories about salps, North Pacific whales, and coral reefs. Other scholars examined his methods of cataloging species and translations of Indigenous languages. English editions of his publications and correspondence appeared in print. His travelogue *A Voyage Around the World with the Romanzov Exploring Expedition in the Years 1815–1818*, originally published in 1836, was issued in English in 1986. It remains unique in the genre of voyage narratives due to its intimate prose and energetic celebration of natural history.[18] The current interest in Chamisso's legacy is multifaceted, but a central attraction is the way his work exhibited the holistic scientific approach of nineteenth-century luminaries such as Alexander von Humboldt. Like Humboldt, Chamisso possessed a deep fascination with the mysteries of the natural world, and he traveled far to observe the things that most intrigued him. He recognized knowledge as something to be shared, because the "naturalist's privilege" resided in an obligation to circulate knowledge to contemporaries and future generations.[19]

In contrast to Chamisso's enduring recognition, Johann Eschscholtz's legacy remains mostly obscure. He published no poetry or stylistic prose to attract a popular audience, nor did his ideas about species lead directly to a new paradigm about their origins, differentiation, or arrangement. Nonetheless, he embraced the practice of natural history with the energy and discipline of a zealot. He published three dozen scholarly studies, trained students who traveled on scientific expeditions, drew his own plates for scientific volumes, and circumnavigated the globe a second time as a chief naturalist. His daily correspondence with colleagues around Europe was almost a full-time job, he informed Chamisso in 1830, and he believed that those communications were imperative to advance the field of natural history.[20]

Eschscholtz embodied the centuries-long naturalist tradition and philosophy that, at its best, "elevated the very concept of life."[21] His work subtly anticipated the environmental sensibility and ecosystem framework of twentieth-century thinkers like Aldo Leopold and Rachel Carson. Eschscholtz studied species down to the level of a singular specimen in a precise habitat. In so doing, he sought to comprehend the specimen's unique characteristics in relation to its environment. He harangued Chamisso for not remembering the exact location of a flower they collected years earlier—how could his friend not recall that moment of discovery? Eschscholtz disregarded the binary of success or failure, instead focusing on the process of conducting investigative work. In one zoological report, he mentioned as an afterthought the massive collection of "2,400 kinds of animals" he "examined" or "collected." More important than the collection itself, Eschscholtz emphasized, was the means by which he acquired the fauna. He noted the expertise of Native "inhabitants" who "enabled us" in collecting species, he recorded the precise location of a specific coral reef where they found "the greatest variety" of zoophytes, and he described the method of "procuring" a "specimen" that just might "form a link between" two other species.[22] It was this scientific process of deliberate observation, collaboration, and measured speculation that he offered to future generations of naturalists.

Ludwig Choris's expedition culminated in his creation of a unique format to narrate the voyage: a visual travelogue. He surely could not imagine producing a volume like *Voyage pittoresque autour du monde* when he joined the expedition as a twenty-year-old artist in 1815. He, like the others, had read narratives and viewed the botanical and ethnographic illustrations produced by previous voyage artists. Choris was also acquainted with Spain's decades-long Royal Botanical Expedition to the New Kingdom of Granada (1783–1817), which resulted in a rich archive of scientific illustrations.[23] The *Rurik's* personnel instructed him to produce coastal views and botanical illustrations. He spent the three years at sea sketching and painting with watercolors, like all voyage artists. But his artistic life took a dramatic turn when he moved to Paris in 1819. Once there, Choris imagined a new voyage medium for natural history—a comprehensive visual account of an entire voyage rendered with the novel printing technology of lithography.

For an era in which most natural history illustrations existed in a stable format and specific publication, Choris's work circulated before and after his death as reproductions and replicas in many venues. His sketch of King Kamehameha was copied and distributed to viewers before the *Rurik* left the Pacific Ocean. His watercolors of various figures and specific landscapes—turned into prints by printmakers hired by publishers—appeared in other writers' publications as he refined his own lithographs in Paris. Subsequent voyagers and travel writers reused Choris's prints in their own volumes, in large part because his images captured actual scenes and ethnographic information. Many of his lithographs appear today in scholarly and popular publications precisely because they document a specific time, locale, group of people, or representation of Indigenous material culture.

Choris's artistic illustrations were intentionally unstable in another way. The popularity of lithography resulted from its relative ease, affordability, high level of detail, and reproducibility. However, the reproduction process also allowed for variations in color, the addition of new elements in a particular view, and, for Choris, the ability to personalize a bound volume of prints for a specific customer.[24] Each extant copy of *Voyage pittoresque autour du monde* found today in an archive or private collection reveals variations that take the viewer back two centuries to decisions made by the artist in his Paris studio and the lithographic printshop located at rue de l'Abbaye #4. Some differences are subtle, such as the deeper red complexion given to a group portrait of Indigenous Californians in one lithograph, or the ethereal greenish tint that appears in one version of *Femme des iles Sandwich*, or the additional shading in a specific print of Kadu that significantly alters his countenance. Other variations are more significant. The portrait of Kamehameha in one copy of *Voyage pittoresque* shows the king with a considerably different facial expression and background, while in this same volume the image of an Aleut hunter's visor is printed in reverse and contains the additional element of an oddly shaped blade.[25] These alterations were all the result of choices made by Choris, and, perhaps in some cases, they were informed by the small group of collaborators with whom he worked.

To some degree Choris must have considered the variations and instability of his lithographs from the *Rurik* expedition as a reflection of natural history itself. If nature constantly changed, species contained countless variations, and human populations were strikingly diverse, how could his visual representations of human and non-human nature not imitate nature's sublime variability? He encountered the sublimity of nature on many occasions during the voyage. Early one morning in 1816, Choris strolled the ship's tidy deck encircled by the fog-shrouded Arctic Sea. As the fog rose, "we saw the sea covered with walrus that were playing on the surface; whales, surrounded the ship and blew water into the air through their blowholes," he wrote. "It was a singular spectacle to see all these huge animals gathered together in a crowd in these unfrequented parts." Surrounded by the quiet sea, Choris watched the sea creatures with a sense of wonder. The panorama was too overwhelming for the artist to capture in a single illustration, or at least no extant sketch of it has survived to this day. But Choris broke apart the scene for use in various lithographs: the marine mammals, the whales, the calm sea, and the seemingly infinite horizon.

Some moments in nature were too immense or wonderful for naturalists to understand, much less for an artist to render on paper.

This sense of wonder may best encapsulate the work conducted on the *Rurik* and during the expedition's productive afterlife. Practitioners of natural history—for this group of individuals and for everyone committed to the vocation—embrace the opportunity to discover what they did not already know and to relish the sense of awe. It was a deeply personal pursuit of finding something new and, at its best, sharing that discovery with like-minded individuals. The grand discovery of a northern passage was a fine ambition for empires and their representatives, but those people who pursued the wonders of nature operated on a lower frequency, where the mystery of creation could reveal itself.

All Species of Knowledge: A Voyage of Discovery, Failure, and Natural History in the Pacific Ocean. David Igler, Oxford University Press. © Oxford University Press 2026. DOI: 10.1093/9780197777718.003.0007

INTRODUCTION

1. Otto von Kotzebue, *A Voyage of Discovery, Into the South Sea and Beering's Straits, for the Purpose of Exploring a North-East Passage Undertaken in the Years 1815–1818, at the Expense of His Highness the Chancellor of the Empire, Count Romanzoff, in the Ship Rurick, Under the Command of the Lieutenant in the Russian Imperial Navy, Otto von Kotzebue*, trans. H. E. Lloyd, 3 vols. (London: Longman, 1821), 1: 207.

2. Ludwig Choris frequently combined spelling from different languages in his journal. "Baydarre" referred to the *baidarka* used by Aleut hunters. See Ludwig Choris, *Journals des Malers Ludwig York Choris*, ed. Niklaus R. Schweizer (New York: Peter Lang, 1999), 236, 237, 266.

3. Kotzebue, *A Voyage of Discovery*, 1: 208.

4. Bathsheba Demuth, *Floating Coast: An Environmental History of the Bering Strait* (New York: W. W. Norton & Co., 2019): xiii–xiv.

5. On the ways that Indigenous sentiment appears in European voyage accounts, see Bronwen Douglas, "In the Event: Indigenous Countersigns and the Ethnohistory of Voyaging," in *Oceanic Encounters: Exchange, Desire, Violence*, eds. Margaret Jolly, Serge Tcherkezoff, and Darrell Tryon (Canberra: ANU Press, 2009), 175–198. On countersigns in relation to groups in the North Pacific, see Marie-Theres Federhofer, "Messy Episodes: Indigenous Countersigns in Ludwig Choris's Diary and Ethnographic Portraits of Kamchadal, Aleut and Chukchi, 1822," *History and Anthropology* (April 2023): 1–22. On Chamisso's collecting of skulls, see Matthias Glaubrecht, Nils Seethaler, Barbara Tebman, and Katrin Koel-Abt, "The Potential of Biohistory: Re-discovering Adelbert von Chamisso's Skull of an Aleut Collected during the '*Rurik*' Expedition 1815–1818 in Alaska," *Zoosystematics and Evolution* 89 (September 2013): 317–336.

6. Adelbert von Chamisso, *A Voyage Around the World with the Romanzov Exploring Expedition in the Years 1815–1818 in the Brig Rurik, Captain Otto von Kotzebue*, trans. and ed. Henry Kratz (Honolulu: University of Hawai`i Press, 1986 [1836]): 85, 86.

7. Chamisso, *A Voyage Around the World*, 88, 89.

8. This translation of Ludwig Choris's writing appears in James W. Vanstone, "An Early Nineteenth-Century Artist in Alaska: Louis Choris and the First Kotzebue Expedition," *Pacific Northwest Quarterly* 51 (October 1960), 150.

9. Louis [Ludwig] Choris, *Voyage pittoresque autour du monde:avec des portraits de sauvages d'Amérique, d'Asie, d'Afrique, et des îles due Grand océan; des paysages, des vues maritimes, et plusieurs objets de'histoire naturelle* (Paris: Impr. de Firmin Didot, 1822). On the ways that Indigenous sentiment and knowledge appears in European voyage accounts, see Douglas, "In the Event," 175–198.

10. I appreciate this perspective on scholarly research. Years ago, I listened to a young and very successful research scientist address an audience of graduate students, who were visibly shaken when she boldly announced the usual outcome of scientific experimentation: "You have to realize that most of the time we fail!" I took note of her statement and keep it posted in my office. For a thoughtful approach to early English exploration and colonization failures, see Peter C. Mancall, "The Age of Failures," *Early American Literature* 56 (2021): 23–50.

11. John Barrow, "Ross's *Voyage of Discovery*," *Quarterly Review* 21 (January 1819), 213.

12. On Indigenous claims, voyaging, and settlement, see Paul D'Arcy, *The People of the Sea: Identity, Environment, and History in Oceania* (Honolulu: University of Hawai`i Press, 2005); Joshua L. Reid, *The Sea Is My Country: The Maritime World of the Makah* (New Haven, CT: Yale University Press, 2015); Emalani Case, *Everything Ancient Was Once New: Indigenous Persistence from Hawai`i to Kahiki* (Honolulu: University of Hawai`i Press, 2021); David A. Chang, *The World and All Things upon It: Native Hawaiian Geographies of Exploration* (Minneapolis: University of Minnesota Press, 2016); K. R. Howe, *Vaka Moana Voyages of the Ancestors: The Discovery and Settlement of the Pacific* (Honolulu: University of Hawai`i Press, 2006); Patrick Kirch, *A Shark Going Inland Is My Chief: The Island Civilization of Ancient Hawai`i* (Berkeley: University of California Press, 2012); David Armitage and Allison Bashford (eds.), *Pacific Histories: Ocean, Land, People* (New York: Palgrave Macmillan, 2014), 1–74.

13. On knowledge production and European voyages, I've been especially influenced by Anne Salmond, *The Trial of the Cannibal Dog: The Remarkable Story of Captain Cook's Encounters in the South Seas* (New Haven, CT: Yale University Press, 2003); Ryan Tucker Jones, *Empire of Extinction: Russians and the North Pacific's Strange Beasts of the Sea, 1741–1867* (New York: Oxford University Press, 2014); Patricia Fara, *Sex, Botany, and Empire: The Story of Carl Linnaeus and Joseph Banks* (New York: Columbia University Press, 2003); and J. Gascoigne, *Science in the Service of Empire: Joseph Banks, the British State, and the Uses of Science in the Age of Revolution* (New York: Cambridge University Press, 1998).

14. The literature here is extensive, including Kapil Raj, *Relocating Modern Science: Circulation and the Construction of Knowledge in South Asia and Europe, 1650–1900* (New York: Palgrave Macmillan, 2007); Daniela Bleichmar, "Visible Empire: scientific expeditions and visual culture in the Hispanic enlightenment," *Postcolonial Studies* 12 (2009): 441–466; *Colonial Botany: Science, Commerce, and Politics in the Early Modern World*, eds. Londa Schiebinger and Claudia Swan (Philadelphia: University of Pennsylvania Press, 2005).

15. Roald Amundsen, *Roald Amundsen's "The North West passage": being the record of a voyage of exploration of the ship "Gjoa" 1903-1907* (London: Constable and Co., 1908). On the search for the Northwest Passage, see Glyn Williams, *Voyages of Delusion: The Quest for the Northwest Passage* (New Haven, CT: Yale University Press, 2002); and most recently, David L. Nicandri, *Discovering Nothing: In Pursuit of an Elusive Northwest Passage* (Vancouver: University of British Columbia Press, 2024).

16. Here I'm drawing on the term *unpacking* used by Anne Greenwood MacKinney and Matthias Glaubrecht, "Unpacking a(nother) voyage round the world: Adelbert von Chamisso's donation of the *Rurik* collection to Berlin's natural history museums," *Journal of the History of Collections* 34 (July 2022): 259–274.

17. For example, see Glaubrecht, et al., "The Potential of Biohistory," 317–336; Federhofer, "Messy Episodes," 1–22; Bronwen Douglas and Elena Gover, "Eponymy, Encounters, and Local Knowledge in Russian Place Naming in the Pacific Islands, 1804–1830," *Historical Review* 62 (2019), 709–740.

18. This term originates with J. C. Beaglehole's characterization of James Cook's voyages. See Beaglehole, *The Life of Captain James Cook* (Palo Alto, CA: Stanford University Press, 1974), 293; Richard Sorrenson, "The Ship as a Scientific Instrument in the Eighteenth Century," *Osiris* 11 (1996): 221–236; Helen M. Rozwadowski, "Small World: Forging a Scientific Maritime Culture for Oceanography," *Isis* 87 (September 1996): 409–429; Warwick Anderson, "Hybridity, Race, and Science: The Voyage of the Zaca, 1934–1935," *Isis* 103 (June 2012): 229–253. For recent studies that focus on a specific ship, see Martin Dusinberre, *Mooring the Global Archive: A Japanese Ship and Its Migrant Histories* (Cambridge: Cambridge University Press, 2023); David Grann, *The Wager: A Tale of Shipwreck, Mutiny, and Murder* (New York: Doubleday, 2023); and Brett L. Walker, *Yukikaze's War: The Unsinkable Japanese Destroyer and World War II in the Pacific* (Cambridge: Cambridge University Press, 2024).

19. Epeli Hauʻofa, "Our Sea of Islands," *Contemporary Pacific* 6, no. 1 (Spring 1994): 153.

20. I am grateful for conversations and personal correspondence with a number of navigation and canoe-building experts and elders from the Caroline, Marshall, and Mariana Islands, including H. Larry Raigetal of the organization "Waʻagey" in Guam; Alson Kelen, who co-founded the "Waan Aelon in Majel Project" (These Islands) in the Marshall Islands; Christian Anien Lehman at the University of Notre Dame; and members of the Marshallese Educational Center.

21. August Mahr argues that Rumiantsev designed the expedition to investigate "the dying organism of the Spanish colonial empire," with a particular goal of Russian advances in Alta California. The northern exploration, according to Mahr, was a "well-fitted scientific drapery" to cover this strategic "scheme." While Rumiantsev was certainly interested in geopolitical matters, he was far more focused on the other outcomes of the *Rurik* expedition. See August Mahr, *The Visit of the "Rurik" to San Francisco in 1816* (Stanford, CA: Stanford University Press, 1932), 23.

22. On the Russian empire and its relations with European nations, see Matthew P. Romaniello, *Enterprising Empires: Russia and Britain in Eighteenth-Century Eurasia* (Cambridge: Cambridge University Pres, 2019). On Russia's eastward expansion in

the eighteenth century, see George V. Lantzeff and Richard A. Pierce, *Eastward to Empire: Exploration and Conquest on the Russian Open Frontier, to 1750* (Montreal: McGill-Queen's University Press, 1973); and James Forsyth, *A History of the Peoples of Siberia: Russia's North Asian Colony, 1581–1991* (Cambridge: Cambridge University Press, 1992). For an excellent discussion among historians of Russian commerce in Central Asia and beyond, see the online conversation regarding Erika Monahan's book *The Merchants of Siberia: Trade in Early Modern Eurasia* (Ithaca, NY: Cornell University Press, 2016), on the "Russian History Blog": https://russian-historyblog.org/2016/09/the-merchants-of-siberia-a-blog-conversation/. For a nuanced account of twentieth-century Russian historiography on the North Pacific, see Andrei V. Grinev, "The Plans for Russian Expansion in the New World and the North Pacific in the Eighteenth and Nineteenth Centuries," *European Journal of American Studies* 5 (2010): 1–27. On the Russian American Company as separate from the imperial government, see Ilya Vinkovetsky, "The Russian-American Company as a Corporation," *The Russian Review* 81 (July 2022): 421–439.

23. Douglas, "In the Event;" Bronwen Douglas, *Science, Voyages, and Encounters in Oceania, 1511–1850* (Basingstoke: Palgrave Macmillan, 2014).

24. I cite the relevant literature throughout this study, including monographic studies by Matt Matsuda, Ryan Tucker Jones, Lilikalā Kameʻeleihiwa, J. Kehaulani Kauanui, Bronwen Douglas, David Chang, and others. For the most recent and comprehensive collection of chapters devoted to Pacific Studies, see *The Cambridge History of the Pacific Ocean*, general editor Paul D'Arcy, 2 vols. (Cambridge: Cambridge University Press, 2022).

25. On Rumiantsev, see Vladimir Svyatoslavovich Kusov, "Count Nikolai Rumiantsev and Russian Exploration of Alaska and North America," *Western Association of Map Libraries Information Bulletin* 25 (November 1993): 11–22; Alexandra Bekasova, "Voyaging towards the Future: The Brig Rurik in the North Pacific and the Emerging Science of the Sea," *British Journal for the History of Science* 53 (December 2020): 469–495; Simon Sebag Montfiore, *The Romanovs: 1613–1918* (New York: Knopf, 2016), 292.

26. James A. Bayard, "European Diary," January 25, 1814, *The Papers of James A. Bayard, 1795–1815*, 2 vols. (Washington, D. C.: Annual Report of the American Historical Association for the Year 1913, 1915), 495; Adam von Krusenstern, "Introduction," in Kotzebue, *A Voyage of Discovery*, 1: 11.

27. The American consul described him as "[t]all and possessing a good figure, mild in his countenance, and courtly in his manners." Bayard, "European Diary," July 24, 1813, *The Papers of James A. Bayard*, 417.

28. Alexey Postnikov and Marvin Falk, *Exploring and Mapping Alaska: The Russian America Era, 1741–1867*, trans. Lydia Black (Fairbanks: University of Alaska Press, 2015), 233, 261; James R. Gibson, *Imperial Russia in Frontier America: The Changing Geography of Supply of Russian America, 1784–1867* (New York: Oxford University Press, 1976), 159.

29. Andrei Ia. Dashkov to James Monroe, February 20, 1815, in *The United States and Russia: The Beginning of Relations, 1765–1815*, eds. Nina N. Bashkina et al. (Washington: U. S. Government Printing Office, 1980), 1110.

30. John Quincy Adams to Nikolai P. Rumiantsev, October 7, 1812, in Dashkov, *The United States and Russia*, 887; Peter Dobell to Adam Johann von Krusenstern, October 19, 1812, in Dashkov, *The United States and Russia*, 890, 892. Dobell authored the widely published and translated book *Travels in Kamchatka and Siberia: With a Narrative of a Residence in China* (London: Henry Colburn, 1830).

31. Mahr, *The Visit of the "Rurik" to San Francisco*, 22–24.

32. Nikolai Rumiantsev to Adam Krusenstern, October 2, 1817; quoted in Bekasova, "Voyaging towards the Future," 474.

33. On Baltic Germans in the eighteenth and nineteenth centuries, see Willard Sunderland, *The Baron's Cloak: A History of the Russian Empire in War and Revolution* (Ithaca, NY: Cornell University Press, 2014), 25–35; A. V. Grinev, "Germans in the History of Russian America," *Journal of the West* 47 (Spring 2008): 32–43. On Krusenstern's vision for Russian maritime exploration, see *Russia Engages the World, 1453–1825*, ed. Cynthia Hyla Whittaker (Cambridge, MA: Harvard University Press, 2003): 107–113.

34. Glynn Barratt, "Russian Activity among the Cook Islands, to 1820," *New Zealand Slavonic Journal* (1998): 46; http://www.jstor.org/stable/40921980, accessed November 10, 2018.

35. A. J. Krusenstern, *Voyage Round the World, in the years 1803, 1804, 1805, & 1806, by order of His Imperial Majesty Alexander the First, on board the ships Nadezhda and Neva, under the command of Captain A. J. von Krusenstern*, trans. Richard Belgrave Hoppner, 3 vols. (London: J. Murray, 1813).

36. John Barrow to Sir Joseph Banks, February 16, 1820; in Niel Chambers (ed.), *The Indian and Pacific Correspondence of Sir Joseph Banks*, vol. 8, 337–338.

37. Krusenstern, *Voyage Round the World*, 1: xi.

38. Glynn Barratt, *Russia in Pacific Waters, 1715–1825: A Survey of the Origins of Russia's Naval Presence in the North and South Pacific* (Vancouver: University of British Columbia Press, 1981), 178.

39. Krusenstern, "Introduction," in Kotzebue, *A Voyage of Discovery*, 1: 2, 6, 7, 11.

40. Krusenstern, "Introduction," 1: 14.

41. Joseph Banks to Sir Charles Blagden, April 1, 2017; in Banks, *The Scientific Correspondences of Sir Joseph Banks, 1765–1820*, ed. Neil Chambers, 6 vols. (London: Pickering & Chatto, 2007), 6: 228.

42. Chamisso, *A Voyage Around the World*, 27.

43. Barratt, "Russian Activity among the Cook Islands, to 1820," 59.

44. Kotzebue, *A Voyage of Discovery*, 1: 99; Krusenstern, "Introduction," 16–18.

45. Barratt, "Russian Activity among the Cook Islands, to 1820," 65.

46. On Linnaean science as a collaborative enterprise, see Hanna Hodacs, et al., "Introduction: de-centring and re-centring Linnaeus," in *Linnaeus, natural history, and the circulation of knowledge*, eds. Hanna Hodacs, et al. (Oxford: Oxford University Press, 2018), 1.

47. Chamisso, *A Voyage Around the World*, 30.

48. Digitized material on Chamisso's literary and scientific works can be found at Berlin's State Library, http://kalliope.staatsbibliothek-berlin.de/en/index.html. For the extensive German scholarship on Chamisso, see Anne MacKinney and Matthias

Glaubrecht, "Academic practice par excellent: Martin Hinrich Lichtenstein's role in Adelbert von Chamisso's career as naturalist," *Internationales Archiv für Sozialgeschichte der deutschen Literatur* 42, no. 2 (2017): 322–347. https://doi.org/10.1515/iasl-2017-0016. For Chamisso's life, see Werner Feudel, *Adelbert von Chamisso: Leben und Werk* (Leipzig: P. Reclam, 1988); Harry Liebersohn, *A Travelers' World: Europe in the Pacific* (Cambridge, MA: Harvard University Press, 2006): 58–72; Henry Kratz's "Introduction" to Chamisso, *A Voyage Around the World*, xi–xxiv; Richard G. Beidleman, *California's Frontier Naturalists* (Berkeley: University of California Press, 2006), 48–51; and Adelbert von Chamisso, *The Alaska Diary of Adelbert von Chamisso: Naturalist on the Kotzebue Voyage 1815–1818*, ed. and trans. Robert Fontuine (Anchorage: Cook Inlet Historical Society, 1986), 1–6.

49. Chamisso, *A Voyage Around the World*, 13.

50. Adelbert von Chamisso, *Peter Schlemihl*, ed. Wulf Koepke (Columbia, SC: Camden House, 1993 [1814]), 32, 107, 112, 122.

51. Liebersohn, *The Travelers' World*, 3–4.

52. Chamisso, *A Voyage Around the World*, 13; Chamisso to Hitzig, February 25, 1816; in Adelbert von Chamisso, *Werke*, ed. Julius Hitzig (Leipzig, 1839), 6: 39.

53. Tatiana Arkadevna Lukina, *Johann Friedrich Eschscholtz, 1793–1831*, trans. Wilma C. Follette (unpublished manuscript), 9. Lukina's biography contains extensive primary documents from Russian and Estonian archives, including correspondence with Chamisso following the voyage. Originally published as Lukina, *Logann Fridrikh Eschol'ts, 1793–1831* (Leningrad: Nauka Leningradskoe otdelnie, 1975), the philologist and botanist Wilma Follette translated this marvelous study for the noted California marine biologist Joel Hedgpeth. I am grateful to the University of California, Berkeley, for retaining a copy of the unpublished translation.

54. Krusenstern, "Introduction," 1: 24. For an interesting approach to the value of illustrations in natural history, see Bleichmar, "Visible Empire," 441–446.

55. On Choris, see Federhofer, "Messy Episodes," 5–7; Choris, *Journals des Malers*; Schweizer, "'At Last He Fell Asleep': Choris, Chamisso, and Kamehameha I in Hawai'i," in Irmengard Rauch and Richard K. Seymour, eds., *Across the Oceans: Studies from East to West in Honor of Richard K. Seymour* (Honolulu: University of Hawai'i Press, 1995), 17–25. For the best treatment of Choris's career and work as an expedition artist, see Ron Tyler, "Entirely New and Very Interesting Things: Louis Choris and the Kotzebue Expedition, 1815–1818," *Imprint* 42 (Fall 2017), 2–43; and Tyler, "The Role of the Exploration Artist: Louis Choris and the Kotzebue Expedition, 1815–1818," *Studii Și Cercetări de Istoria Artei. Seria Artă Plastică* 11, no. 55 (January 2021): 43–76. I appreciate Ron Tyler's suggestions regarding Choris's body of work.

56. Kotzebue, *A Voyage of Discovery*, 90; Chamisso, *A Voyage Around the World*, 20.

57. See Harriet Guest, *Empire, Barbarism, and Civilization: James Cook, William Hodges, and the Return to the Pacific* (Cambridge: Cambridge University Press, 2007); Bernard Smith, *European Vision and the South Pacific* (New Haven, CT: Yale University Press, 1985, 2nd edition).

58. Chamisso, *A Voyage Around the World*, 20.

59. Tiya Miles, *All That She Carried: The Journey of Ashley's Sack, A Black Family's Keepsake* (New York: Random House, 2021), 253. On the process of writing about

historical individuals who produced few (or no) documents in their own hand, see Marisa J. Fuentes, *Dispossessed Lives: Enslaved Women, Violence, and the Archive* (Philadelphia: University of Pennsylvania Press, 2018); Paul E. Johnson, "The Modernization of Mayo Greenleaf Patch: Land, Family, and Marginality in New England, 1766–1818," *New England Quarterly* 55 (December 1982), 488–516. For an evaluation of Kadu's significance, see Chunjie Zhang, "The Islander Kadu and Adelbert von Chamisso," *The Eighteenth Century* 59 (Spring 2017): 79–98.

60. Indigenous research methodologies highlight the significance of reclaiming voices like Kadu's from the colonialist historical records. See Shawn Wilson, *Research Is Ceremony: Indigenous Research Methods* (Halifax, Canada: Fernwood Publishing, 2008), esp. 6–15; Linda Tuhiwai Smith, *Decolonizing Methodologies: Research and Indigenous Peoples* (London: Zed Books, 2021), 1–10; Bagele Chilisa, *Indigenous Research Methodologies* (London: Sage Publications, 2020).

61. This phrase comes from a Yapese chant recited by master canoe builder H. Larry Raigetal during the symposium "The Role of Canoe Building and Navigation in Yapese and Marshallese Seafaring Systems," December 7, 2022, Stanford University. I appreciate the translation of this chant offered by Mr. Raigetal in personal correspondence to author, December 8, 2022.

62. Chamisso, *A Voyage Around the World*, 264. Chamisso provides the most extensive commentary on Kadu, who seems to be a primary reason for his published recollections in 1836. The other writers on the *Rurik* agree on the main points of his story. The best secondary source on Kadu is Liebersohn, *A Travelers' World*, 158–162.

63. On Indigenous guides, travelers, and intermediaries, see *The Brokered World: Go-Betweens and Global Intelligence, 1770–1820*, eds. Simon Schaffer, et al. (Sagamore Beach, MA: Watson Publishing International, 2009); *Indigenous Intermediaries: New Perspective on Exploration Archives*, eds. Shino Konishi, Maria Nugent, and Tiffany Shellam (Canberra: ANU Press, 2015); *Brokers and Boundaries: Colonial Exploration in Indigenous Territory*, eds. Tiffany Shellam, Maria Nugent, Shino Konishi, and Allison Cadzow (Canberra: ANU Press, 2016); Kapil, Raj, "Go-betweens, travelers, and cultural translators," in *A Companion to the History of Science*, ed. Bernard Lightman (Malden, MA: John Wiley and Sons, 2016), 39–57; David Igler, "Indigenous Maritime Travelers and Knowledge Production," in *A World at Sea: Maritime Practices and Global History*, eds. Lauren Benton and Nathan Perl-Rosenthal (Philadelphia: University of Pennsylvania Press, 2020), 108–132. I appreciate the forthcoming work of Josh Reid for what he calls the "routedness" of Indigenous explorers.

64. Krusenstern, "Introduction," 11–12; 12.

65. Kotzebue, *A Voyage of Discovery*, 93.

CHAPTER 1

1. Kotzebue, *A Voyage of Discovery*, 1: 98; Chamisso, *A Voyage Around the World*, 29.

2. Peter Simon Pallas, *Travels Through the Southern Provinces of the Russian Empire in the Years 1793 and 1794* (London: T.N. Longman & O. Reis, 1802); Johann Georg Gmelin, *Flora Sibirica sive Historia plantarum Sibiriae*, 4 vols. (St. Petersburg, 1747–1769).

3. L.F. Thompson, *Kotzebue: A Survey of His Progress in France, and England* (Paris, Librairie Ancienne Honoré Champion, 1928), 55.

4. Chamisso, *A Voyage Around the World*, 25–26.

5. For one example of instructions to the naturalist, see Joseph Banks, "The Instructions," in *The Endeavour Journal of Joseph Banks, 1768–1771*, ed. J. C. Beaglehole (Sidney: Public Library of New South Wales, 1963): vol. 1, cclxxxii.

6. William Reynolds, *The Private Journal of William Reynolds: United States Exploring Expedition, 1838–1842*, eds. Nathaniel Philbrick and Thomas Philbrick (New York: Penguin Books, 2004): 13. Italics in original.

7. Chamisso, *A Voyage Around the World*, 33, 34.

8. Chamisso, "Remarks and Opinions," in Kotzebue, *A Voyage of Discovery*, 3: 4; Eschscholtz, "General Observations," in Kotzebue, *A Voyage of Discovery*, 3: 323.

9. Louis [Ludwig] Choris, "Traversee de Cronstradt au Chili," in *Voyage pittoresque autour du monde* (Paris: Didot, 1822), 1.

10. Chamisso, "A View of the Great Ocean," in Kotzebue, *A Voyage of Discovery*, vol. 2: 353–406.

11. Tatiana Arkadevna Lukina, *Johann Friedrich Eschscholtz* (Leningrad: Nauka Publishing House, 1975), 15; Chamisso, *A Voyage Around the World*, 33.

12. Luis Ferrer and Ane Pastor, "The Portuguese man-of-war: Gone with the wind," *Regional Studies in Marine Science* 14 (2017): 53–62.

13. Eschscholtz, "General Observations," in Kotzebue, *A Voyage of Discovery*, 3: 321; Adelbert von Chamisso, *Werke*, ed. Julius Hitzig (Leipzig, 1839), vol. 6: 30; Chamisso, *A Voyage Around the World*, 33.

14. For superb research on Chamisso's study of salps, see Matthias Glaubrecht and Wolfgang Dohle, "Discovering the alternation of generations in salps (Tunicata, Thaliacea): Adelbert von Chamisso's dissertation "De Salpa" 1819—its material, origin and reception in the early nineteenth century," *Zoosystematics and Evolution* 88 (October 2012): 317–363.

15. Chamisso, *A Voyage Around the World*, 33. He comments further upon the salp discovery in "Remarks and Opinions," vol. 3, 321–322.

16. L. A. G. Bosc, *Histoire naturelle des vers: contenant leur description et leurs moeurs* (Paris: Deterville, 1802).

17. Glaubrecht and Dohle, "Discovering the alternation of generations in salps," 330.

18. Chamisso, *A Voyage Around the World*, 49, emphasis added; Chamisso, *Werke*, 38.

19. Chamisso, *A Voyage Around the World*, 43; Kotzebue, *A Voyage of Discovery*, 112. On the ritual of crossing the line, see Anne Salmond, *The Trial of the Cannibal Dog: The Remarkable Story of Captain Cook's Encounters in the South Seas* (New Haven, CT: Yale University Press, 2003), 58–59.

20. The following discussion draws information from the incomparable database and website "SlaveVoyages: The Trans-Atlantic Slave Trade Database." http://www.slavevoyages.org/, accessed February 7, 2019. For assistance in navigating this database, I appreciate the guidance of my colleague and database co-editor Alex Borucki.

21. Kotzebue, *A Voyage of Discovery*, vol. 1: 29.

22. See "Regions of Trade for Slave Voyages Outfitted in Rio de Janeiro, 1808–1856," in David Eltis and David Richardson, *Atlas of the Transatlantic Slave Trade* (New Haven, CT: Yale University Press, 2010), 83.

23. Kotzebue, *A Voyage of Discovery*, vol. 1:12, 11; Chamisso, "Remarks and Opinions," v. 3: 5.

24. Eschscholtz, "General Observations," v. 3: 326–327.

25. Kotzebue, *A Voyage of Discovery*, 1: 115; Chamisso, "Remarks and Opinions," 3: 10–11.

26. "Voyages: The Trans-Atlantic Slave Trade Database." http://www.slavevoyages.org/, accessed February 8, 2019.

27. Adam Johann von Krusenstern, *Voyage Round the World, in the years 1803, 1804, 1805, & 1806*, trans. Richard Belgrave Hoppner (London: C. Roworth, 1813): vol. 1, 74.

28. Alexander von Humboldt and Aimé Bonpland, *Personal Narrative of Travels to the Equinoctial Regions of America, 1799–1804*, trans. and ed. Thomasina Ross, 3 vols. (London: George Bell & Sons, 1894), 3: 272.

29. Kotzebue had all the notable late eighteenth-century exploration journals as well as published notes of previous captains and geographers.

30. Kotzebue, *A Voyage of Discovery*, 1: 144.

31. Adam von Krusenstern, "Analysis of the Islands Discovered by the Rurick," in Kotzebue, *A Voyage of Discovery*, 2: 291–313.

32. Kotzebue, *A Voyage of Discovery*, 1: 144–145; 149. Doubtful Island is today known as Tekokota.

33. Choris documented this scene in the lithograph "Débarquement á travers les Récifs de l'Isle de Romanzoff" (Landing through the Reefs of Romanzoff Island). See Louis Choris, *Vues et Paysages des régions équinoxiales* (Paris: Paul Renouard, 1826), 19.

34. Kotzebue, *A Voyage of Discovery*, 1: 154, 157, 159.

35. Kotzebue, *A Voyage of Discovery*, 1: 161.

36. Alexandra Bekasova, "Voyaging towards the Future," 490.

37. Krusenstern, "Analysis of the Islands Discovered by the Rurick," 2: 298, 307.

38. Krusenstern, "Analysis of the Islands Discovered by the Rurick," 2: 311. On this point, see Bronwen Douglas and Elena Govor, "Eponymy, Encounters, and Local Knowledge in Russian Place Naming in the Pacific Islands, 1804–1830," *The Historical Journal* 62 (2019): 709–740.

39. Chamisso offered this comment in specific reference to Kotzebue's naming of "Romanzoff Island," but was clearly making a broader point about the captain's claims. See Chamisso, "Remarks and Opinions," 3: 220.

40. On Chamisso's influences from romanticism, see Harry Liebersohn, "Discovering Indigenous Nobility: Tocqueville, Chamisso, and Romantic Travel Writing," *American Historical Review* 99 (June 1994): 746–766.

41. On "sea people," see Matt K. Matsuda, *Pacific Worlds: A History of Seas, Peoples, and Cultures* (New York: Cambridge University Press, 2012): 9; Paul D'Arcy, *The People of the Sea: Identity, Environment, and History in Oceania* (Honolulu: University of Hawai'i Press, 2005). On Māori creation stories, see Margaret Orbell, *A Concise Encyclopedia of Māori Myth and Legend* (Christchurch, NZ: Canterbury University Press, 1998), 60.

42. Epeli Hau'ofa, "Our Sea of Islands," *Contemporary Pacific* 6 (Spring 1994): 153.

43. Chamisso, *A Voyage Around the World*, 132.

44. Steven Roger Fischer, *Island at the End of the World: The Turbulent History of Easter Island* (London: Reaktion Books, 2005), 73–74; Kotzebue, *A Voyage of Discovery*, 1: 136.

45. Chamisso, "Remarks and Opinions," 3: 261, 314.

46. Chamisso, *A Voyage Around the World*, 73.

47. Otto von Kotzebue, "Voyage de Kotzebue," July 16, 1816; in *Journal des Voyages; Gazette Geographique* (Paris, 1816), 126.

48. Kotzebue, *A Voyage of Discovery*, 1: 183–184.

49. Chamisso, *A Voyage Around the World*, 77.

50. Dorothy Jean Ray, *Aleut and Eskimo Art: Tradition and Innovation in South Alaska* (Seattle: University of Washington Press, 1981), 15.

51. Choris, quoted in "An Early Nineteenth-Century Artist in Alaska: Louis Choris and the First Kotzebue Expedition," ed. James W. Vanstone, *Pacific Northwest Quarterly* 51 (October 1960), 146. Vanstone's essay includes a full translation of Choris's comments on both seasons in the Arctic contained in *Voyage pittoresque*.

52. Choris, *Journals des Malers*, 171.

53. Chamisso, "Remarks and Opinions," 3: 316. For a superb study of the specific skull donated to the Berlin Anatomical Museum by Chamisso, see Matthias Glaubrecht, et al., "The potential of biohistory: Re-discovering Adelbert von Chamisso's skull of an Aleut collected during the 'Rurik' Expedition 1815–1818 in Alaska," *Zoosystematics and Evolution* 89 (2013): 317–336.

54. Choris, in Vanstone, "An Early Nineteenth-Century Artist in Alaska," 150.

55. Chamisso, *A Voyage Around the World*, 80; 81.

56. Kotzebue, *A Voyage of Discovery*, vol. 1, 198; Chamisso, *A Voyage Around the World*, 82.

57. Today Shishmaref is experiencing significant impact from climate change. The island's inhabitants (mostly Inuit) are losing a battle against rising sea levels, diminishing sea ice, and unprecedented high seas that ravage the shoreline. The townspeople of Shishmaref remain divided over the issue of relocating their community, and neither state nor federal officials have made adequate removal funds available. On warming in the Arctic, see Elizabeth Kolbert, *Field Notes from a Catastrophe: Man, Nature, and Climate Change* (New York: Bloomsbury, 2006).

58. On this place and the Iñupiat, see Bathsheba Demuth, *The Floating Coast: An Environmental History of the Bering Strait* (New York: W. W. Norton, 2019), esp. 137–168.

59. Kotzebue, *A Voyage of Discovery*, vol. 1, 207; 241; 209.

60. Kotzebue, *A Voyage of Discovery*, vol. 1, 238.

61. Demuth, *The Floating Coast*, 141–143; Norman Chance and Norman Allee Chance, *The Inupiat and Arctic Alaska: An Ethnography of Development* (New York: Holt, Rinehart & Winston, 1990). The word "Iñupiat" refers to the people, while "Iñupiaq" refers to their spoken language.

62. Choris, in Vanstone, "An Early Nineteenth-Century Artist in Alaska," 151.

63. Choris, in Vanstone, "An Early Nineteenth-Century Artist in Alaska," 151.

64. Choris, in Vanstone, "An Early Nineteenth-Century Artist in Alaska," 151.

65. Erika Monahan, *The Merchants of Siberia: Trade in Early Modern Eurasia* (Ithaca, NY: Cornell University Press, 2016), esp. 175–206.

66. On Choris's attention to detail with cultural artifacts, see Federhofer, "Messy Episodes," 13–14.

67. Many Chukchi villages had been subjugated by Russia's imperial advance during the eighteenth century, but apparently a few coastal villages remained fairly autonomous. See George V. Lantzeff and Richard A. Pierce, *Eastward to Empire: Exploration and Conquest on the Russian Open Frontier, to 1750* (Montreal: McGill-Queen's University Press, 1973), 218–219; James Forsyth, *A History of the Peoples of Siberia: Russia's North Asian Colony, 1581–1991* (Cambridge: Cambridge University Press, 1992), 78–83.

68. Choris, in Vanstone, "An Early Nineteenth-Century Artists in Alaska," 150.

69. Kotzebue, *A Voyage of Discovery*, vol. 1, 259.

70. Chamisso, *A Voyage Around the World*, 90; 91; 92.

71. Chamisso, *A Voyage Around the World*, 92.

72. Choris, in Vanstone, "An Early Nineteenth-Century Artist in Alaska," 152.

CHAPTER 2

1. H. Larry Raigetal offered the translation of this Yapese navigation chant in personal correspondence to author, December 8, 2022. Raigetal's work with present-day canoe builders as well as his scholarship helped inspire this chapter. See Hilary Larry Raigetal, "Revitalizing 'Traditional' Navigation Systems in the Contemporary Pacific," in *The Cambridge History of the Pacific Ocean, Volume 1, The Pacific Ocean to 1800*, eds. Ryan Tucker Jones and Matt K. Matsuda (Cambridge: Cambridge University Press, 2023), 345–366.

2. Chamisso, "Remarks and Opinions of the Naturalist," in Kotzebue, *A Voyage of Discovery*, vol. 3, 312; 92.

3. On the term *dri-belle*, see Julianne M. Walsh, "Imagining the Marshall Islands: Chiefs, Tradition, and the State on the Fringes of United States Empire," PhD dissertation, University of Hawai`i, 2003; Chamisso, *A Voyage Around the World*, 129. For an excellent study of the Marshall Islands in the context of U.S. imperial control, see Lauren Hirshberg, *Suburban Empire: Cold War Militarization in the US Pacific* (Berkeley: University of California Press, 2022).

4. Dennis F. Alessio, "Waan Aelon in Majel: Cultural Development in the Marshall Islands," *Micronesian Journal of the Humanities and Social Sciences* 5 (November 2006), 605. The term *iroij* is alternatively spelled "irooj" in some texts. The spelling of individual names by the *Rurik* personnel was of their own creation and was based on what they heard phonetically.

5. Vicente M. Diaz and J. Kehaulani Kauanui, "Native Pacific Cultural Studies on the Edge," *The Contemporary Pacific* 13 (Fall 2001): 316–317.

6. I draw this conclusion in part from information offered by Alson Kelen, a Marshallese master canoe builder and Director of Waan Aelõñ in Majel (WAM); personal correspondence with author, December 13, 2022.

7. On the "*nontransfer* of important bodies of knowledge," see Londa L. Schiebinger, *Plants and Empire: Colonial Bioprospecting in the Atlantic World* (Cambridge, MA: Harvard University Press, 2009), 3. For an outdated and ultimately condescending interpretation of Kadu's actions aboard the *Rurik*, see Francis X. Hezel, S. J., *The First Taint of Civilization: A History of the Caroline and Marshall Islands in Pre-Colonial Days, 1521–1885* (Honolulu: University of Hawai`i Press, 1983).

8. On Indigenous intermediaries, see Schaffer, ed., *The Brokered World*; Konishi, Nugent, Shellam, eds., *Indigenous Intermediaries*; Shellam, et al., *Brokers and Boundaries*.

9. Chamisso, "Remarks and Opinions," vol. 3, 96.

10. Saul H. Riesenberg, "The Ghost Islands of the Carolines," *Micronesica* 11 (July 1975): 7–33; William H. Alkire, "Systems of Measurement on Woleai Atoll, Caroline Islands," *Anthropos* 65 (1970): 1–73; S[aul]. H. Riesenberg, "Table of Voyages Affecting Micronesian Islands," *Oceania* 36 (December 1965): 155–170; R. T. Simmons, et al., "Blood Group Genetic Variations in Natives of the Caroline Islands and in Other Parts of Micronesia," *Oceania* 36 (December 1965): 132–154.

11. David Hanlon, "The 'Sea of Little Lands': Examining Micronesia's Place in 'Our Sea of Islands,'" *The Contemporary Pacific* 21 (2009): 91–110.

12. Alan Eugene Davis, "Suggestions for Study of the Native Knowledge of Marine Animals in the Eastern Caroline Islands," in *Oceanographic History: The Pacific and Beyond*, eds. Keith R. Benson and Philip F. Rehbock (Seattle: University of Washington Press, 2002): 71–84.

13. H. Larry Raigetal emphasized the navigators' "world of spirits" in his presentation, "The Role of Canoe Building and Navigation in Yapese and Marshallese Seafaring Systems," December 7, 2022, Stanford University. The spiritual realm is central to Indigenous research methodologies, as articulated by recent scholars. See Wilson, *Research Is Ceremony*, esp. 6–15; Tuhiwai Smith, *Decolonizing Methodologies*, 1–10; Chilisa, *Indigenous Research Methodologies*.

14. Alkire, "Systems of Measurement on Woleai Atoll," 37–44.

15. Riesenberg, "The Ghost Islands of the Carolines," 17–20.

16. On the sawei system, see Paul D'Arcy, *The People of the Sea: Environment, Identity, and History in Oceania* (Honolulu: University of Hawai'i Press, 2008): 146–159; M. L. Berg, "Yapese Politics, Yapese Money and the Sawei Tribute Network before World War I," *Journal of Pacific History* 27 (December 1992): 150–164.

17. Damon Salesa, "The Pacific in Indigenous Time," in *Pacific Histories: Ocean, Land, People*, eds. David Armitage and Alison Bashford (New York: Palgrave Macmillan, 2014), 47.

18. D'Arcy, *People of the Sea*, 147; Alkire, "Systems of Measurement," 6–7; Berg, "Yapese Politics, Yapese Money and the *Sawei* Tribute Network," 155–157.

19. On accidental voyages, see "Polynesian Navigation: A Symposium on Sharp's Theory of Accidental Voyages," ed. Jack Golson (Auckland, NZ: Polynesian Society, 1972).

20. Simmons et al., "Blood Group Genetic Variations," 135–136.

21. Paul D'Arcy, "Connected by the Sea: Towards a Regional History of the Western Caroline Islands," *Journal of Pacific History* 36 (August 2010): 173; 178; Riesenberg, "Table of Voyages Affecting Micronesian Islands," 157–160.

22. Raigetal, "The Role of Canoe Building and Navigation in Yapese and Marshallese Seafaring Systems." For a detailed discussion of Woleai canoes, see Alkire, "Systems of Measurement on Woleai Atoll," 23–37.

23. Kevin Dawson, *Undercurrents of Power: Aquatic Culture in the African Diaspora* (Philadelphia: University of Pennsylvania Press, 2018), 192.

24. Diaz and Kauanui, "Native Pacific Cultural Studies on the Edge," 317.

25. Hanlon, "The 'Sea of Little Lands,'" 103.

26. Kadu's information provided rich details for Smithsonian Institution researchers in the twentieth century, who cited him as the historical source for an extensive report of Micronesian voyages stretching back into the late 1700s. The Smithsonian's comprehensive line-map of accidental and intentional voyages looks like a finely spun spider's web delineating hundreds of routes connecting islands between the Marshalls in the east and the Philippines in the west. It clearly illustrated the extent of Indigenous voyages in the Micronesian seas. See Riesenberg, "Table of Voyages Affecting Micronesian Islands," 157; Chamisso, "Remarks and Opinions," 98.

27. Otto von Kotzebue, *A New Voyage Round the World in the Years 1823, 1824, 1825, 1826* (London: Henry Colburn and Richard Bentley, 1830), vol. 1, 217; Kotzebue, *A Voyage of Discovery*, vol. 1, 6; 10. Emphasis added.

28. Chamisso, *A Voyage Around the World*, 130.

29. This discussion draws upon "Foreign Ships in Micronesia," http://micsem.org/pubs/articles/historical/forships/marshalls.htm, accessed May 11, 2021; Walsh, "Imagining the Marshalls," 128–139.

30. The Russian Captain published two maps of the Marshall Islands in his voyage account: "Plan of the Group Called the Romanzoff's Islands," and "Charts of the Islands of Radack and Ralick." See Kotzebue, *Voyage of Discovery*, vol. 2, 435; 436.

31. Greg Dening, *Beach Crossings*, 51. On culture contact and the "zero point," see ed. Lucy P. Mair, *Methods and Study of Culture Contact in Africa* (Oxford: Oxford University Press, 1938).

32. Choris, *Journal*, 236.

33. Chamisso, *A Voyage Around the World*, 132.

34. Ludwig Choris, *Journals des Malers Ludwig York Choris*, ed. Niklaus R. Schweizer (New York: Peter Lang, 1999), 237; Kotzebue, *A Voyage of Discovery*, vol. 2, 41; 69; 83; 48. New "engagements" between Europeans and islanders, writes Warwick Anderson, contained the possibility of a shared "intimacy and understanding," even if this result might be temporary. The *Rurik*'s officers certainly understood their relationships with the Marshall islanders in this benevolent manner. See Warwick Anderson, "Hybridity, Race, and Science: The Voyage of the Zaca, 1934–1935," *Isis* 103 (June 2012), 231.

35. Chamisso, *A Voyage Around the World*, 132; 129.

36. Kotzebue, *Voyage of Discovery*, 76; 86.

37. This dynamic of supplying islanders with weapons and the resulting violence played out in many places, including the Sulu Zone of the Sulu and Celebes Seas. See James Francis Warren, "Saltwater Slavers and Captives in the Sulu Zone, 1768–1878," *Slavery and Abolition* 31 (September 2010), 429–449.

38. Chamisso, *A Voyage Around the World*, 152; "Remarks and Opinions," vol. 3, 166.

39. Chamisso, "Remarks and Opinions of the Naturalist," vol. 3, 166–167.

40. Kotzebue, *A Voyage of Discovery*, vol. 1, 151.

41. Following his second voyage to the Pacific, Kotzebue reports on Kadu's life after the voyage. See Kotzebue, *A New Voyage Round the World in the Years 1823, 1824, 1825, 1826*, vol. 1, 317; 307.

42. Joseph Genz, et al., "Wave Navigation in the Marshall Islands: Comparing Indigenous and Western Scientific Knowledge of the Ocean," *Oceanography* 22 (June 2009): 234–246; Genz, "Navigating the Revival of Voyaging in the Marshall Islands: Predicaments of Preservation and Possibilities of Collaboration," *Contemporary Pacific* 23 (2011): 1–34.

43. Alson Kelen, "The Role of Canoe Building and Navigation in Yapese and Marshallese Seafaring Systems," symposium presentation, December 7, 2022, Stanford University; and personal correspondence with author, December 13, 2022.

44. Chamisso, *A Voyage Around the World*, 159.

45. Celine Carayon, *Eloquence Embodied: Nonverbal Communication Among French and Indigenous Peoples in the Americas* (Chapel Hill: University of North Carolina Press, 2019), 13–18.

46. Kotzebue, *A Voyage of Discovery*, vol. 2, 161–162; Chamisso, "Vocabulary of the Dialects of Chamori (Mariana Islands), and of Eap, Ulea, and Radack," in "Remarks and Opinions," vol. 2, 409–432; quote is on 409.

47. Kotzebue, *A Voyage of Discovery*, vol. 2, 155.

48. Chamisso, "Remarks and Opinions," 102.

49. Chamisso, "Remarks and Opinions," vol. 2, 433.

50. Chamisso, *A Voyage Around the World*, 160; Chamisso, "Remarks and Opinions," vol. 3, 116.

51. On Cantova, see Christophe Descantes, "The Martyrdom of Father Juan Cantova on Ulithi Atoll: The Hegemonic Struggle Between Spanish Colonialism and a Micronesian Island Polity," *Missionalia* 32 (November 2004): 394–418.

52. Chamisso, "Remarks and Opinions," vol. 2, 127; 129.

53. Chamisso, *A Voyage Around the World*, 161.

54. Chamisso, *Voyage*, 161. On phrenology and skull exhibits, see Ann Fabian, *The Skull Collectors: Race, Science, and America's Unburied Dead* (Chicago: University of Chicago Press, 2010); Bronwen Douglas, "Climate to Crania: Science and the Racialization of Human Difference," in ed. Bronwen Douglas and Chris Ballard, *Foreign Bodies: Oceania and the Science of Race, 1850–1940* (Canberra: ANU Press, 2012): 33–96; Nicole Starbuck, " 'Primitive Race,' 'pure race,' 'brown race,' 'every race,': Louis Freycinet's Understanding of Human Difference in Oceania," in ed. John West-Sooby, *Discovery and Empire: The French in the South Seas* (Adelaide, Australia: University of Adelaide Press, 2013): 215–240.

55. Chamisso, *A Voyage Around the World*, 129.

56. Here I specify Indigeneity rather than race, because, unlike many Pacific naturalists or explorers, Chamisso, Eshscholtz, and Choris did not seem interested in advancing ideas of racial categorization and hierarchies. They were deeply curious about the Indigenous cultures they witnessed, while they also attempted to link human characteristics to specific individuals. As Marie-Therese Federhofer argues, the *Rurik* expedition "did not carry out experiments designed to demonstrate racial distinction." See Federhofer, "Messy Episodes," 4.

57. Choris, *Voyage pittoresque*, 18–22.

58. Chamisso, "Remarks and Opinions," vol. 3, 127. For a discussion of European fascination with cannibalism, see Anne Salmond, *The Trial of the Cannibal Dog: The*

Remarkable Story of Captain Cook's Encounters in the South Seas (New Haven, CT: Yale University Press, 2003).

59. According to Choris, this discussion took place over the course of a few days after their departure from the Marshall Islands. See Choris, *Journal*, 262–264; Chamisso, "Remarks and Opinions," vol. 3, 122, 178, 215, 216.

60. Chamisso, "Remarks and Opinions," vol. 3, 178, 127.

61. Gathering correct and incorrect information sheds critical light on the methods of researching Indigenous cultures. See Smith, *Decolonizing Methodologies*, esp. 1–10; Chilisa, *Indigenous Research Methodologies*, 6–15.

62. Richard Sorrenson, "The Ship as a Scientific Instrument in the Eighteenth Century," *OSIRIS* 11 (1996), 227. Captain James Cook used the term *crank* in 1772 in reference to modifications needed for the *Resolution* prior to departure from England.

63. Kotzebue, *A Voyage of Discovery*, vol. 2, 158–159.

64. Jules S-C Dumont D'Urville, *Two Voyages to the South Seas*, trans. and ed. Helen Rosenman (Honolulu: University of Hawai`i Press, 1987), vol. 1, 22.

65. Choris, in Vanstone, "An Early Nineteenth-Century Artist in Alaska," 152.

66. Chamisso quotes this passage from his journal in *A Voyage Around the World*, 163.

67. Chamisso, *A Voyage Around the World*, 164.

68. Frederick Eschscholtz, "On the Diseases of the Crew During the Three-Year Voyage," in Kotzebue, *A Voyage of Discovery*, vol. 2, 332.

69. Chamisso, *A Voyage Around the World*, 164; 163.

70. Kotzebue, *A Voyage of Discovery*, vol. 2, 161; 162.

71. Kotzebue, *A Voyage of Discovery*, vol. 2, 161–162.

72. Eschscholtz, "On the Diseases of the Crew," 332; Chamisso, *A Voyage Around the World*, 164; Kotzebue, *A Voyage of Discovery*, vol. 2, 162.

73. Vanstone, "An Early Nineteenth-Century Artist in Alaska," 158; Kotzebue, *A Voyage of Discovery*, vol. 2, 165; 166.

74. Kotzebue, *A Voyage of Discovery*, vol. 2, 175–76.

75. Kotzebue, *A Voyage of Discovery*, vol. 2, 176–77.

76. Eschscholtz, "On the Diseases of the Crew," 336.

77. Chamisso, *A Voyage Around the World*, 174; 175.

78. John Barrow, review of *A Voyage of Discovery into the South Sea and Beering's Straits*, in *The Quarterly Review* 26 (January 1822), 363.

CHAPTER 3

1. Chamisso, *A Voyage Around the World*, 190.

2. On travel literature and the publishing industry in Britain, see Innes M. Keighren, Charles W. J. Withers, and Bill Bell, *Travels in Print: Exploration, Writing, and Publishing with John Murray, 1773–1859* (Chicago: University of Chicago Press, 2015).

3. Frederic Shoberl, *The World in Miniature: Africa* (London: R. Ackermann, 1821); see also K. E. Attar, "Russia Revealed: A Senate House Library Case Study of Special Collection Promotion," *SCONUL Focus* 50 (January 2021): 79–83.

4. Daniella Bleichmar draws this connection in "The cabinet and the world: Non-European objects in early modern European collections," *Journal of the History of Collections* 33 (2021), 435.

5. Frederic Shoberl, *The World in Miniature: The South Sea Islands*, 2 vols. (London: R. Ackermann, 1824), vol. 1, iii; iv; v.

6. Kadu may have also considered it a reasonable theory, given his own experience of drifting to the Marshall Islands. Shoberl, *The World in Miniature: the South Sea Islands*, vol. 1, 8.

7. Shoberl, *The World in Miniature: the South Sea Islands*, iv; vii.

8. For a contemporaneous example involving a French expedition, see Starbuck, "'Primitive race,'" 215–240. On the shift to racial characteristics and race theory, see Douglas, "Climate to Crania," 33–96.

9. On Russian debates about the empire's role in the North Pacific, see Andrei V. Grinev, "The Plans for Russian Expansion in the New World and the North Pacific in the Eighteenth and Nineteenth Centuries," *European Journal of American Studies* 5 (2010): 1–27.

10. Chamisso, *A Voyage Around the World*, 178.

11. Ilya Vinkovetsky, *Russian America: An Overseas Colony of a Continental Empire, 1804–1867* (New York: Oxford University Press, 2011): 142–149; Andrei V. Grinev, "Natives and Creoles of Alaska in the Maritime Service in Russian America," *The Historian* 82 (2020): 328–345. On the RAC as a corporation distinct from the Russian government, see Vinkovetsky, "The Russian-American Company as a Corporation," *The Russian Review* 81 (July 2022): 421–439.

12. Ray Hudson and Rachel Mason, *Lost Villages of the Eastern Aleutians* (Washington, D.C.: National Parks Service, 2014), 58.

13. Ryan Tucker Jones, *Empire of Extinction: Russians and the North Pacific's Strange Beasts of the Sea, 1741–1867* (New York: Oxford University Press, 2014), 11. On Aleut language and ethnography, see Hudson and Mason, *Lost Villages of the Eastern Aleutians*, 3–5; Roza G. Liapunova, *Essays on the Ethnography of the Aleuts*, trans. Jerry Shelest (Fairbanks: University of Alaska Press, 1996), 140–144; Ryan Tucker Jones, "Kelp Highways, Siberian Girls in Maui, and Nuclear Walruses: The North Pacific in a Sea of Islands," *Journal of Pacific History* 48 (December 2014), 379–381.

14. Matthew P. Romaniello, *Enterprising Empires: Russia and Britain in Eighteenth-Century Eurasia* (Cambridge: Cambridge University Pres, 2019), 262.

15. Lydia T. Black, *Russians in Alaska, 1732–1867* (Fairbanks: University of Alaska Press, 2004): 89. On the practice of taking captives, see David Igler, *The Great Ocean: Pacific Worlds from Captain Cook to the Gold Rush* (New York: Oxford University Press, 2013), 73–97.

16. Jones, *Empire of Extinction*, 84; Ilya Vinkovetsky, *Russian America: An Overseas Colony of a Continental Empire, 1804–1867* (New York: Oxford University Press, 2011), 18.

17. Igler, *The Great Ocean*, 105–111.

18. Admiralty to Golovnin, August 13, 1817; in *The Russian American Colonies: A Documentary Record, 1798–1867*, eds. Basil Dmytryshyn, E. A. P. Crownhart-Vaughan, and Thomas Vaughan (Portland: Oregon Historical Society Press, 1989), vol. 3: 288.

19. Louis Choris, *Journal des Malers Ludwig Choris*, ed. Niklaus R. Schweizer (New York: Lang, 1999), 268.

20. Chamisso, "Remarks and Opinions," vol. 3, 315; Chamisso, *A Voyage Around the World*, 92.

21. Kotzebue, *A Voyage of Discovery*, vol. 1, 273.

22. For a brilliant review of Rumiantsev's activities, see Alexandra Bekasova, "Voyaging towards the Future," 469–495. As early as 1808 Rumiantsev was suggesting a new course for the RAC. See his letters dated April 20 and May 20, 1808, in *The Russian American Colonies*, 156–158; 163–164.

23. Chamisso, *A Voyage Around the World*, 267; Choris, *Journal*, 268. This remark is difficult to decipher in Choris's journal, and here I'm relying on the translation in Federhofer, "Messy Episodes."

24. Choris, in Vanstone, "An Early Nineteenth-Century Artist in Alaska," 155–156. Choris's diary entries at this point in the voyage are filled with commentary about Kadu. Choris was actively gathering information about Kadu's beliefs as well as his reactions to the different people they encounter in the North. See Choris, *Journal*, 264–269.

25. Choris, in Vanstone, "An Early Nineteenth Century Artist in Alaska," 156.

26. Choris, in Vanstone, "An Early Nineteenth-Century Artist in Alaska," 156.

27. Choris, in Vanstone, "An Early Nineteenth-Century Artist in Alaska," 156.

28. Historian Ron Tyler suggests that his careful human renderings were intended to assist the "science" of physiognomy. See Tyler, "Entirely New and Very Interesting Things," 19–20.

29. Chamisso, *A Voyage Around the World*, 98; 100. On the maritime traffic in Alta California, see Igler, *The Great Ocean*, 17–42.

30. Dmytryshyn, et al., eds., *The Russian American Colonies: A Documentary Record*, vol. 3: 109; 212.

31. Grinev, "The Plans for Russian Expansion in the New World and the North Pacific in the Eighteenth and Nineteenth Centuries," 1–27.

32. Dmytryshyn, et al., eds., *The Russian American Colonies: A Documentary Record*, vol. 3: 222; 223; 235.

33. See "A Letter from the Directors of the Russian American Company to Andrei IA. Dashkov, Russian Consul-General to the United States, Concerning John Jacob Astor, Trade and the Columbia River," 16 October 1814, in Dmytryshyn, et al., eds., *The Russian American Colonies*, vol. 3: 216–221. For American and English trading on the Northwest Coast, see Igler, *The Great Ocean*, 33–36.

34. Dmytryshyn, et al., eds., *The Russian American Colonies*, vol. 3: 251.

35. Jones, *Empire of Extinction*, 220.

36. Dmytryshyn, et al., eds., *The Russian American Colonies*, vol. 3: 257.

37. Chamisso, *A Voyage Around the World*, 106; Chamisso, "Remarks and Opinions," vol. 3, 43; 42.

38. Luis Arguello to Governor Don Vicente de Sola, October 2, 1816; in August Mahr, *The Visit of the "Rurik" to San Francisco*, 108.

39. The following discussion is based on Chamisso, "Remarks and Opinions," vol. 3, 38–52; Chamisso, *A Voyage Around the World*, 241–247; 346–347.

40. Chamisso, "Remarks and Opinions," vol. 3, 42–46; Chamisso, *A Voyage Around the World*, 242.

41. Chamisso, "Remarks and Opinions," vol. 3, 47; 48; 49; Chamisso, *A Voyage Around the World*, 102; 348.

42. Louis Choris, *San Francisco One Hundred Years Ago*, trans. Porter Garnett (San Francisco: A. M. Robertson, 1913), 3. This volume provides an English translation of Choris's narrative for the month spent in San Francisco.

43. I was surprised to find Choris's "Dance of the Inhabitants of Mission San Francisco" included as part of the AP U.S. History curriculum. See David M. Kennedy and Lizabeth Cohen, *The American Pageant* (Boston: Cengage Publishing, 2015), 16th edition, 378.

44. Choris, in *San Francisco One Hundred Years Ago*, 9–10. Emphasis added.

45. On Native California mourning rituals, see Lee M. Panich, " 'Sometimes They Bury the Deceased's Clothes and Trinkets': Indigenous Mortuary Practices and Mission Santa Clara de Asis," *Historical Archaeology* 49 (2015), 110–129; Panich, "Death, Mourning, and Accommodation in the Missions of Alta California," in *Franciscans and American Indians in Pan-Borderland Perspective: Adaptation, Negotiation, and Resistance*, eds. Jeffrey M. Burns and Timothy J. Johnson (Gainesville: University Press of Florida, 2018), 251–264.

46. Tyler, "Entirely New and Very Interesting Things," 35.

47. Choris, *San Francisco One Hundred Years Ago*, 11–12.

48. Chamisso, "Remarks and Opinions," 51; Chamisso, *A Voyage Around the World*, 109.

49. Seth Archer, *Sharks Upon the Land: Colonialism, Indigenous Health, and Culture in Hawaii, 1778–1855* (Cambridge: Cambridge University Press, 2018); Igler, *The Great Ocean*, 43–71.

50. Kotzebue, *A Voyage of Discovery*, vol. 1, 298.

51. Kotzebue, *A Voyage of Discovery*, vol. 1, 315.

52. Chamisso, *A Voyage Around the World*, 190. Kotzebue also severely criticized the influence of Protestant missionaries following his second voyage. See Kotzebue, *A New Voyage Round the World in the Years 1823, 1824, 1825, 1826*.

53. Ludwig Choris, as quoted in *Through Alien Eyes: The Visit of the Russian Ship Rurik to San Francisco in 1816 and the Men Behind the Visit*, ed. Edward Mornin (Oxford: P. Lang, 2002), 47, 49.

54. Choris, in Vanstone, "An Early Nineteenth-Century Artist in Alaska," 153.

CHAPTER 4

1. On the significance of mobility and travel for natural history and Linnaean science, see Hanna Hodacs, Kenneth Nyberg, and Stéphanie van Damme, "Introduction: de-centring and re-centring Linnaeus," in *Linnaeus, natural history, and the circulation of knowledge*, eds. Hanna Hodacs, Kenneth Nyberg, and Stéphanie van Damme (Oxford: Voltaire Foundation, 2018), 4–5. For useful introductions to the large body of literature on natural history and seaborne naturalists, see Glyn Williams, *Naturalists at Sea: Scientific Travellers from Dampier to Darwin* (New Haven, CT: Yale University Press, 2013); Patricia Fara, *Sex, Botany, and Empire: The Story of Carl Linnaeus and Joseph Banks* (New York: Columbia University Press, 2003).

2. This section draws on the discussion in David Igler, "Trading Nature in the Pacific: Ecological Exchange Prior to 1900," in *Cambridge History of the Pacific Ocean, Vol. II: The Pacific Ocean Since 1800*, eds. Paul D'Arcy, Anne Perez-Hattori, and Jane Samson (Cambridge: Cambridge University Press, 2023), 369–388.

3. Jennifer Newell, *Trading Nature: Tahitians, Europeans, and Ecological Exchange* (Honolulu: University of Hawai`i Press, 2010). For an excellent accounting of these species introductions, see Appendix B, 213–224; 224.

4. Newell, *Trading Nature*, 195.

5. On the biological impact faced by Tahitians and other Pacific islanders, see P. V. Kirch and J. L. Rallu, eds., *The Growth and Collapse of Pacific Island Societies: Archaelogical and Demographic Perspectives* (Honolulu: University of Hawai`i Press, 2007); Newell, *Trading Nature*, 113.

6. On plants in Hawai`i, see K. Nagata, "Early Plant Introductions in Hawai`i," *The Hawaiian Journal of History* 19 (1985), 35–61.

7. Daniel Lewis, *Belonging on an Island: Birds, Extinction, and Evolution in Hawai`i* (New Haven, CT: Yale University Press, 2018), Lewis, *Belonging on an Island*, 10.

8. Lewis, *Belonging on an Island*, 37–39.

9. Kotzebue, *A Voyage of Discovery*, vol. 2, 37

10. Alfred Crosby, *Ecological Imperialism: The Biological Expansion of Europe, 900–1900* (Cambridge: Cambridge University Press, 1986), 270.

11. George Forster, quote in Newell, *Trading Nature*, ix.

12. For histories that address the global dimensions of the breadfruit transplantation, see Anne Salmond, *Bligh: William Bligh in the South Seas* (Berkeley: University of California Press, 2011); and E. DeLoughrey, "Globalizing the Routes of Breadfruit and Other Bounties," *Journal of Colonialism and Colonial History* 8 (Winter 2007), https://muse.jhu.edu/, accessed September 6, 2018.

13. On these themes of science, empire, and commerce, see P. Fara, *Sex, Botany, and Empire: The Story of Carl Linnaeus and Joseph Banks* (New York: Columbia University Press, 2003); and J. Gascoigne, *Science in the Service of Empire: Joseph Banks, the British State, and the Uses of Science in the Age of Revolution* (New York: Cambridge University Press, 1998).

14. Salmond, *Bligh*, 108.

15. Brian Edwards, cited in DeLoughrey, "Globalizing the Routes of Breadfruit and Other Bounties," 11.

16. Salmond, *Bligh*, 393; 395.

17. Salmond, *Bligh*, 431.

18. Salmond, *Bligh*, 472.

19. Banks, *Endeavour Journal*, vol. 1, 428.

20. For further details of this incident, see Anne Salmond, *Two Worlds: First Meetings Between Māori and Europeans, 1642–1772* (Auckland, NZ: Viking, 1991), 87.

21. James L. Reveal, "Douglas-fir: A Nomenclatural Morass." https://lewis-clark.org/, accessed September 27, 2022.

22. In a recent study on naturalists in Oceania, Leah Lui-Chivizhe and Jenny Newell write: "To know a place as a naturalist, with a classificatory eye, and a collecting bag, is to know in a way external to oneself." I tend to agree with this sentiment in regard

to the mentality of European naturalists traveling abroad, and yet it strikes me that all people interested in natural diversity would experience the same separation from nature whenever they left their home environs. See Lui-Chivezhe and Jenny Newell, "Reflections: On Engagements with Indigenous Knowledge and Collections," in *Naturalist Histories: Making Nature, Knowledge, and People in Oceania*, edited by Jamon Alex Halvaksz and Joshua A. Bell (Honolulu: University of Hawai`i Press, 2024), 266.

23. Adelbert von Chamisso, "Ex Plantis, in expeditione Romanzoffiana detectis, genera tria nova," *Horae physicae Berolinenses* (Bonn, 1820), 69–105.

24. Chamisso, *A Voyage Around the World*, 242; 345 n. 6.

25. Despite the large collection of California plants gathered by Eschscholtz, Chamisso regretted that "the season [for collecting] was not the most favorable one for us." Chamisso, *A Voyage Around the World*, 242.

26. Anne Greenwood MacKinney and Matthias Glaubrecht, "Unpacking a(nother) voyage round the world, 270.

27. Eschscholtz to Chamisso, 9 June–6 July 1820, in Lukina, *Eschscholtz*, 132–133.

28. "Flora named as a result of Russian American Activities," n.a., (Jenner: California History Center, 1984), 4.

29. Lydia T. Black, "Whaling in the Aleutians," *Etudes/Inuit/Studies* 11 (1987), 21.

30. Chamisso, "Remarks and Opinions of the Naturalist of the Expedition," in Kotzebue, *A Voyage of Discovery*," vol. 3, 290; 304; 261.

31. Chamisso, "Remarks and Opinions," vol. 3, 307; 309.

32. Eschscholtz wrote several reports that Chamisso appended to his "Remarks and Opinions." They included his studies of minerals, butterflies, coral islands, rocks, and general observations. On his study of sea turtles, see Oscar Flores-Villela, et al., "Identity of Three New Sea Turtles Named by J. Friedrich Eschscholtz," *Chelonian Conservation and Biology* 15 (2016), 157–162.

33. Eschscholtz, "On the Coral Islands," in Kotzebue, *A Voyage of Discovery*, vol. 3, 331–333.

34. David R. Stoddart, "'This Coral Episode': Darwin, Dana, and the Coral Reefs of the Pacific," in *Darwin's Laboratory: Evolutionary Theory and Natural History in the Pacific*, eds. Roy MacLeod and Philip F. Rehbock (Honolulu: University of Hawai`i Press, 1994); Lukina, *Johann Friedrich Eschscholtz*, 51.

35. Londa Schiebinger, *Plants and Empire: Colonial Bioprospecting in the Atlantic World* (Cambridge, MA: Harvard University Press, 2007), 11.

36. Nikolai Rumiantsev to Vasilii Golovnin, October 28, 1818; and Nikolai Rumiantsev to Petr Ricord, February 13, 1817; as quoted in Alexandra Bekasova, "Voyaging towards the Future," 475; 474.

37. Kotzebue, *A Voyage of Discovery*, vol. 2, 166; Chamisso, *A Voyage Around the World*, 268.

38. Chamisso, *A Voyage Around the World*, 266.

39. Chamisso, *A Voyage Around the World*, 267.

40. Ludwig Choris, *Journal*, 239; 398.

41. Chamisso, *A Voyage Around the World*, 130.

42. Chamisso used this term interchangeably for the Marshall Islands and the larger region of Micronesia. It suggests his belief that the region between the Hawaiian Islands and the Philippines was relatively untouched by Europeans.

43. Chamisso gives no name for this island and describes is as sparsely inhabited. The people apparently remained at a distance from the European visitors, but this reticence would change in the coming days and weeks. Chamisso, *A Voyage Around the World*, 134–135.

44. Chamisso, *A Voyage Around the World*, 140; 141.

45. Gleb Shishmaref, "Report of Lieutenant Schishchmareff," in Kotzebue, *A Voyage of Discovery*, vol. 2, 23.

46. Shishmaref, "Report of Lieutenant Schishchmareff," 25–26.

47. Chamisso, *A Voyage Around the World*, 140.

48. Kotzebue, *A New Voyage Round the World in the Years 1823, 1824, 1825, and 1826*, 294–330.

49. Carol E. Harrison, "Planting Gardens, Planting Flags: Revolutionary France in the South Pacific," *French Historical Studies* 34 (Spring 2011), 244.

50. Tatiana Arkadevna Lukina, *Johann Friedrich Eschscholtz, 1793–1831*, trans. Wilma C. Folette (Leningrad: Nauka Publishing House, 1975), 151.

51. Chamisso, *A Voyage Around the World*, 263.

52. On this episode, see Ryan Tucker Jones, "Running into Whales: The History of the North Pacific from Below the Waves," *American Historical Review* 118 (April 2013): 349–377.

53. Tatiana Arkadevna Lukina mentions the four Aleut hunters in her biography of Johann Friedrich Eschscholtz, noting at the voyage's end that they "were assigned to the disposal of the Russian-American trading company." See Lukina, *Johann Friedrich Eschscholtz*, 41. Chamisso, *A Voyage Around the World*, 175.

54. Adelbert von Chamisso, "Cetaceorum maris Kamtschatici imagines, ab Aleutis e lingo fictas," *Nova Acta Academiae Caesarae Leopoldino-Carolinae Germanicae naturae Curiosorum* 12 (1824), 251–263. The Latin translation was completed by Giuseppe Catanzaro. I appreciate the research assistance provided by Emily Willrich and the thoughtful suggestions offered by Marie-Theres Federhofer.

55. On North Pacific Indigenous whaling, see Joshua L. Reid, *The Sea Is My Country: The Maritime World of the Makah* (New Haven, CT: Yale University Press, 2015); Bathsheba Demuth, *Floating Coast: An Environmental History of the Bering Strait* (New York: W.W. Norton and Company, 2019); Jones, *Empire of Extinction*, 9–12; Ryan Tucker Jones, *Red Leviathan: The Secret History of Soviet Whaling* (Chicago: University of Chicago Press, 2022), 10–13; and Black, "Whaling in the Aleutians," 7–50.

56. Black, "Whaling in the Aleutians," 10.

57. Jones, *Red Leviathan*, 11.

58. Black, "Whaling in the Aleutians," 18.

59. Robert F. Heizer, "Aconite Poison Whaling in Asia and America: An Aleutian Transfer to the New World," *Bureau of American Ethnology Bulletin* 133 (1944), 415–468; Black, "Whaling in the Aleutians," 19–20.

60. Chamisso, *A Voyage Around the World*, 94.
61. Choris, in Vanstone, "An Early Nineteenth-Century Artists in Alaska," 151; *The Alaska Diary of Adelbert von Chamisso: Naturalist on the Kotzebue Voyage, 1815–1818*, trans. Robert Fortuine (Anchorage, AK.: Cook Inlet Historical Society, 1986), 29.
62. Chamisso, "Cetaceorum maris Kamtschatici imagines, ab Aleutis e lingo fictas," 251; 258.
63. Chamisso, "Cetaceorum maris Kamtschatici imagines, ab Aleutis e lingo fictas," 251.
64. Jones, *Empire of Extinction*, 12; Chamisso, "Cetaceorum maris Kamtschatici imagines, ab Aleutis e lingo fictas," 258.
65. Chamisso, "Cetaceorum maris Kamtschatici imagines, ab Aleutis e lingo fictas," 251–251; 259.
66. Chamisso, "Cetaceorum maris Kamtschatici imagines, ab Aleutis e lingo fictas," 256; 260; 257; 258.
67. Joel Asaph Allen, *Mammalian Orders of Cete and Sirenia* (Washington, D.C.: U.S. Government Printing Office, 1882), 516.
68. Allen, *Mammalian Orders*, 516.
69. Chamisso, "Cetaceorum maris Kamtschatici imagines, ab Aleutis e lingo fictas," 251; 257.
70. Douglas, "In the Event," 175–207.
71. Lukina, *Johann Friedrich Eschscholtz*, 109.
72. Chamisso published this comment in the journal *Isis* following his first article on salps. See Lukina, *Johann Friedrich Eschscholtz*, 102.
73. Eschscholtz to Chamisso, June 9, 1820; in Lukina, *Johann Friedrich Eschscholtz*, 130–136.

CHAPTER 5

1. John Barrow, *A Chronological History of Voyages into the Arctic Regions* (London: John Murray, 1818), 357–365.
2. On the Russian state and the Russian American Company in the early nineteenth century, see Matthew P. Romaniello, *Enterprising Empires: Russia and Britain in Eighteenth-Century Eurasia* (Cambridge: Cambridge University Pres, 2019), 257–263. On the early modern Russian state, education, and commerce, see Igor Fedyukin, *The Enterprisers: The Politics of School in Early Modern Russia* (New York: Oxford University Press, 2019); and Erika Monahan, *The Merchants of Siberia: Trade in Early Modern Eurasia* (Ithaca, NY: Cornell University Press, 2016).
3. Ludwig Choris, *Journals des Malers Ludwig York Choris*, ed. Niklaus R. Schweizer (New York: Peter Lang, 1999), 278.
4. Chamisso, *A Voyage Around the World*, 195. For Kotzebue's account of Kadu's decision, see Kotzebue, *A Voyage of Discovery*, vol. 2, 208–210.
5. Choris, *Journal*, 278; Chamisso, *A Voyage Around the World*, 270.
6. Both Kotzebue and Chamisso comment on the changes in hierarchy and inter-island violence. On escalating violence in the Marshall Islands, also see Richard V. Williamson and Donna K. Stone, *Anthropological Survey of the Marshall*

Islands (Majuro Atoll: Republic of Marshall Islands: Historic Preservation Office, 2001), 6; Julianne M. Walsh, "Imagining the Marshall Islands: Chiefs, Tradition, and the State on the Fringes of United States Empire," PhD dissertation, University of Hawaiʻi, 2003, 135–138; and Paul D'Arcy, "Connected by the Sea: Towards a Regional History of the Western Caroline Islands," *Journal of Pacific History* 36 (August 2010), 163–182.

7. Kotzebue, *A Voyage of Discovery*, vol. 2, 209.

8. Kotzebue, *A Voyage of Discovery*, vol. 2, 192; Chamisso, *Voyage*, 119–120.

9. Chamisso, *A Voyage Around the World*, 181.

10. Chamisso, *A Voyage Around the World*, 181.

11. Chamisso, *A Voyage Around the World*, 152–153

12. Johann Eschscholtz to Adelbert von Chamisso, October 25, 1826; in Tatiana Arkadevna Lukina, *Johann Friedrich Eschscholtz, 1793–1831*, 151.

13. Kotzebue, *A New Voyage Round the World in the Years 1823, 1824, 1825, 1826*, vol 1, 307; 317.

14. Chamisso, *A Voyage Around the World*, 199; 367; 199.

15. On their relationship and Kadu's contributions to "European discourses," see Chunjie Zhang, "The Islander Kadu and Adelbert von Chamisso: Relations in Oceania," *The Eighteenth Century* 58 (Spring 2017): 79–98.

16. Kotzebue, *A New Voyage of Discovery*, vol. 1, 297.

17. William Lay's account, published three years before Paulding's *Journal*, offers a chilling story of the mutiny led by Samuel Comstock, who murdered the captain of the *Globe* and several other sailors. According to Lay, the nine sailors who made it ashore at Mili decided to kill Comstock, which they did shortly before the islanders attacked them, killing all except for Lay and Hussey. See William Lay and Cyrus Hussey, *A Narrative of the Mutiny on Board the Ship Globe* (New London, CT: Wm. Lay, and C. M. Hussey, 1828).

18. Hiram Paulding, *Journal of the Cruise of the United States Schooner Dolphin* (New York: G. & C. & H. Carvill, 1831), 134–135.

19. Kotzebue, *A New Voyage of Discovery*, 311.

20. Chamisso's second account of the voyage included the message to "my dear Kadu, [who] made the better choice" by remaining in the Marshall Islands. Chamisso, *A Voyage Around the World*, 198.

21. Jules Dumont d'Urville, *Voyage Pittoresque Autor du Monde*, 2 Volumes (Paris: L. Tenre Er H Dupoy, 1834–35), vol. 2, 527–529.

22. On the role of individuals in "global microhistory," see Tonio Andrade, "A Chinese Farmer, Two African Boys, and a Warlord: Toward a Global Microhistory," *Journal of World History* 21 (December 2010), 575.

23. For information on this network, see the superb work by historian Alexandra Bekasova; Bekasova, "Voyaging towards the Future," 474. On the larger context of Russia attempting to involve itself with European endeavors, see Cynthia Hyla Whittaker, ed., *Russia Engages the World, 1453–1825* (Cambridge, MA: Harvard University Press, 2003).

24. Innes M. Keighren, Charles W. J. Withers, and Bill Bell, *Travels in Print: Exploration, Writing, and Publishing with John Murray, 1773–1859* (Chicago: The University

of Chicago Press, 2015), 4; Janice Cavell, "Who Discovered the Northwest Passage?" *Arctic* 71 (September 2018), 292. Also see Cavell, *Tracing the Connected Narrative: Arctic Exploration in British Print Culture, 1818–1860* (Toronto: University of Toronto Press, 2008).

25. Bekasova, "Voyage towards the Future," 480.

26. Cavell, *Tracing the Connected Narrative*, 62; Keighren, *Travels into Print*, 5.

27. Barrow, *A Chronological History of Voyages*, 357, 358.

28. Barrow, review of *A Voyage of Discovery into the South Sea and Beering's Straits*, 341–364.

29. Barrow, *A Chronological History of Voyages*, 360; 361.

30. Yuri Shur, et al., "Yedoma Permafrost Genesis: Over 150 Years of Mystery and Controversy," *Frontiers in Earth Science* 9 (January 2022), 3–4.

31. For example, see the *London Moderator and National Advisor*, July 15, 1818. London newspapers also covered the arrival of the *Rurik* in St. Petersburg in September.

32. The voyage of the *Rurik* was covered by some American newspapers in 1815. See the *Alexandria Gazette*, August 5, 1815. Krusenstern and Rumiantsev publicized Captain Kotzebue's initial dispatch from Kamchatka in 1816, and some version of it appeared in the *Portland Gazette and Maine Advertiser* on May 13, 1817. A number of newspapers picked up the story about the iceberg and putrefying mammoth in 1818, including the *Portland Gazette* (September 8, 1818), the *Rhode Island Republican* (September 9, 1818), and the *Edwardsville Spectator* (June 19, 1819). This is only a brief sampling of American newspapers covering the story of the *Rurik*.

33. On Jefferson's interest in American natural history, see Andrea Wulf, *Founding Gardeners: The Revolutionary Generation, Nature, and the Shaping of the American Nation* (New York: Vintage, 2012).

34. On this point, see Bekasova, "Voyaging towards the Future," 470.

35. Shur, et al., "Yedoma Permafrost Genesis: Over 150 Years of Mystery and Controversy."

36. Vladimir Svyatoslavovich Kusov, "Count Nikolai Rumiantsev and Russian Exploration of Alaska and North America," *Western Association of Map Libraries Information Bulletin* 25 (November 1993): 20; Bekasova, "Voyaging towards the Future," 482.

37. Romaniello, *Enterprising Empires*, 261.

38. For an insightful analysis of the Russian political landscape at this moment, see Erki Tammiksaar and Tarmo Kiik, "Origins of the Russian Antarctic Expedition, 1819–1821," *Polar Record* 49 (2013), 185; 182. Gleb Shishmaref's voyage to the Arctic received very little attention, and his account of the expedition was not published until 1950 (only in the Soviet Union).

39. Glynn Barratt, "Russian Activity among the Cook Islands, to 1820," *New Zealand Slavonic Journal* (1998): 46; http://www.jstor.org/stable/40921980, accessed November 10, 2018.

40. Erika Monahan, *The Merchants of Siberia: Trade in Early Modern Eurasia* (Ithaca, NY: Cornell University Press, 2016), vi.

41. Gerhard Kortum, "Germania in Pacifico: Humboldt, Chamisso and Other Early German Contributions to Pacific Research, 1741–1876," in Keith R. Bengtsson and

Philip F. Rehbock, eds., *Oceanographic History: the Pacific and Beyond* (Seattle: University of Washington Press, 2002), 115.

42. Chamisso, *A Voyage Around the World*, 115. The other two men he included on this list were Sir Joseph Banks and the Marquis de Lafayette.

43. Chamisso, quoted in MacKinney and Glaubrecht, "Unpacking a(nother) voyage round the world, 341.

44. These circumstances are thoroughly examined in MacKinney and Glaubrecht, "Academic practice par excellence," 340-346; and MacKinney and Glaubrecht, "Unpacking a(nother) voyage round the world," 263-268.

45. Chamisso, *A Voyage Around the World*, 233-234.

46. Adelbert von Chamisso, "Voyage de Kotzebue," *Journals des Voyages, Découvertes et Navigations Modernes* (1818), 201-208. Chamisso likely wrote this letter during the *Rurik*'s stop in Portsmouth, England.

47. Adelbert von Chamisso, in *Journals des Voyages*, 202; 203; 202; 205; 207; 208. I am grateful to Ian Coller for assistance with this translation.

48. Monica Sproll, "World knowledge and aesthetic identity: characteristics of a Schlemihl generation in the scientific letters of Adelbert von Chamisso," in *Letters around 1800—On the mediality of generation*, eds. Selma Jahnke and Sylvie Le Moël S (Berlin: Berliner Wiss.-Verl, 2015): 103-134; cited in MacKinney and Glaubrecht, "Academic practice par excellence," 347.

49. MacKinney and Glaubrecht, "Academic practice par excellence," 339; 345.

50. Johann Eschscholtz to Karl Ledebour, September 15, 1817; cited in Lukina, trans. Wilma C. Follette, *Johann Friedrich Eschscholtz*, 15-16.

51. Adelbert von Chamisso, "De animalibus quibusdam e classe Vermium Linnaeana, Auct. De Chamisso. De Salpa," *Isis* 2 (1820): 273-276. On Chamisso's salps research, see Matthias Glaubrecht and Wolfgang Dohle, "Discovering the alternation of generations in salps (Tunicata, Thaliacea): Adelbert von Chamisso's dissertation "De Salpa" 1819—its material, origin and reception in the early nineteenth century," *Zoosystematics and Evolution* 88 (October 2012), 317-363.

52. Glaubrecht and Dohle, "Discovering the alternation of generations in salps," 351.

53. Glaubrecht and Dohle discuss the rejection and later acceptance of Chamisso's theory in "Discovering the alternation of generations in salps," 348-360; quote at 360.

54. Chamisso, *A Voyage Around the World*, 33.

55. Following his appointment at the University of Berlin, Chamisso married Antonie Piaste, the foster-daughter of his close friend and publisher, Eduard Hitzig. They had seven children before Chamisso died in 1838.

56. See Kortum, "Germania in Pacifico," 114. The first comprehensive bibliography of Chamisso's work was Gunther Schmid, *Chamisso als Naturforscher, eine Bibliographie* (Leipzig: K. F. Koehler, 1942).

57. For the contemporary German scholarship on Chamisso, see MacKinney and Glaubrecht, "Academic practice par excellence," 323.

58. Adelbert von Chamisso, *Uber die Hawaiische sprache von Adelbert v. Chamisso* (Leipzig: In der Weidmannischen Buchhandlung, 1837). *Reise um die Welt* appears as the first two volumes of Chamisso's *Werke*, ed. Julius Eduard Hitzig, 6 vols. (Leipzig: Weidmannsche Buchhandlung, 1836-1839).

59. Chamisso, "A View of the Great Ocean, of its Islands, and its Coasts," in Kotzebue, *A Voyage of Discovery*, vol. 2, 387.

60. Johann Eschscholtz to Adelbert von Chamisso, September 7, 1819; June 9, 1820; in Lukina, *Johann Friedrich Eschscholtz*, 118; 136.

61. Johann Eschscholtz to Adelbert von Chamisso, September 7, 1819, in Lukina, *Johann Friedrich Eschscholtz*, 118.

62. On the debate between these two thinkers, see Phillip R. Sloan, "The Buffon-Linnaeus Controversy," *Isis* 67 (September 1976): 356–375; Paul L. Farber, "Buffon and the Concept of Species," *Journal of the History of Biology* 5 (Fall 1972): 259–284; quote at 262.

63. Johann Friedrich Eschscholtz, *Ideen zur Aneinanderreihung der rückgrathigen Thiere* (Dorpat: Schünmann, 1819).

64. Lukina, *Johann Friedrich Eschscholtz*, 54–55.

65. Eschscholtz to Chamisso, June 9, 1820; in Lukina, *Johann Fredrich Eschscholtz*, 131.

66. Lukina, *Johann Friedrich Eschscholtz*, 55, 59.

67. See the discussion of Dumont D'urville in Harry Liebersohn, *The Travelers' World: Europe to the Pacific* (Cambridge, MA: Harvard University Press, 2006), 225–230.

68. Lukina, *Johann Friedrich Eschscholtz*, 59–60.

69. Eschscholtz to Chamisso, January 4–7, 1820, in Lukina, *Johann Friedrich Eschscholtz*, 128.

70. Johann Eschscholtz, *System der Acalephen* (Berlin, 1829); quoted in Lukina, *Johann Friedrich Eschscholtz*, 104–106.

71. Johann Eschscholtz to Karl Ledebour, September 15, 1817; quoted in Lukina, *Johann Friedrich Eschscholtz*, 13.

72. Johann Eschscholtz, "Review of the Zoological Collection," in Kotzebue, *A New Voyage Round the World*, vol. 2, 362.

73. Seppo Koponen and Pekka Niemelä, "Johann Friedrich Gustav von Eschscholtz—a pioneer naturalist and explorer of the Pacific Islands and Western North America," *Memoranda Soc. Fauna Flora Fennica* 96 (2020), 57–64; Lukina, *Johann Friedrich Eschscholtz*, 123.

74. Johann Eschscholtz, *Zoologischer Atlas* (Berlin: G. Reimer, 1833).

75. "Instructions from the Main Administration of the Russian American Company to Aleeksandr A. Baranov Concerning Education for Creoles," March 22, 1817, in Dmytryshyn, et al., eds., *The Russian American Colonies: A Documentary Record*, 244–245.

76. On the *Rurik*'s return and Choris's work in Paris, see Ron Tyler, "Entirely New and Very Interesting Things: Louis Choris and the Kotzebue Expedition, 1815-1818," *Imprint* 42 (Fall 2017), 27–30. Also See Tyler, "The Role of the Exploration Artist: Louis Choris and the Kotzebue Expedition, 1815-1818," *Studii Şi Cercetări de Istoria Artei. Seria Artă Plastică* 11, no. 55 (January 2021): 43–76.

77. The following discussion of professional contacts draws from various sources, including Barratt, "Russian Activity Among the Cook Islands," 63–65; Tyler, "Entirely New and Very Interesting Things," 28–30; Bekasova, "Voyaging towards the Future," 492–493; and Federhofer, "Messy Episodes," 1–22.

78. Matthias Glaubrecht, Nils Seethaler, Barbara Tebman, and Katrin Koel-Abt, "The Potential of Biohistory: Re-discovering Adelbert von Chamisso's Skull of an Aleut Collected during the 'Rurik' Expedition 1815–1818 in Alaska," *Zoosystematics and Evolution* 89 (September 2013), 317–336.

79. Choris, quoted in Federhofer, "Messy Episodes," 16.

80. On the different methods of lithography, see Michael Twyman, *Lithography: 1800–1850: The Techniques of Drawing on Stone in England and France and their Application in Works of Topography* (New York: Oxford University Press, 1970).

81. Elizabeth Robins Pennell, *Lithography and Lithographers: Some Chapters in the History of the Art* (London: T. Fisher Unwin, 1915), 53. On the rapid growth of lithographic printers in France, see Michael Twyman, *Breaking the Mould: The First Hundred Years of Lithography* (London: British Library, 2001), 28–35.

82. Michael Twyman, "The Illustration Revolution," in *The Cambridge History of the Book in Britain*, vol. 6, *1830–1914*, ed. David McKitterick (Cambridge: Cambridge University Press, 2009), 127.

83. Tyler, "Entirely New and Very Interesting Things," 29. Choris produced most of his own lithographs, but as Tyler observes, a number of collaborators assisted with parts of the lithographic work.

84. On the methods of lithography, see Twyman, "Breaking the mould," 64–77.

85. Different versions of *Voyage pittoresque* range in production quality from fully hand-colored to simple black-and-white lithographs. Among the best volumes are those held by the Turnbull Library (Wellington, New Zealand), the Alaska State Archives (Juneau), and the Beinecke Library (Yale University). On the pricing of the *livraisons* and the completed book, see Tyler, "Entirely New and Very Interesting Things," 30; and Tyler, "The Role of the Exploration Artist: Louis Choris and the Kotzebue Expedition, 1815–1818," 73.

86. Twyman, *Lithography, 1800–1850*, 231.

87. Chamisso made this comment in his review of Choris's *Voyage pittoresque*; cited in Federhofer, "Messy Episodes," 13.

88. Choris to Chamisso, March 26, 1821; quoted in Federhofer, "Messy Episodes," 13. "[I]t is worth noting that neither Franz Joseph Gall nor Choris uses the word 'race' at any point in *Voyage pittoresque*," Federhofer observes. While correct about the word *race*, Choris clearly made reference to skin color in his journal, and occasionally his preference for lighter skin tones. See Choris, *Journal*, 368.

89. Art historian Jean Charlot provides interesting, though dated, analysis of this lithograph in *Choris and Kamehameha* (Honolulu, HI: Bishop Museum Press, 1958). "As published," Charlot writes, "the woman acquires a gentle dignity—a native virtue expressed by the Hawaiian word 'olu'olu [pleasant or gracious]—that, paired with nudity, recaptures the flavor of a pagan culture unmarred by foreign inroads" (6).

90. Choris, *Journal*, 366. This passage relies on a translation completed by Doris Lonk.

91. Charlot, *Choris and Kamehameha*, 35–44. Charlot provides extensive detail and analysis of Choris's sketches, tracings, and watercolors from the moment he began drawing the King to the ultimate lithographs and aquatints.

92. Kotzebue, *A Voyage of Discovery*, vol. 1, 331.

93. Charlot, *Choris and Kamehameha*, 44.
94. Choris contrasted the King's humility with the bearing of his son and heir, Liholiho, who, he stated, "acted all arrogant and barely seemed to take notice of us." Choris, *Journals des Malers*, 369.
95. Choris, *Journals des Maler*, 369.
96. Choris compared his own limited knowledge to those Europeans who had lived for years or even decades among Indigenous communities. In Hawai`i, he noted with admiration the British sailor John Young, who arrived in 1790 and spent the rest of his life as an advisor to Kamehameha. Choris, *Journals des* Malers, 370–371.
97. Federhofer, "Messy Episodes," 3.
98. E.-T. Hamy, "Le Second Voyage et la Mort au Mexique de Louis Choris, Peintre et Naturalist, Correspondent du Muséum (1827–1828)," *Bulletin du Muséum d'histoire naturelle* (1906), 2.
99. Alexander von Humboldt to Adelbert von Chamisso, n.d. [1836], quoted in Liebersohn, *The Travelers' World*, 137.

CONCLUSION

1. Innes M. Keighren, Charles W. J. Withers, and Bill Bell, *Travels in Print: Exploration, Writing, and Publishing with John Murray, 1773–1859* (Chicago: The University of Chicago Press, 2015).
2. Barrow, *A Chronological History of Voyages*, 357.
3. John Barrow, review of *A Voyage of Discovery into the South Sea and Beering's Straits*, in *The Quarterly Review* 26 (January 1822), 341; 345; 346.
4. Barrow, "A Voyage of Discovery," 348; 349; 353.
5. Barrow, "A Voyage of Discovery," 361; 353; 363.
6. Barrow, *A Chronological History of Voyages*, 357; 358; 360.
7. Barrow, *A Chronological History of Voyages*, 360.
8. Barrow, "A Voyage of Discovery," 346.
9. Hobbles Danaiyarri, "The Saga of Captain Cook," eds. Deryck M. Schreuder and Stuart Ward, *Australia's Empire* (New York: Oxford University Press, 2010), 28; Maria Nugent, "A failure to say hello: how Captain Cook blundered his first impression with Indigenous people," *The Conversation*, April 28, 2020.
10. On the use of *terra nullius* in Australia, see Stuart Banner, *Possessing the Pacific: Land, Settlers, and Indigenous People from Australia to Alaska* (Cambridge, MA: Harvard University Press, 2007), 13–46.
11. Peter Mancall, "The Age of Failure," *Early American Literature* 56 (2021), 24.
12. Stephanie E. Smallwood, "Reflections on Settler Colonialism, the Hemispheric Americas, and Chattel Slavery," *The William and Mary Quarterly* 76 (2021), 407–419.
13. John Marra, *Journal of the Resolution's Voyage in 1772, 1773, 1774, and 1775, on discovery to the southern hemisphere, by which the Non-Existence of an undiscovered Continent, between the equator and the 50th degree of Southern latitude, is demonstrably proved* (Dublin: printed for Caleb Jenkin and John Beatty, 1776).
14. Here I refer to the American midshipman William Reynolds, Alfred Wallace, and Kadu.

15. On the Marshall Islands in the era of U.S. colonialism and atomic testing, see Lauren Hirshberg, *Suburban Empire: Cold War Militarization in the US Pacific* (Berkeley: University of California Press, 2022).

16. E. O. Wilson, *Biophilia* (Cambridge, MA: Harvard University Press, 1984), 22.

17. See the scholars of Chamisso cited throughout this study, including Marie-Theres Federhofer, Matthias Glaubrecht, Wolfgang Dohle, Anne Greenwood MacKinney, Monica Sproll, Harry Liebersohn, Ryan Tucker Jones, Gerhard Kortum, Nils Seethaler, Barbara Tebman, and Katrin Koel-Abt.

18. Chamisso, *A Voyage Around the World*.

19. Wilson, *Biophilia*, 28.

20. Johann Eschscholtz to Adelbert von Chamisso, August 5, 1830; in Lukina, *Johann Friedrich Eschscholtz, 1793–1831*, 157.

21. Wilson, *Biophilia*, 22. Wilson was most enamored with those involved in Darwinian debates of the mid-1800s, including Asa Gray, Louis Agassiz, John Dalton Hooker, and Darwin.

22. Johann Eschscholtz, "Review of the Zoological Collection of Fr. Eschscholtz," in Kotzebue, *A New Voyage Round the World in the Years 1823, 1824, 1825, 1826*, vol. 2, 362; 336; 338; 361.

23. Bleichmar, "Visible Empire," *Postcolonial Studies* 12 (2009), 441–466.

24. On Choris's production of *livraison* or serial sections of the volume, see Tyler, "Entirely New and Very Interesting Things," 13.

25. These variations became apparent after viewing a dozen copies of *Voyage pittoresque* in different archives across the United States and the world. The copy held by the Autry Museum of the American West stands out for the unique differences in some of the lithographs, including the altered portrait of Kamehameha, the Aleut visor, and an image of two skulls. This copy of Choris's book was given to the Autry by the landscape watercolorist Eva Scott Fényes, who in the early twentieth century lived four blocks from my home in Pasadena. This fact has no significance beyond the coincidence that my favorite copy of Choris's work was once housed so close to my current residence. I thank Autry librarian Katlynn Friedman for digging up this information.

BIBLIOGRAPHY

PRIMARY SOURCES

Allen, Joel Asaph. *Mammalian Orders of Cete and Sirenia*. Washington, D.C.: U.S. Government Printing Office, 1882.

Amundsen, Roald. *Roald Amundsen's "The North West passage": being the record of a voyage of exploration of the ship "Gjoa" 1903–1907*. London: Constable and Co., 1908.

Banks, Joseph. *The Endeavour Journal of Joseph Banks, 1768–1771*. Edited by J. C. Beaglehole, 3 vols. Sidney: Public Library of New South Wales, 1963.

Banks, Joseph. *The Indian and Pacific Correspondence of Sir Joseph Banks*. Edited by Neil Chambers. London: Imperial College Press, 2000.

Banks, Joseph. *The Scientific Correspondences of Sir Joseph Banks, 1765–1820*. Edited by Neil Chambers. London: Pickering & Chatto, 2007.

Barrow, John. *A Chronological History of Voyages into the Arctic Regions*. London: John Murray, 1818.

Barrow, John. "Ross's *Voyage of Discovery*." *The Quarterly Review* 21 (January 1819), 213–214.

Barrow, John. *A Voyage of Discovery into the South Sea and Beering's Straits*. Review in *The Quarterly Review* 26 (January 1822), 341–364.

Bayard, James A. *The Papers of James A. Bayard, 1795–1815*, 2 vols. Washington, D.C.: Annual Report of the American Historical Association for the Year 1913, 1915.

Bosc, L. A. G. *Histoire naturelle des vers: contenant leur description et leurs moeurs*. Paris: Deterville, 1802.

Chamisso, Adelbert von. "Voyage de Kotzebue." *Journals des Voyages, Découvertes et Navigations Modernes*. Paris, 1818, 201–208.

Chamisso, Adelbert von. "De animalibus quibusdam e classe Vermium Linnaeana, Auct. De Chamisso. De Salpa." *Isis* 2 (1820): 273–276.

Chamisso, Adelbert von. "Ex Plantis, in expeditione Romanzoffiana detectis, genera tria nova." *Horae physicae Berolinenses* (Bonn, 1820): 69–105.

Chamisso, Adelbert von. "Remarks and Opinions of the Naturalist." In Otto von Kotzebue, *A Voyage of Discovery, Into the South Sea and Beering's Straits, for the Purpose of Exploring a North-East Passage Undertaken in the Years 1815–1818, at the*

Expense of His Highness the Chancellor of the Empire, Count Romanzoff, in the Ship Rurick, Under the Command of the Lieutenant in the Russian Imperial Navy, Otto von Kotzebue, 3 vols. Translated by H. E. Lloyd. London: Longman, 1821.

Chamisso, Adelbert von. "Cetaceorum maris Kamtschatici imagines, ab Aleutis e lingo fictas." *Nova Acta Academiae Caesarae Leopoldino-Carolinae Germanicae naturae Curiosorum* 12 (1824): 251–263.

Chamisso, Adelbert von. *Uber die Hawaiische sprache von Adelbert v. Chamisso*. Leipzig: In der Weidmannischen Buchhandlung, 1837.

Chamisso, Adelbert von. *Werke*. Edited by Julius Eduard Hitzig, 6 vols. Leipzig: Weidmannsche Buchhandlung, 1836–1839.

Chamisso, Adelbert von. *A Voyage Around the World with the Romanzov Exploring Expedition in the Years 1815–1818 in the Brig Rurik, Captain Otto von Kotzebue*. Translated and edited by Henry Kratz. Honolulu: University of Hawai`i Press, 1986 [1836].

Chamisso, Adelbert von. *The Alaska Diary of Adelbert von Chamisso: Naturalist on the Kotzebue Voyage 1815–1818*. Edited and translated by Robert Fontuine. Anchorage: Cook Inlet Historical Society, 1986.

Chamisso, Adelbert von. *Peter Schlemihl*. Edited by Wulf Koepke. Columbia, SC: Camden House, 1993 [1814].

Choris, Louis. *Voyage pittoresque autour du monde: avec des portraits de sauvages d'Amérique, d'Asie, d'Afrique, et des îles due Grand océan; des paysages, des vues maritimes, et plusieurs objets de'histoire naturelle*. Paris: Impr. de Firmin Didot, 1822.

Choris, Louis. *Vues et paysages des régions équinoxiales*. Paris: Paul Renouard, 1826.

Choris, Louis. *San Francisco One Hundred Years Ago*. Translated by Porter Garnett. San Francisco: A. M. Robertson, 1913.

Choris, Louis. *Journals des Malers Ludwig York Choris*. Edited by Niklaus R. Schweizer. New York: Peter Lang, 1999.

Dobell, Peter. *Travels in Kamchatka and Siberia: With a Narrative of a Residence in China*. London: Henry Colburn, 1830.

D'Urville, Jules S-C Dumont. *Two Voyages to the South Seas*. Translated and edited by Helen Rosenman, 3 vols. Honolulu: University of Hawai`i Press, 1987.

Eschscholtz, Johann Friedrich. *Ideen zur Aneinanderreihung der rückgrathigen Thiere*. Dorpat: Schünmann, 1819.

Eschscholtz, Johann Friedrich. *System der Acalephen: eine aus führliche Beschreibung aller medusenartigen Strahlthiere*. Berlin, F. Dummler, 1829.

Gmelin, Johann Georg. *Flora Sibirica sive Historia plantarum Sibiriae*, 4 vols. St. Petersburg: Ex Typographia Academiae Scientarium, 1747–1769.

Humboldt, Alexander von, and Aimé Bonpland. *Personal Narrative of Travels to the Equinoctial Regions of America, 1799–1804*, 3 vols. Translated and edited by Thomasina Ross. London: George Bell & Sons, 1894.

Kotzebue, Otto von. "Voyage de Kotzebue." *Journal des Voyages; Gazette Geographique* July 16, 1816 (Paris, 1816): 126–127.

Kotzebue, Otto von. *A Voyage of Discovery, Into the South Sea and Beering's Straits, for the Purpose of Exploring a North-East Passage Undertaken in the Years 1815–1818, at the Expense of His Highness the Chancellor of the Empire, Count Romanzoff, in the Ship*

Rurick, Under the Command of the Lieutenant in the Russian Imperial Navy, Otto von Kotzebue, 3 vols. Translated by H. E. Lloyd. London: Longman, 1821.

Kotzebue, Otto von. *A New Voyage Round the World in the Years 1823, 1824, 1825, 1826*, 3 vols. London: Henry Colburn and Richard Bentley, 1830.

Krusenstern, Adam Johann von. *Voyage Round the World, in the years 1803, 1804, 1805, & 1806, by order of His Imperial Majesty Alexander the First, on board the ships Nadezhda and Neva, under the command of Captain A. J. von Krusenstern*, 3 vols. Translated by Richard Belgrave Hoppner. London: J. Murray, 1813.

Lay, William, and Cyrus Hussey. *A Narrative of the Mutiny on Board the Ship Globe*. New London, CT: Wm. Lay, and C. M. Hussey, 1828.

Marra, John. *Journal of the Resolution's Voyage in 1772, 1773, 1774, and 1775, on discovery to the southern hemisphere, by which the Non-Existence of an undiscovered Continent, between the equator and the 50th degree of Southern latitude, is demonstrably proved*. Dublin: printed for Caleb Jenkin and John Beatty, 1776.

Pallas, Peter Simon. *Travels Through the Southern Provinces of the Russian Empire in the Years 1793 and 1794*. London: T.N. Longman & O. Reis, 1802.

Paulding, Hiram. *Journal of the Cruise of the United States Schooner Dolphin*. New York: G. & C. & H. Carvill, 1831.

Reynolds, William. *The Private Journal of William Reynolds: United States Exploring Expedition, 1838–1842*. Edited by Nathaniel Philbrick and Thomas Philbrick. New York: Penguin Books, 2004.

Shoberl, Frederic. *The World in Miniature: Africa*. London: R. Ackermann, 1821.

Shoberl, Frederic. *The World in Miniature: the South Sea Islands*, 2 vols. London: R. Ackermann, 1824.

Veniaminov, Ivan. *Notes on the Islands of the Unalaska District*. Translated by L. T. Black and R. H. Geoghegan; edited by R. A. Pierce. Kingston, ON: Limestone Press, 1984.

SECONDARY SOURCES

Alessio, Dennis F. "Waan Aelon in Majel: Cultural Development in the Marshall Islands." *Micronesian Journal of the Humanities and Social Sciences* 5 (November 2006): 605–612.

Alkire, William H. "Systems of Measurement on Woleai Atoll, Caroline Islands." *Anthropos* 65 (1970): 1–73.

Anderson, Warwick. "Hybridity, Race, and Science: The Voyage of the Zaca, 1934–1935." *Isis* 103 (June 2012): 229–253.

Andrade, Tonio. "A Chinese Farmer, Two African Boys, and a Warlord: Toward a Global Microhistory." *Journal of World History* 21 (December 2010): 573–591.

Archer, Seth. *Sharks Upon the Land: Colonialism, Indigenous Health, and Culture in Hawai`i, 1778–1855*. Cambridge: Cambridge University Press, 2018.

Armitage, David, and Allison Bashford, eds. *Pacific Histories: Ocean, Land, People*. New York: Palgrave Macmillan, 2014.

Attar, K. E. "Russia Revealed: A Senate House Library Case Study of Special Collection Promotion." *SCONUL Focus* 50 (January 2021): 79–83.

Banner, Stuart. *Possessing the Pacific: Land, Settlers, and Indigenous People from Australia to Alaska*. Cambridge, MA: Harvard University Press, 2007.

Barratt, Glynn. *Russia in Pacific Waters, 1715–1825: A Survey of the Origins of Russia's Naval Presence in the North and South Pacific*. Vancouver: University of British Columbia Press, 1981.

Barratt, Glynn. "Russian Activity among the Cook Islands, to 1820." *New Zealand Slavonic Journal* (1998): 34–98. http://www.jstor.org/stable/40921980.

Beaglehole, J. C. *The Life of Captain James Cook*. Palo Alto, CA: Stanford University Press, 1974.

Beidleman, Richard G. *California's Frontier Naturalists*. Berkeley: University of California Press, 2006.

Bekasova, Alexandra. "Voyaging towards the Future: The Brig Rurik in the North Pacific and the Emerging Science of the Sea." *British Journal for the History of Science* 53 (December 2020): 469–495.

Berg, M. L. "Yapese Politics, Yapese Money and the Sawei Tribute Network before World War I." *Journal of Pacific History* 27 (1992): 150–164.

Black, Lydia T. "Whaling in the Aleutians." *Etudes/Inuit/Studies* 11 (1987): 7–50.

Black, Lydia T. *Russians in Alaska, 1732–1867*. Fairbanks: University of Alaska Press, 2004.

Bleichmar, Daniela. "Visible Empire: Scientific Expeditions and Visual Culture in the Hispanic Enlightenment." *Postcolonial Studies* 12 (2009): 441–466.

Bleichmar, Daniela. "The Cabinet and the World: Non-European Objects in Early Modern European Collections." *Journal of the History of Collections* 33 (2021): 435–445.

Carayon, Celine. *Eloquence Embodied: Nonverbal Communication among French and Indigenous Peoples in the Americas*. Chapel Hill: University of North Carolina Press, 2019.

Case, Emalani. *Everything Ancient Was Once New: Indigenous Persistence from Hawai`i to Kahiki*. Honolulu: University of Hawai`i Press, 2021.

Cavell, Janice. *Tracing the Connected Narrative: Arctic Exploration in British Print Culture, 1818–1860*. Toronto: University of Toronto Press, 2008.

Chance, Norman, and Norman Allee Chance. *The Inupiat and Arctic Alaska: An Ethnography of Development*. Fort Worth, TX: Holt, Rinehart & Winston, 1990.

Chang, David A. *The World and All Things upon It: Native Hawaiian Geographies of Exploration*. Minneapolis: University of Minnesota Press, 2016.

Charlot, Jean. *Choris and Kamehameha*. Honolulu, HI: Bishop Museum Press, 1958.

Chilisa, Bagele. *Indigenous Research Methodologies*. London: Sage Publications, 2020.

Crosby, Alfred. *Ecological Imperialism: The Biological Expansion of Europe, 900–1900*. Cambridge: Cambridge University Press, 1986.

Danaiyarri, Hobbles. "The Saga of Captain Cook." In *Australia's Empire*, edited by Deryck M. Schreuder and Stuart Ward, 26–32. Oxford: Oxford University Press, 2008.

D'Arcy, Paul. *The People of the Sea: Identity, Environment, and History in Oceania*. Honolulu: University of Hawai`i Press, 2005.

D'Arcy, Paul. "Connected by the Sea: Towards a Regional History of the Western Caroline Islands." *Journal of Pacific History* 36 (August 2010): 163–182.

D'Arcy, Paul., ed. *The Cambridge History of the Pacific Ocean*, 2 vols. Cambridge: Cambridge University Press, 2022.

Davis, Alan Eugene. "Suggestions for Study of the Native Knowledge of Marine Animals in the Eastern Caroline Islands." In *Oceanographic History: The Pacific and Beyond*, edited by Keith R. Benson and Philip F. Rehbock, 71–84. Seattle: University of Washington Press, 2002.

Dawson, Kevin. *Undercurrents of Power: Aquatic Culture in the African Diaspora.* Philadelphia: University of Pennsylvania Press, 2018.

DeLoughrey, E. "Globalizing the Routes of Breadfruit and Other Bounties." *Journal of Colonialism and Colonial History* 8 (Winter 2007). https://muse.jhu.edu/, accessed September 6, 2018.

Demuth, Bathsheba. *Floating Coast: An Environmental History of the Bering Strait.* New York: W. W. Norton & Co., 2019.

Dening, Greg. *Beach Crossings: Voyaging Across Times, Cultures, Self.* Philadelphia: University of Pennsylvania Press, 2004.

Diaz, Vicente M., and J. Kehaulani Kauanui. "Native Pacific Cultural Studies on the Edge." *The Contemporary Pacific* 13 (Fall 2001): 315–342.

Dmytryshyn, Basil, E. A. P. Crownhart-Vaughan, and Thomas Vaughan, eds. *The Russian American Colonies: A Documentary Record, 1798–1867*, 3 vols. Portland: Oregon Historical Society Press, 1989.

Douglas, Bronwen. "In the Event: Indigenous Countersigns and the Ethnohistory of Voyaging." In *Oceanic Encounters: Exchange, Desire, Violence*, edited by Margaret Jolly, Serge Tcherkezoff, and Darrell Tryon, 175–198. Canberra: ANU Press, 2009.

Douglas, Bronwen. "Climate to Crania: Science and the Racialization of Human Difference." In *Foreign Bodies: Oceania and the Science of Race, 1850–1940*, edited by Bronwen Douglas and Chris Ballard, 33–96. Canberra: ANU Press, 2012.

Douglas, Bronwen. *Science, Voyages, and Encounters in Oceania, 1511–1850.* Basingstoke: Palgrave Macmillan, 2014.

Douglas, Bronwen, and Elena Gover. "Eponymy, Encounters, and Local Knowledge in Russian Place Naming in the Pacific Islands, 1804–1830." *Historical Review* 62 (2019): 709–740.

Dusinberre, Martin. *Mooring the Global Archive: A Japanese Ship and its Migrant Histories.* Cambridge: Cambridge University Press, 2023.

Eltis, David, and David Richardson. *Atlas of the Transatlantic Slave Trade.* New Haven, CT: Yale University Press, 2010.

Fabian, Ann. *The Skull Collectors: Race, Science, and America's Unburied Dead.* Chicago: University of Chicago Press, 2010.

Fara, Patricia. *Sex, Botany, and Empire: The Story of Carl Linnaeus and Joseph Banks.* New York: Columbia University Press, 2003.

Farber, Paul L. "Buffon and the Concept of Species." *Journal of the History of Biology* 5 (Fall 1972): 259–284.

Federhofer, Marie-Theres. "Messy Episodes: Indigenous Countersigns in Ludwig Choris's Diary and Ethnographic Portraits of Kamchadal, Aleut and Chukchi, 1822." *History and Anthropology* 35:4 (April 2023): 1–22.

Fedyukin, Igor. *The Enterprisers: The Politics of School in Early Modern Russia.* New York: Oxford University Press, 2019.

Ferrer, Luis, and Ane Pastor. "The Portuguese man-of-war: Gone with the wind." *Regional Studies in Marine Science* 14 (2017): 53–62.

Feudel, Werner. *Adelbert von Chamisso: Leben und Werk*. Leipzig: P. Reclam, 1988.

Fischer, Steven Roger. *Island at the End of the World: The Turbulent History of Easter Island*. London: Reaktion Books, 2005.

Flores-Villela, Oscar, et al. "Identity of Three New Sea Turtles Named by J. Friedrich Eschscholtz." *Chelonian Conservation and Biology* 15 (2016): 157–162.

Forsyth, James. *A History of the Peoples of Siberia: Russia's North Asian Colony, 1581–1991*. Cambridge: Cambridge University Press, 1992.

Fuentes, Marisa J. *Dispossessed Lives: Enslaved Women, Violence, and the Archive*. Philadelphia: University of Pennsylvania Press, 2018.

Gamble, Lynn H. *The Chumash World at European Contact: Power, Trade, and Feasting Among Complex Hunter-Gatherers*. Berkeley: University of California Press, 2011.

Gascoigne, J. *Science in the Service of Empire: Joseph Banks, the British State, and the Uses of Science in the Age of Revolution*. New York: Cambridge University Press, 1998.

Genz, Joseph. "Wave Navigation in the Marshall Islands: Comparing Indigenous and Western Scientific Knowledge of the Ocean." *Oceanography* 22 (June 2009): 234–246.

Genz, Joseph. "Navigating the Revival of Voyaging in the Marshall Islands: Predicaments of Preservation and Possibilities of Collaboration." *Contemporary Pacific* 23 (2011): 1–34.

Gibson, James R. *Imperial Russia in Frontier America: The Changing Geography of Supply of Russian America, 1784–1867*. New York: Oxford University Press, 1976.

Glaubrecht, Matthias, Nils Seethaler, Barbara Tebman, and Katrin Koel-Abt. "The Potential of Biohistory: Re-discovering Adelbert von Chamisso's Skull of an Aleut Collected during the 'Rurik' Expedition 1815–1818 in Alaska." *Zoosystematics and Evolution* 89 (September 2013): 317–336.

Glaubrecht, Matthias, and Wolfgang Dohle. "Discovering the alternation of generations in salps (Tunicata, Thaliacea): Adelbert von Chamisso's dissertation "De Salpa" 1819— its material, origin and reception in the early nineteenth century." *Zoosystematics and Evolution* 88 (October 2012): 317–363.

Golson, Jack. *Polynesian Navigation: A Symposium on Sharp's Theory of Accidental Voyages*. Auckland: Polynesian Society, 1972.

Grann, David. *The Wager: A Tale of Shipwreck, Mutiny, and Murder*. New York: Doubleday, 2023.

Grinev, Andrei V. "Germans in the History of Russian America." *Journal of the West* 47 (Spring 2008): 32–43.

Grinev, Andrei V. "The Plans for Russian Expansion in the New World and the North Pacific in the Eighteenth and Nineteenth Centuries." *European Journal of American Studies* 5 (2010): 1–27.

Grinev, Andrei V. "Natives and Creoles of Alaska in the Maritime Service in Russian America." *The Historian* 82 (2020): 328–345.

Guest, Harriet. *Empire, Barbarism, and Civilization: James Cook, William Hodges, and the Return to the Pacific*. Cambridge: Cambridge University Press, 2007.

Hackel, Steven W. *Children of Coyote, Missionaries of Saint Francis: Indian-Spanish Relations in Colonial California, 1769–1850*. Chapel Hill: University of North Carolina Press, 2005.

Halvaksz, Jamon Alex, and Joshua A. Bell, eds. *Naturalist Histories: Making Nature, Knowledge, and People in Oceania.* Honolulu: University of Hawai`i Press, 2024.

Hanlon, David. "The 'Sea of Little Lands': Examining Micronesia's Place in 'Our Sea of Islands.'" *The Contemporary Pacific* 21 (2009): 91–110.

Harrison, Carol E. "Planting Gardens, Planting Flags: Revolutionary France in the Pacific." *French Historical Studies* 34 (Spring 2011): 243–277.

Haúofa, Epeli. "Our Sea of Islands," *Contemporary Pacific* 6 (Spring 1994): 148–161.

Heizer, Robert F. "Aconite Poison Whaling in Asia and America: An Aleutian Transfer to the New World." *Bureau of American Ethnology Bulletin* 133 (1944): 415–468.

Hezel, Francis X. S. J. *The First Taint of Civilization: A History of the Caroline and Marshall Islands in Pre-Colonial Days, 1521–1885.* Honolulu: University of Hawai`i Press, 1983.

Hirshberg, Lauren. *Suburban Empire: Cold War Militarization in the US Pacific.* Berkeley: University of California Press, 2022.

Hodacs, Hanna, et al., eds. *Linnaeus, Natural History, and the Circulation of Knowledge.* Oxford: Oxford University Press, 2018.

Howe, K. R. *Vaka Moana Voyages of the Ancestors: The Discovery and Settlement of the Pacific.* Honolulu: University of Hawai`i Press, 2006.

Hudson, Ray, and Rachel Mason. *Lost Villages of the Eastern Aleutians.* Washington, D.C.: National Parks Service, 2014.

Igler, David. *The Great Ocean: Pacific Worlds from Captain Cook to the Gold Rush.* New York: Oxford University Press, 2013.

Igler, David. "Indigenous Maritime Travelers and Knowledge Production." In *A World at Sea: Maritime Practices and Global History*, edited by Lauren Benton and Nathan Perl-Rosenthal, 108–132. Philadelphia: University of Pennsylvania Press, 2020.

Igler, David. "Trading Nature in the Pacific: Ecological Exchange Prior to 1900." In *Cambridge History of the Pacific Ocean, Vol. II: The Pacific Ocean since 1800*, edited by Paul D'Arcy, Anne Perez-Hattori, and Jane Samson, 369–388. Cambridge: Cambridge University Press, 2023.

Johnson, Paul E. "The Modernization of Mayo Greenleaf Patch: Land, Family, and Marginality in New England, 1766–1818." *New England Quarterly* 55 (December 1982): 488–516.

Jones, Ryan Tucker. "Running into Whales: The History of the North Pacific from Below the Waves." *American Historical Review* 118 (April 2013): 349–377.

Jones, Ryan Tucker. *Empire of Extinction: Russians and the North Pacific's Strange Beasts of the Sea, 1741–1867.* New York: Oxford University Press, 2014.

Jones, Ryan Tucker. "Kelp Highways, Siberian Girls in Maui, and Nuclear Walruses: The North Pacific in a Sea of Islands." *Journal of Pacific History* 48 (December 2014): 373–395.

Jones, Ryan Tucker. *Red Leviathan: The Secret History of Soviet Whaling.* Chicago: University of Chicago Press, 2022.

Keighren, Innes M., Charles W. J. Withers, and Bill Bell. *Travels in Print: Exploration, Writing, and Publishing with John Murray, 1773–1859.* Chicago: University of Chicago Press, 2015.

Kelen, Alson. "The Role of Canoe Building and Navigation in Yapese and Marshallese Seafaring Systems." Symposium presentation, December 7, 2022, Stanford University.

Kirch, Patrick. *A Shark Going Inland Is My Chief: The Island Civilization of Ancient Hawai`i*. Berkeley: University of California Press, 2012.

Kirch, P. V., and J. L. Rallu, eds. *The Growth and Collapse of Pacific Island Societies: Archaelogical and Demographic Perspectives*. Honolulu: University of Hawai`i Press, 2007.

Kolbert, Elizabeth. *Field Notes from a Catastrophe: Man, Nature, and Climate Change*. New York: Bloomsbury, 2006.

Konishi, Shino, Maria Nugent, and Tiffany Shellam, eds. *Indigenous Intermediaries: New Perspective on Exploration Archives*. Canberra: ANU Press, 2015.

Koponen, Seppo, and Pekka Niemelä. "Johann Friedrich Gustav von Eschscholtz—a pioneer naturalist and explorer of the Pacific Islands and Western North America." *Memoranda Societatis Fauna Flora Fennica* 96 (2020): 57–64.

Kortum, Gerhard. "Germania in Pacifico: Humboldt, Chamisso and Other Early German Contributions to Pacific Research, 1741–1876." In *Oceanographic History: The Pacific and Beyond*, edited by Keith R. Bengtsson and Philip F. Rehbock, 110–121. Seattle: University of Washington Press, 2002.

Kusov, Vladimir Svyatoslavovich. "Count Nikolai Rumiantsev and Russian Exploration of Alaska and North America." *Western Association of Map Libraries Information Bulletin* 25 (November 1993): 11–22.

Lantzeff, George V., and Richard A. Pierce. *Eastward to Empire: Exploration and Conquest on the Russian Open Frontier, to 1750*. Montreal: McGill-Queen's University Press, 1973.

Lewis, Daniel. *Belonging on an Island: Birds, Extinction, and Evolution in Hawai`i*. New Haven, CT: Yale University Press, 2018.

Liapunova, Roza G. *Essays on the Ethnography of the Aleuts*. Translated by Jerry Shelest. Fairbanks: University of Alaska Press, 1996.

Liebersohn, Harry. "Discovering Indigenous Nobility: Tocqueville, Chamisso, and Romantic Travel Writing." *American Historical Review* 99 (June 1994): 746–766.

Liebersohn, Harry. *A Travelers' World: Europe in the Pacific*. Cambridge, MA: Harvard University Press, 2006.

Lukina, Tatiana Arkadevna. *Johann Friedrich Eschscholtz, 1793–1831*. Translated by Wilma C. Follette. Originally published as Lukina, *Logann Fridrikh Eschol'ts, 1793–1831*. Leningrad: Nauka Leningradskoe otdelnie, 1975.

MacKinney, Anne Greenwood, and Matthias Glaubrecht. "Academic practice par excellence: Martin Hinrich Lichtenstein's role in Adelbert von Chamisso's career as naturalist." *Internationales Archiv für Sozialgeschichte der deutschen Literatur* 42, no. 2 (2017): 322–347.

MacKinney, Anne Greenwood, and Matthias Glaubrecht. "Unpacking a(nother) voyage round the world: Adelbert von Chamisso's donation of the *Rurik* collection to Berlin's natural history museums." *Journal of the History of Collections* 34 (July 2022): 259–274.

Mahr, August. *The Visit of the "Rurik" to San Francisco in 1816*. Stanford, CA: Stanford University Press, 1932.

Mair, Lucy P. *Methods and Study of Culture Contact in Africa*. Oxford: Oxford University Press, 1938.

Malloy, Mary. *Souvenirs of the Fur Trade: Northwest Coast Indian Art and Artifacts Collected by American Mariners 1788–1844*. Cambridge, MA: Harvard University Press, 2000.

Mancall, Peter C. "The Age of Failures." *Early American Literature* 56 (2021): 23–50.

Matsuda, Matt K. *Pacific Worlds: A History of Seas, Peoples, and Cultures*. New York: Cambridge University Press, 2012.

Miles, Tiya. *All That She Carried: The Journey of Ashley's Sack, A Black Family's Keepsake*. New York: Random House, 2021.

Monahan, Erika. *The Merchants of Siberia: Trade in Early Modern Eurasia*. Ithaca, NY: Cornell University Press, 2016.

Montfiore, Simon Sebag. *The Romanovs: 1613–1918*. New York: Knopf, 2016.

Mornin, Edward, ed. *Through Alien Eyes: The Visit of the Russian Ship Rurik to San Francisco in 1816 and the Men behind the Visit*. Oxford: P. Lang, 2002.

Nagata, K. "Early Plant Introductions in Hawai`i." *The Hawaiian Journal of History* 19 (1985): 35–61.

Newell, Jennifer. *Trading Nature: Tahitians, Europeans, and Ecological Exchange*. Honolulu: University of Hawai`i Press, 2010.

Nicandri, David L. *Discovering Nothing: In Pursuit of an Elusive Northwest Passage*. Vancouver: University of British Columbia Press, 2024.

Nugent, Maria. "A failure to say hello: how Captain Cook blundered his first impression with Indigenous people." *The Conversation*, April 28, 2020.

Orbell, Margaret. *A Concise Encyclopedia of Māori Myth and Legend*. Christchurch, NZ: Canterbury University Press, 1998.

Panich, Lee M. "'Sometimes They Bury the Deceased's Clothes and Trinkets': Indigenous Mortuary Practices and Mission Santa Clara de Asis." *Historical Archaeology* 49 (2015): 110–129.

Panich, Lee M. "Death, Mourning, and Accommodation in the Missions of Alta California." In *Franciscans and American Indians in Pan-Borderland Perspective: Adaptation, Negotiation, and Resistance*, eds. Jeffrey M. Burns and Timothy J. Johnson, 251–264. Gainesville: University Press of Florida, 2018.

Pennell, Elizabeth Robins. *Lithography and Lithographers: Some Chapters in the History of the Art*. London: T. Fisher Unwin, 1915.

Postnikov, Alexey, and Marvin Falk. *Exploring and Mapping Alaska: The Russian America Era, 1741–1867*. Translated by Lydia Black. Fairbanks: University of Alaska Press, 2015.

Raigetal, Hilary Larry. "The Role of Canoe Building and Navigation in Yapese and Marshallese Seafaring Systems." Symposium presentation, Stanford University, December 7, 2022.

Raigetal, Hilary Larry. "Revitalizing 'Traditional' Navigation Systems in the Contemporary Pacific." In *The Cambridge History of the Pacific Ocean, Volume I, The Pacific Ocean to 1800*, edited by Ryan Tucker Jones and Matt K. Matsuda, 345–366. Cambridge: Cambridge University Press, 2023.

Raj, Kapil. *Relocating Modern Science: Circulation and the Construction of Knowledge in South Asia and Europe, 1650–1900*. New York: Palgrave Macmillan, 2007.

Raj, Kapil. "Go-Betweens, Travelers, and Cultural Translators." In *A Companion to the History of Science*, edited by Bernard Lightman, 39–57. Malden, MA: John Wiley and Sons, 2016.

Ray, Dorothy Jean. *Eskimo Art: Tradition and Innovation in North Alaska*. Seattle: University of Washington Press, 1977.

Ray, Dorothy Jean. *Aleut and Eskimo Art: Tradition and Innovation in South Alaska*. Seattle: University of Washington Press, 1981.

Reid, Joshua L. *The Sea Is My Country: The Maritime World of the Makah*. New Haven, CT: Yale University Press, 2015.

Riesenberg, Saul H. "Table of Voyages Affecting Micronesian Islands." *Oceania* 36 (December 1965): 155–170.

Riesenberg, Saul H. "The Ghost Islands of the Carolines." *Micronesica* 11 (July 1975): 7–33.

Romaniello, Matthew P. *Enterprising Empires: Russia and Britain in Eighteenth-Century Eurasia*. Cambridge: Cambridge University Pres, 2019.

Rozwadowski, Helen N. "Small World: Forging a Scientific Maritime Culture for Oceanography." *Isis* 87 (September 1996): 409–429.

Salesa, Damon. "The Pacific in Indigenous Time." In *Pacific Histories: Ocean, Land, People*, edited by David Armitage and Alison Bashford, 31–52. New York: Palgrave Macmillan, 2014.

Salmond, Anne. *Two Worlds: First Meetings Between Māori and Europeans, 1642–1772*. Auckland, NZ: Viking, 1991.

Salmond, Anne. *The Trial of the Cannibal Dog: The Remarkable Story of Captain Cook's Encounters in the South Seas*. New Haven, CT: Yale University Press, 2003.

Salmond, Anne. *Bligh: William Bligh in the South Seas*. Berkeley: University of California Press, 2011.

Schiebinger, Londa L. *Plants and Empire: Colonial Bioprospecting in the Atlantic World*. Cambridge, MA: Harvard University Press, 2009.

Schiebinger, Londa, and Claudia Swan, eds. *Colonial Botany: Science, Commerce, and Politics in the Early Modern World*. Philadelphia: University of Pennsylvania Press, 2005.

Schmid, Gunther. *Chamisso als Naturforscher, eine Bibliographie*. Leipzig: K. F. Koehler, 1942.

Schweizer, Niklaus. "'At Last He Fell Asleep': Choris, Chamisso, and Kamehameha I in Hawai`i." In *Across the Oceans: Studies from East to West in Honor of Richard K. Seymour*, edited by Irmengard Rauch and Richard K. Seymour, 17–25. Honolulu: University of Hawai`i Press, 1995.

Shaffer, Simon, ed. *The Brokered World: Go-Betweens and Global Intelligence, 1770–1820*. Sagamore Beach, MA: Watson Publishing International, 2009.

Shellam, Tiffany, ed. *Brokers and Boundaries: Colonial Exploration in Indigenous Territory*. Canberra: ANU Press, 2016.

Shur, Yuri, et al. "Yedoma Permafrost Genesis: Over 150 Years of Mystery and Controversy." *Frontiers in Earth Science* 9 (January 2022). https://doi.org/10.3389/feart.2021.757891.

Simmons, R. T. "Blood Group Genetic Variations in Natives of the Caroline Islands and in Other Parts of Micronesia." *Oceania* 36 (December 1965): 132–154.

Sloan, Phillip R. "The Buffon-Linnaeus Controversy." *Isis* 67 (September 1976): 356–375.

Smallwood, Stephanie E. "Reflections on Settler Colonialism, the Hemispheric Americas, and Chattel Slavery." *The William and Mary Quarterly* 76 (2021): 407–419.

Smith, Bernard. *European Vision and the South Pacific*. New Haven, CT: Yale University Press, 1985, 2nd edition.

Smith, Linda Tuhiwai. *Decolonizing Methodologies: Research and Indigenous Peoples*. London: Zed Books, 2021.

Sorrenson, Richard. "The Ship as a Scientific Instrument in the Eighteenth Century." *Osiris* 11 (1996): 221–236.

Starbuck, Nicole. " 'Primitive Race,' 'pure race,' 'brown race,' 'every race,': Louis Freycinet's Understanding of Human Difference in Oceania." In *Discovery and Empire: The French in the South Seas*, edited by John West-Sooby, 215–240. Adelaide, Australia: University of Adelaide Press, 2013.

Stoddart, David R. " 'This Coral Episode': Darwin, Dana, and the Coral Reefs of the Pacific." In *Darwin's Laboratory: Evolutionary Theory and Natural History in the Pacific*, edited by Roy MacLeod and Philip F. Rehbock, 19–48. Honolulu: University of Hawai`i Press, 1994.

Sunderland, Willard. *The Baron's Cloak: A History of the Russian Empire in War and Revolution*. Ithaca, NY: Cornell University Press, 2014.

Tammiksaar, Erki, and Tarmo Kiik, "Origins of the Russian Antarctic Expedition, 1819–1821." *Polar Record* 49 (2013): 180–192.

Thompson, L. F. *Kotzebue: A Survey of His Progress in France, and England*. Paris: Librairie Ancienne Honoré Champion, 1928.

Turner, Lucien M. *An Aleutian Ethnography*. Edited by Raymond L. Hudson. Fairbanks: University of Alaska Press, 2008.

Twyman, Michael. *Lithography: 1800–1850: The Techniques of Drawing on Stone in England and France and their Application in Works of Topography*. London: Oxford University Press, 1970.

Twyman, Michael. *Breaking the Mould: The First Hundred Years of Lithography*. London: British Library, 2001.

Twyman, Michael. "The Illustration Revolution." In *The Cambridge History of the Book in Britain*, vol. 6, *1830–1914*, edited by David McKitterick, 117–143. Cambridge: Cambridge University Press, 2009.

Tyler, Ron. "Entirely New and Very Interesting Things: Louis Choris and the Kotzebue Expedition, 1815–1818." *Imprint* 42 (Fall 2017): 2–43.

Tyler, Ron. "The Role of the Exploration Artist: Louis Choris and the Kotzebue Expedition, 1815–1818." *Studii Si Cercetari de Istoria Artei. Seria Arta Plastica* 11, no. 55 (January 2021): 43–76.

Vanstone, James W. "An Early Nineteenth-Century Artist in Alaska: Louis Choris and the First Kotzebue Expedition." *Pacific Northwest Quarterly* 51 (October 1960), 145–158.

Vinkovetsky, Ilya. *Russian America: An Overseas Colony of a Continental Empire, 1804–1867*. New York: Oxford University Press, 2011.

Vinkovetsky, Ilya. "The Russian-American Company as a Corporation." *The Russian Review* 81 (July 2022), 421–439.

Walker, Brett L. *Yukikaze's War: The Unsinkable Japanese Destroyer and World War II in the Pacific*. Cambridge: Cambridge University Press, 2024.

Walsh, Julianne M. "Imagining the Marshall Islands: Chiefs, Tradition, and the State on the Fringes of United States Empire." PhD dissertation, University of Hawai`i, 2003.

Warren, James Frances. "Saltwater Slavers and Captives in the Sulu Zone, 1768–1878." *Slavery and Abolition* 31 (September 2010): 429–449.

Whittaker, Cynthia Hyla, ed. *Russia Engages the World, 1453–1825*. Cambridge, MA: Harvard University Press, 2003.

Williams, Glyn. *Voyages of Delusion: The Quest for the Northwest Passage*. New Haven, CT: Yale University Press, 2002.

Williams, Glyn. *Naturalists at Sea: Scientific Travellers from Dampier to Darwin*. New Haven, CT: Yale University Press, 2013.

Williamson, Richard V., and Donna K. Stone. *Anthropological Survey of the Marshall Island*. Majuro Atoll: Republic of Marshall Islands: Historic Preservation Office, 2001.

Wilson, E. O. *Biophilia*. Cambridge, MA: Harvard University Press, 1984.

Wilson, Shawn. *Research Is Ceremony: Indigenous Research Methods*. Halifax, Canada: Fernwood Publishing, 2008.

Wulf, Andrea. *Founding Gardeners: The Revolutionary Generation, Nature, and the Shaping of the American Nation*. New York: Vintage, 2012.

Zhang, Chunjie. "The Islander Kadu and Adelbert von Chamisso." *The Eighteenth Century* 59 (Spring 2017): 79–98.

For the benefit of digital users, indexed terms that span two pages (e.g., 52–53) may, on occasion, appear on only one of those pages.